How Documentaries Went Mainstream

How Documentaries Went Mainstream

A History, 1960–2022

NORA STONE

OXFORD
UNIVERSITY PRESS

Oxford University Press is a department of the University of Oxford. It furthers
the University's objective of excellence in research, scholarship, and education
by publishing worldwide. Oxford is a registered trade mark of Oxford University
Press in the UK and certain other countries.

Published in the United States of America by Oxford University Press
198 Madison Avenue, New York, NY 10016, United States of America.

© Oxford University Press 2023

All rights reserved. No part of this publication may be reproduced, stored in
a retrieval system, or transmitted, in any form or by any means, without the
prior permission in writing of Oxford University Press, or as expressly permitted
by law, by license, or under terms agreed with the appropriate reproduction
rights organization. Inquiries concerning reproduction outside the scope of the
above should be sent to the Rights Department, Oxford University Press, at the
address above.

You must not circulate this work in any other form
and you must impose this same condition on any acquirer.

Library of Congress Cataloging-in-Publication Data
Names: Stone, Nora, author.
Title: How documentaries went mainstream: a history, 1960–2022 / by Nora Stone.
Description: New York, NY: Oxford University Press, [2023] |
Includes bibliographical references.
Identifiers: LCCN 2022060620 (print) | LCCN 2022060621 (ebook) |
ISBN 9780197557297 (hardback) | ISBN 9780197557303 (paperback) |
ISBN 9780197557327 (epub)
Subjects: LCSH: Documentary films—United States—History and criticism.
Classification: LCC PN1995.9.D6 S8275 2023 (print) |
LCC PN1995.9.D6 (ebook) | DDC 070.1/8—dc23/eng/20230126
LC record available at https://lccn.loc.gov/2022060620
LC ebook record available at https://lccn.loc.gov/2022060621

DOI: 10.1093/oso/9780197557297.001.0001

For my parents

Contents

Acknowledgments	ix
Introduction: How Documentaries Went Mainstream	1
1. Direct Cinema Blossoms, but Little Support for Documentary Films in Theaters (1960 to 1977)	9
2. A Rising Tide: How the Independent Film Movement Boosted Documentaries (1978 to 1989)	39
3. Fighting for a Place on Public Television: Independent Filmmakers Lobby (1978 to 1990)	68
4. Television or Cinema? Redefining Documentary for Prestige and Profit (1990 to 1999)	88
5. The Docbuster Era (2000 to 2007)	116
6. Streaming Video Drives Documentary Production Trends and Private Investment (2008 to 2022)	151
Conclusion: Documentary Film Inches Closer to the Center, but Core Tensions Remain	188
Bibliography	197
Index	203

Acknowledgments

First, I must acknowledge my professors in the Department of Communication Arts at the University of Wisconsin–Madison. Their commitment to the highest ideals of scholarship has been a guiding light in my life. They taught me how to be a better scholar, writer, and teacher than I thought possible. Without the sterling education I received at Madison, this book would not have come to fruition.

Kelley Conway, Vance Kepley, and J. J. Murphy were particularly transformative mentors. Their gentle guidance and good humor kept me on track over the many years of this project, from seminar paper to dissertation to monograph. I aspire to their insight, tenacity, and impact on the field. When he was a new professor, Eric Hoyt advised graduate students to build something that other scholars could use. My hope is that this book fulfills that mandate.

As I followed my interest in documentary film and the mechanisms of distribution, I found likeminded folks: Tanya Goldman and Josh Glick. They are superlative colleagues and friends. A phone call with one of them always renews my excitement to research and theorize about documentaries.

Writing is a lonely sport. It is a comfort to look across a coffee shop table and see a friendly face, engaged in their own struggle with ideas and words. I treasure the time I spent crafting early versions of this manuscript alongside Maureen Rogers, Matt Connolly, and Caroline Leader.

My family has made the writing of this book possible. My parents, Steve and Julie Stone, are an unceasing source of strength and encouragement. Their emotional and material support made space for me to continue my scholarship. I am so grateful to them. Lily Stone and Will Chim kept my spirits up during the weeks and months of writing during the pandemic. Their admiration touches my heart. My in-laws, Bookie and Ray Ginter, Ryan and Bri Colvin, are an unexpected blessing. Their love and acceptance fortify me.

A profound thanks to my partner in all things, Brandon Colvin. He is my favorite person, and the person I admire most. His faith in me is a beacon.

If I need help, he is there, helping me untangle problems and express myself more clearly. If I need motivation, he is there, reminding me of my passion for research and filmmaking. If I need comfort, he is there, delighting and embracing me every single day. This book, and my life, would be much poorer without him by my side.

Introduction

How Documentaries Went Mainstream

Documentary feature films have historically existed on the margins of mainstream media. In the United States, enterprising documentarians have spent most of the past sixty years struggling to find a larger, broader audience for their films. Often negatively associated with long-form television journalism and tedious educational programming, documentaries have rarely escaped their perceived status as "cultural vegetables"—good for you, but relatively unappealing. Recently, this marginal status has shifted quite dramatically. Nearly unthinkable a decade ago, documentary films have become reliable earners at the US box office. In 2018 alone, *Won't You Be My Neighbor?* made almost $23 million, *They Shall Not Grow Old* and *Free Solo* each earned almost $18 million, *RBG* netted $14 million, and *Three Identical Strangers* earned $12 million. In addition to their theatrical presence, documentary films are ubiquitous on cable channels and streaming video services, which have made documentary programming a key component of their offerings to subscribers. In 2019, Netflix paid the highest price for a documentary out of the Sundance Film Festival: $10 million for *Knock Down the House*, about four working-class women, including Alexandria Ocasio-Cortez, running for Congress in the 2018 midterm elections. Longtime documentary champion and former head of HBO Documentary Sheila Nevins said that Netflix was playing with "Monopoly money" by acquiring the documentary at such a high price, but she also granted that this was a trend across the board.[1] Industry journalists took note. This surge in popularity had made documentaries nearly ubiquitous. In 2019, think pieces from CBS News, NPR, the *Los Angeles Times*, and *The Ringer* all simultaneously proclaimed a new golden age of documentary.[2] With broad public interest and robust

---

[1] Mandalit del Barco, "The Documentary Is in—and Enjoying—an 'Undeniable Golden Age,'" *NPR.org*, February 19, 2019, https://www.npr.org/2019/02/19/696036323/the-documentary-is-in-and-enjoying-an-undeniable-golden-age.

[2] "The Golden Age of Documentary Filmmaking," CBS News, March 3, 2019, https://www.cbsnews.com/news/the-golden-age-of-documentary-filmmaking/; del Barco, "The Documentary

investment in their production, documentary films are definitively more popular and prestigious than ever before.

Although the commercial ascension of documentary films might seem meteoric, it is the culmination of decades-long efforts on the part of innovative, intrepid filmmakers; risk-taking, often socially committed distribution companies; and institutions like public television stations, cable networks, film festivals, and contemporary streaming services that have developed and fortified the audience for documentary features. The commercialization of documentary filmmaking has transformed it into a media sector that promises sufficient financial stability and growth potential to attract sizable, consistent private investment—a remarkable inflection point in a history alternately defined by scrappy entrepreneurs and nonprofit advocates.

Three core tensions recur in this history. The first is documentary film's dual foundation in the worlds of television and cinema. Television has been a persistent funding source and exhibition outlet for documentary films over the past sixty years, but this association has, at times, prevented documentaries from being seen as vital, engaging cinema. Releasing a film in theaters keeps it in the media cycle for a longer period than does a television broadcast, allowing it to accrue more reviews from critics, features from journalists, and word of mouth from audiences. Labeling a documentary a "film" also conveys a higher level of prestige and import. These differences in release structure and perception have contributed to documentary film's commercial and discursive transition.

The second core tension is between the isolated entrepreneur and the organized institution. No matter the broader landscape for documentary, there are filmmakers who do whatever it takes to make documentaries and bring them to viewers—they fund production with personal favors and credit cards, self-distribute their work, form distribution collectives, publish films for free streaming over the internet. As documentary films' commercial potential and connection with the commercial media industry have grown, so too have the number of commercial and nonprofit entities invested in them. It may appear that these institutions would eliminate the need for activist, entrepreneurial documentarians, but this development has in no way sidelined them. Instead, their persistent presence over time demonstrates

---

Is In"; Amy Kaufman, "'Three Identical Strangers,' 'RBG' Directors and Others Look Back on Documentary's Big Year," *Los Angeles Times*, January 4, 2019; Sean Fennessey, "We Are Living through a Documentary Boom," *The Ringer*, July 24, 2018.

that documentary retains a grassroots spirit and a connection to maverick American independent cinema.

Finally, and most crucially, there is the ambiguity surrounding what the "market" for documentary films even is or should be. This tension extends throughout the history of documentary film in the United States and strikes at the heart of the difficulty of tracing documentary film's commercialization. For documentary films, there is more to the market than a rationalized system of commodity exchange. The feature documentary market has a parallel and symbiotic element to it: the concept of public service. Some agents of this market, like distributors, are explicitly interested in documentary features as commodities that can be exchanged for profit like fiction features. Other agents, like government agencies, public broadcasters, and nonprofit organizations, are more interested in producing and circulating documentary features as a form of public service—a way to promote alternative ideas and cultural forms. Documentary filmmakers come to the market with a mix of these goals and must navigate each stage of the documentary world with an eye toward often-contradictory principles and imperatives. The intertwining of commodity exchange and public service is especially tight once a film begins to circulate through various exhibition sites and windows; documentaries supported by grants or by public TV, for instance, increasingly circulate through commercial spaces like theaters and streaming services.

The commercialization process traced in the book is not separate from, nor does it replace, the public service element of the documentary film market. Rather, the balance between these elements has changed over time. The public service aspect of documentary film has been diluted, compared to the 1960s and 1970s, but is still present and significant. Currently, the most commercial documentary films are generally apolitical and barely invested in public service, if at all. For example, see the recent theatrically released documentaries *Biggest Little Farm* (2019) and *Apollo 11* (2019), and documentaries popular on streaming services, *Miss Americana* (2020) and *Tiger King: Murder, Mayhem, and Madness* (2020). Barring a handful of exceptions, this has always been the case. But the public service element of documentary film still benefits from ballooning interest and investment in popular documentary forms. The commercialization of documentary film has expanded the audience size of documentaries, making them broadly accessible in more entertainment-oriented venues, like movie theaters, cable television, and streaming services.

Explaining the Commercialization of Documentary

This book enriches the history of documentary film by foregrounding production funding mechanisms, distribution norms, and discourses, with a resulting greater explanatory power. In extant studies, there has been little attention to how industrial and institutional changes affect what documentary films are made and which audiences view them. Instead, chronological histories often highlight major film movements and trumpet stylistic advances.[3] Such scholarship traces crucial developments in the art of documentary film, but it suggests little about how documentarians related to the broader world of commercial media. At the same time, most histories of American cinema and television barely gesture to documentary film, because documentary's commercial and cultural significance is presumed to be insignificant in comparison to Hollywood tentpole films or even indie fiction films. This history concentrates on documentary film industry and institutions in order to account for both extraordinarily successful documentaries that break into the zeitgeist and the simultaneous persistence of conventional films and release strategies. Drawing on archival documents, interviews with filmmakers and film distributors, industry trade journals, and popular press, the book illuminates how documentary features have become more plentiful, popular, and profitable than ever before.

This work joins histories that clarify the material conditions affecting how documentary films are made and what happens when audiences encounter them. Much recent scholarship has analyzed the activist power of documentary film in the networked media age.[4] These authors discuss how the affordances of streaming video and online community have allowed people to form communities and take action based on documentary film. But the commercial valance of many films and distribution platforms goes unexplored. In this way, the public service value of documentary film, particularly political documentary, has received far more scholarly attention than the commercial side. Texts on individual documentarians offer hints about the

---

[3] Stephen Mamber, *Cinema Verite in America: Studies in Uncontrolled Documentary* (Cambridge, MA: MIT Press, 1974); Richard Barsam, *Nonfiction Film: A Critical History, Revised and Expanded* (Bloomington: Indiana University Press, 1992); Betsy McLane, *A New History of Documentary Film*, 2nd ed. (London: Continuum, 2012).

[4] Angela Aguayo, *Documentary Resistance: Social Change and Participatory Media* (New York: Oxford University Press, 2019); Caty Borum Chattoo, *Story Movements: How Documentaries Empower People and Inspire Social Change* (New York: Oxford University Press, 2020); Tanya Horeck, *Justice on Demand: True Crime in the Digital Streaming Era* (Detroit: Wayne State University Press, 2019).

documentary film market. For example, David Resha's *The Cinema of Errol Morris* and multiple essays in Jeff Jaeckle and Susan Ryan's edited collection *ReFocus: The Films of Barbara Kopple* discuss how filmmakers financed and distributed their productions.[5] But an account of the wider system and its change over time remains elusive.

This history is attentive to the transmedia relationships that supported and grew the commercial potential of documentary film. While academic areas divide up the study of particular media, documentary filmmakers cannot isolate themselves to a single medium; they must consider and navigate the whole documentary ecosystem.[6] Consequently, the book illuminates networks of production and circulation that transcend conceptual categories, like film and television, commercial and nonprofit media, theatrical distribution and nontheatrical circulation. It identifies key institutions for documentary film that have not been clearly identified or related to one another before. Highlighting transmedia means I elaborate the history not only of documentary film, but also cable television, public television, home video, and video streaming services. To help me triangulate the place of documentary film in the commercial media industry, I rely on texts that trace shifting industrial logics and those that foreground agents like festival programmers, film distributors, and television and streaming service executives.[7]

---

[5] David Resha, *The Cinema of Errol Morris* (Middletown, CT: Wesleyan University Press, 2015); Jeff Jaeckle and Susan Ryan, eds., *ReFocus: The Films of Barbara Kopple* (Edinburgh: Edinburgh University Press, 2019). Other examples include Douglas Kellner and Dan Streible, *Emile de Antonio: A Reader* (Minneapolis: University of Minnesota Press, 2000); P. J. O'Connell, *Robert Drew and the Development of Cinema Verite in America* (Carbondale: Southern Illinois University Press, 1992); Gary Edgerton, *Ken Burns' America* (New York: Palgrave, 2001); Jonathan Vogels, *The Direct Cinema of David and Albert Maysles* (Carbondale: Southern Illinois University Press, 2005); Matthew H. Bernstein, ed., *Michael Moore: Filmmaker, Newsmaker, Cultural Icon* (Ann Arbor: University of Michigan Press, 2010); Keith Beattie, *D.A. Pennebaker* (Urbana: University of Illinois Press, 2011).

[6] *Los Angeles Documentary and the Production of Public History, 1958–1977*, is a notable exception to this rule. The author explicitly shows the connections and the movement back and forth between television documentaries and alternate documentaries. Joshua Glick, *Los Angeles Documentary and the Production of Public History, 1958–1977* (Berkeley: University of California Press, 2018).

[7] Tino Balio, ed., *Hollywood in the Age of Television* (Boston: Unwin Hyman, 1990); Paul McDonald and Janet Wasko, eds., *The Contemporary Hollywood Film Industry* (Hoboken, NJ: Wiley-Blackwell, 2008); Marc Leverette, Brian L. Ott, and Cara Louise Buckley, eds., *It's Not TV: Watching HBO in the Post-television Era* (New York: Routledge, 2008); Gary R. Edgerton and Jeffrey P. Jones, eds., *The Essential HBO Reader* (Lexington: University Press of Kentucky, 2008); Travis Vogan, "ESPN Films and the Construction of Prestige in Contemporary Sports Television," *International Journal of Sport Communication* 5, no. 2 (June 2012), 137–52, https://doi.org/10.1123/ijsc.5.2.137; Yannis Tzioumakis, *Hollywood's Indies: Classics Divisions, Specialty Labels, and American Independent Cinema* (Edinburgh: Edinburgh University Press, 2012); Alisa Perren, *Indie, Inc.: Miramax and the Transformation of Hollywood in the 1990s* (Austin: University of Texas Press, 2012); Dina Iordanova, "The Film Festival as an Industry Node," *Media Industries Journal* 1, no. 3 (January 1, 2015), https://doi.org/10.3998/mij.15031809.0001.302; Amanda Lotz, *We Now Disrupt This Broadcast: How Cable Transformed Television and the Internet Revolutionized It All* (Cambridge, MA: MIT Press, 2018);

In this book, I foreground distribution and circulation as the locus of meaning and value for documentaries. Centering distribution means attending to business strategy and changing delivery technology, as well as interrogating how commodity and public service value are invoked in different contexts. A number of texts published in the last fifteen years have attended to emerging distribution methods in the media industry, especially those that blur the boundaries between film and television. In *Reinventing Cinema: Movies in the Age of Media Convergence*, Chuck Tryon compares different services and practices of circulation in the digital era.[8] Like Tryon, I attend to the interplay between circulation practices and the discourse surrounding a text, but I narrow my scope to one specific genre. Julia Knight and Peter Thomas's *Reaching Audiences: Distribution and Promotion of Alternative Moving Image* shows how changes in public policy and technology affected alternative film distribution in the United Kingdom.[9] The essays in Derek Johnson's *From Networks to Netflix: A Guide to Changing Channels* detail television and video streaming services' programming and branding strategies. This book is in conversation with the above by cutting across individual channels and services to show how documentary films have been used across the media landscape.[10]

The growing commercialization of documentary film has not gone unnoticed, but it has not been sufficiently explained. Journalistic accounts of documentary's rise usually offer one or two causes—Netflix streaming and growing interest in reality TV and other stories about the real world. But these accounts, published consistently over the past twenty years whenever a documentary enters the cultural conversation or breaks a box-office record, do not grapple with the overlapping causal mechanisms that have commercialized documentary film. Nor do they offer meaningful periodization of the commercialization of documentary film, only a snapshot from an endless march of progress. I refine these rough accounts through a robust synoptic history of the market for documentary films, using knowledge of film

---

Patricia Aufderheide, "Documentary Filmmaking and US Public TV's Independent Television Service, 1989–2017," *Journal of Film and Video* 71, no. 4 (2021), 3–14.

[8] Chuck Tryon, *Reinventing Cinema: Movies in the Age of Media Convergence* (Piscataway, NJ: Rutgers University Press, 2009).

[9] Julia Knight and Peter Thomas, *Reaching Audiences: Distribution and Promotion of Alternative Moving Image* (Bristol: Intellect, 2011).

[10] Derek Johnson, ed., *From Networks to Netflix: A Guide to Changing Channels* (London: Routledge, 2018).

economics and the norms of industry discourse to tell a richer story. This periodization will allow scholars to compare the commercialization of documentary film with other genres. It adds reference points to a complex history of change.

Moving chronologically, each chapter engages with a few significant elements of the documentary film ecosystem, including theatrical distribution, public television, cable television, film festivals, nonprofit and governmental granting agencies, home video, and video streaming services. Using individual films' distribution histories as case studies, I analyze how these elements affected the commercialization of documentary film.

Chapter 1 covers 1960 to 1977, a time when the commercial possibilities for documentary film were being redefined. Television networks funded the production of documentaries, but Direct Cinema documentarian Robert Drew and his associates had ambitions beyond the scope of broadcast and the limits of journalism. They looked for a new context and new audiences for their work, and found it at film festivals, in experimental film culture, and, marginally, within the art-house film market. More successful on the art-house circuit were touristic documentaries like *Mondo Cane* (1963), which were marketed like the foreign films that dominated the art-house box office. Direct Cinema filmmakers finally hit upon a winning formula by making documentaries about popular music and youth culture, like *Dont Look Back* (1967) and *The Endless Summer* (1966). Simultaneously, politically committed filmmakers sought to circumvent the existing commercial infrastructure by creating their own collectives for producing and distributing alternative documentaries.

In Chapters 2 and 3, I contend with the two infrastructural anchors that increased the commercial value and cultural currency of documentary film in the 1980s: the rise and solidification of the American indie film movement and the maturation of the national Public Broadcasting Service. Chapter 2 explores how American independent film culture and institutions led to greater support for documentary film. New independent distribution companies and studio classics divisions acquired documentary films, particularly those with a music or performance element, like *Say Amen Somebody* (1982) and *Stop Making Sense* (1984). At the same time, documentarians extended the DIY practices of political filmmaking collectives by self-distributing their films, like *Word Is Out* (1978) *The War at Home* (1979), and *The Atomic Cafe* (1982). Chapter 3 traces how documentary filmmakers lobbied for access to PBS funding and airtime. While

PBS had some mechanisms for supporting documentary production, independent filmmakers used the community and institutions formed through the American indie cinema movement to fight for more. The result was funding through the Independent Television Service and regular airtime through *P.O.V.*, both of which persist to this day.

Chapter 4 covers the 1990s, a period in which some documentaries, including *Paris Is Burning* (1991) and *When We Were Kings* (1996), earned higher grosses at the box office. But this escalation in commercial value led to a widening gap between powerful distribution companies that occasionally picked up documentaries and smaller distributors that distributed the majority of documentary films. The increasing commercial prospects also brought the conflict over documentary films as cinema or television to a head. The Academy of Motion Picture Arts and Sciences tried to enshrine the distinction with a rule change, decreeing that documentary films must have a regular theatrical release in order to qualify for Academy Awards nominations. This led to HBO shifting its strategy surrounding documentary films.

Chapter 5 details the "docbuster" era, a time of heightened visibility and popularity for documentary films. The years 2000 to 2007 saw a higher concentration of documentaries succeeding in theaters than ever before, with standouts like *Fahrenheit 9/11* (2004), *March of the Penguins* (2005), and *Capturing the Friedmans* (2003). At the same time, the growth of the DVD market provided a new ancillary market for documentary films, and more cable television channels began funding the production of documentaries. While film festivals are often seen as a haven from the hypercommercial concerns of Hollywood, major film festivals became more imbricated with the industry than ever during this time.

The trend toward commercialization in the docbuster years intensified in the streaming era. Chapter 6 covers the contemporary moment, beginning in 2008. That year Netflix founded its streaming service and made documentary films a key part of its brand identity. This chapter explores how Netflix's strategy around documentary shifted between 2008 and 2020. These shifts profoundly affected the documentary film industry—they drove production trends, caused filmmakers to adjust their mode of production, sent small theatrical distributors into a tailspin, and inspired numerous other streamers and portals to imitate Netflix's strategy. With more outlets eager to acquire documentaries, the risk of investment lowered substantially, and companies began large-scale private investing in documentary projects for the first time ever.

1
Direct Cinema Blossoms, but Little Support for Documentary Films in Theaters (1960 to 1977)

Salesman (1969, dirs. Albert Maysles, David Maysles, Charlotte Zwerin) is a groundbreaking observational documentary film about door-to-door Bible salesmen. The film captures the mundane lives of the salesmen, nicknamed the Badger, the Bull, the Gipper, and the Rabbit, as they attend a sales team meeting, live in threadbare motel rooms, and knock on doors to sell expensive, illustrated Bibles. Shot on low-contrast 16 mm film, the mobile camera offers sincere, unflinching attention to men delivering sales pitch after sales pitch. The possibility of failure hangs over every interaction with those who open their door to the salesmen, building up suspense in each scene.

Salesman is recognized as a masterpiece, a revolutionary Direct Cinema film that showed how affecting a slice of life of ordinary people can be. The film was selected for the National Film Registry of the Library of Congress and parodied on the series *Documentary Now!* But the circumstances of *Salesman*'s production and circulation did not predict the esteem and influence the film would come to hold. Instead, the Maysles produced *Salesman* independently, at a budget between $100,000 and $200,000. They then formed their own distribution company to release the film. They premiered *Salesman* in New York City in April 1969, with a benefit for Cesar Chavez's grape pickers union.[1] They also sneaked the film onto television stations in other areas, in an effort to boost box-office returns. *Salesman* garnered rave reviews and played at prestigious festivals, including Berlin, Venice, and Mannheim. But the film was "relatively unsuccessful in limited playoffs in New York and other major cities," according to *Variety*.[2] After about seven

---

[1] Kent E. Carroll, "Maysles Bros. Bible-Selling 'Salesman' Proves a Tough Sell for Producers," *Variety*, April 16, 1969, 7.
[2] "'Salesman' Rings Bell in Offbeat Playoff Dates," *Variety*, November 12, 1969, 38.

How Documentaries Went Mainstream. Nora Stone, Oxford University Press. © Oxford University Press 2023.
DOI: 10.1093/oso/9780197557297.003.0002

months, the Maysles sold *Salesman* to a nontheatrical distributor, National Talent Service. NTS listed the rental for a $500 guarantee, plus $50 of the gate. The first nine months of *Salesman*'s nontheatrical release earned $50,000, while likely bearing lower overhead costs than a theatrical release would have.

Salesman's release is emblematic of this period because the Maysles bought into the hopes for theatrical release of documentaries. But in the end, they sold the rights to *Salesman* to a nontheatrical distributor, tacitly acknowledging that the market did not yet support theatrical release of most documentary films.

The Fragmentary Market for Documentary Film

From 1960 to 1977 the commercial status of the feature documentary was radically redefined. Previously established types of documentaries, including newsreels and war documentaries, were essentially wiped out in the 1950s. US documentary production shifted almost completely to journalistic television. Some television documentarians, like Robert Drew and his associates, had larger ambitions. Their ideas and experiments exceeded the scope of broadcast and the limits of journalism, forcing them to find a new context and audience for their work. These Direct Cinema pioneers found such an audience at film festivals, in experimental film culture, and on the fringes of the art house market.

At the same time, one type of documentary film thrived in theaters: the touristic documentary. Films like *Mondo Cane* promised to shock and amaze viewers by showing exotic landscapes and lifestyles. Spectacle and titillation appealed to audiences, who bought tickets to see something they could not see on television. Direct Cinema documentaries also figured out a formula that attracted audiences: documentaries about popular music and youth culture. Film can capture musical performances with thrilling intimacy and aural fidelity, and in the 1960s and 1970s, documentarians harnessed this power in groundbreaking rockumentaries. To this day, documentaries about pop musicians, among other performers, are among the most commercially viable.

Although the trailblazing successes of films like *Dont Look Back* proved to be harbingers of future commercial strategies, they did little to address the distribution and exhibition challenges facing the numerous politically oriented documentary filmmakers whose public-service agenda did not aim to replicate the profit-driven model of circulation. Instead, such filmmakers experimented with various models of self- and collective distribution by focusing their energies on nontheatrical exhibition within college campuses and along activist circuits. Without the spectacle of foreign sights or musical performances, there was little opportunity to generate interest for audiences.

Documentary on Television: Clip Shows, Investigative Journalism, and Observational Documentary

World War II was a significant time for documentary film in America. Major Hollywood directors like John Ford, Frank Capra, and William Wyler made documentaries about the war for the federal government.[3] These and other documentary films were exhibited widely to American citizens and military personnel alike. In large cities, entire cinemas were devoted to showing newsreels and war-related nonfiction. But once the war was over, interest in documentaries shrank. At the same time, television began to broadcast news programs, which soon supplanted newsreels. The most highly regarded newsreel, *March of Time*, ceased production in 1951. And while schools and community organizations regularly rented nonfiction films, few documentaries were released theatrically.

The rapid spread of television and the growth of the television industry provided a substantial shift in the financing and exhibition of documentary media in the United States. Television became the center for nonfiction films. Throughout the 1950s, American television networks were reliable producers of news documentaries and nonfiction entertainment shows.[4] But these documentaries and documentary series were made exclusively for television, and they had little contact with other exhibition contexts or with film culture.

Though live television was highly regarded during the medium's first decade, American television networks soon sought to exercise more control and reap the financial rewards of syndication by producing prefilmed programs. Documentaries were a key part of that strategy. Television

---

[3] *The Battle of Midway* (1942, dir. John Ford), *Why We Fight* (seven films, made between 1942 and 1945, dirs. Frank Capra and Anatole Litvak), *Memphis Belle* (1944, dir. William Wyler).
[4] Michael Curtin, *Redeeming the Wasteland: Television Documentary and Cold War Politics* (New Brunswick, NJ: Rutgers University Press, 1995).

networks produced both hard-hitting journalistic shows like *See It Now!* and compilation-style documentaries about celebrities and history (*Victory at Sea* series [1952–53], *Project XX* [1954–62], *Air Power* [1956–57]). The typical journalistic documentary was anchored by a correspondent-host and covered a problem of national or international import. This correspondent introduced the episode's topic, interviewed experts, and presented actuality footage. Produced by the network news divisions, journalistic documentaries were loss leaders, winning over critics but struggling to find both sponsors and audiences. On the other hand, the lighter fare was quite popular. Vance Kepley points out, "An NBC survey of *Project XX*'s commercial performance over its first decade indicated that the specials often generated strong ratings comparable to those of entertainment rather than public service programming."[5] While documentaries are often seen as sober affairs—the opposite of commercial television—nonfiction television programming incorporated a variety of tones, styles, and rhetorical strategies as early as the 1950s.[6]

The networks' interest in documentary programming peaked in 1961 and 1962. Mounting criticism of quiz-show fixing and rampant commercialism led to threats of tighter regulations on the broadcasting industry. In order to maintain control, network heads met with Federal Communications Commission chairman John Doerfer as early as 1959.[7] Both parties preferred self-regulation of broadcast television to further government interference, so they made a plan to demonstrate the networks' willingness to correct course without new outside regulations. Under the Doerfer Plan, each network promised to air two hours of public service programming in prime time each week.[8] Documentary was the primary vehicle for these aims. This briefly opened up opportunities for more independently made nonfiction

---

[5] Vance Kepley Jr., "The Origins of NBC's Project XX in Compilation Documentaries," *Journalism Quarterly* 61, no. 1 (1984), 25.

[6] This strategy continued in the 1960s, when independent producer David Wolper made numerous nonfiction series for syndication (*Biography* [1962] and *The Story Of* [1962]) and for national network broadcast (*Hollywood: The Golden Years, Hollywood: The Fabulous Era, Hollywood: The Great Stars*, made for NBC). Contemporary critic William Bluem observed, "Wolper found that there were some documentaries which networks, too, would carry—so long as they could be classed as 'entertainment' documentaries and thus not conflict with the networks' direct supervision of their public-affairs programming." A. William Bluem, *Documentary in American Television: Form, Function, Method* (New York: Hastings House Publishers, 1965), 177. For more on Wolper's work and how it shaped public history, see Joshua Glick, *Los Angeles Documentary and the Production of Public History, 1958–1977* (Berkeley: University of California Press, 2018).

[7] Curtin, *Redeeming the Wasteland*.

[8] James Lewis Baughman, "ABC and the Destruction of American Television, 1953–1961," *Business and Economic History* 12 (1983), 62.

television, including the Drew Associates' Direct Cinema documentaries that purposefully defied the conventions of television journalism.

In the early 1950s, *Life* magazine correspondent Robert Drew was looking for a way to make the filmic equivalent of *Life*'s photojournalism. In 1954, Drew made a pilot for NBC for a nonfiction series called *Key Picture*, but the network was unable to find a sponsor for this program, a prototype of the visually driven documentaries he would later make. Later in the decade, Drew took a different tack and convinced Time, Inc. / *Life* magazine to fund his filmmaking endeavors. The idea was that his documentaries would promote *Life* magazine, as the newsreel series *The March of Time* had done for *Time* magazine. With backing from Time, Inc., Drew put together a crew that included Richard Leacock—who had worked with Robert Flaherty—as well as younger filmmakers D. A. Pennebaker, David and Albert Maysles, and Hope Ryden.

Drew had limited success with his first documentaries. His early short efforts played on popular network television shows: *Zero Gravity* (1958) ran as a segment on the *Ed Sullivan Show* and on CBS News. *Bullfight at Malaga* (1958) was supposed to be a special on ABC, but because ABC affiliates worried about the violence toward an animal, a shortened version ran as a segment on the *Tonight Show* on NBC. None of the early Drew programs gained much attention or critical acclaim; it seemed Drew's idea for candid film journalism might die on the vine. Drew Associates continued to make films with production financing from Time, Inc., but finding a consistent distribution and exhibition channel proved much more difficult. Even *Primary* (1960), the Direct Cinema classic that follows John F. Kennedy and Hubert Humphrey as they battle for Wisconsin in the Democratic primary, passed without support from the networks or notice from critics. While it is now considered a landmark documentary, none of the three national networks broadcast the film. Instead, a few stations owned by Time-Life and RKO-General, as well as some independent stations, broadcast the film in major cities.

Despite the paltry showing of *Primary*, Drew had better luck selling his next ideas to the networks for national broadcast. Drew produced *On the Pole* (1960) as a sports special for CBS. Then ABC hired Drew Associates to make episodes of its documentary series *Close-Up!* Because its news department was understaffed and lacked a well-known correspondent to host its series, ABC turned to outside producer Drew to supply episodes for *Close-Up!* This decision incensed the head of ABC's news department, who thought it wrong to surrender editorial control to an outside producer. Here the question about what Drew was making came into sharp relief: were the films journalism, or were they something else? Drew trained as a journalist at *Life* magazine and in the Nieman Fellowship at Harvard University, but he and his associates worked independently of the networks' news divisions. They purposefully defied the conventions of network news documentaries, like reporters' voice-over narration and interviews with experts, by employing an observational style. Yet they relied on the television networks to broadcast their work. This struggle for independence and access to the airwaves would continue, even after Drew Associates dissolved.

Soon the early members of Drew Associates broke off to form their own production entities. Many figures now celebrated as indisputably innovative pioneers of Direct Cinema continued in vain to try to work with networks. Ricky Leacock and Joyce Chopra made *Happy Mother's Day* in 1963, for ABC. However, sponsors rejected it, and the network reedited it before air. Granada TV, a British television production company, commissioned David and Albert Maysles to make *What's Happening: The Beatles in the USA*. When Granada licensed it to CBS, the network edited it and added narration by Carol Burnett. Later in the decade, D. A. Pennebaker and Ricky Leacock made *Monterey Pop* with backing from ABC. However, the network decided not to air it, so the filmmakers bought the rights from the network and distributed it through their theatrical distribution company. Though Direct Cinema pioneers were consistently frustrated by their dealings with American television networks, by the end of the 1960s, the former Drew Associates would forge the theatrical market for documentaries.

Feature Documentaries and Film Culture

Certain organizations and cultural movements set the stage for documentaries to grow in status and interest in the 1960s. Cinema 16, a film society based in New York, fostered cinephilia in the postwar years. Increased interest in foreign films swelled the number of distributors handling alternative films and screens exhibiting them. Finally, a number of American filmmakers, including former Drew Associates and critics, formed a community that would welcome the documentarians working in the next decade.

Cinema 16 was an important legitimizing outlet for documentaries, programming and exhibiting them alongside the most prestigious cinematic fare. Incorporated in 1947, this nontheatrical club's regular series and special programs created an eclectic context where documentaries were shown alongside classic, foreign, and experimental works. Cinema 16 also sent out programs of work to film societies (distribution began in 1948). Though it is better remembered for circulating avant-garde films and fostering cinephilia around classic Hollywood studio films during the 1950s, documentaries were central to its mission. In addition, Robert Flaherty, the father of American documentary film, helped with the club's initial membership drive. Some Cinema 16 programs were all documentaries, such as the June 1950 program "Film and Reality," described in the program notes as "A history of the documentary film as shown in the works of Sergei Eisenstein, John Grierson, Andre Gide, Jean Vigo, Robert Flaherty, Jean Painleve, Pare Lorentz, Louis de Rochemont, and accompanied by an authoritative commentary. Selected by Alberto Cavalcanti (*Dead of Night*)."[9] Cinema 16 also showed individual contemporary documentaries, like *The Quiet One* (1948, dir. Sidney Meyers), shown 1952–53, and *All My Babies* (1953, dir. George Stoney) shown in early 1953. In May 1953, "A Program of Restricted Nazi Propaganda Films," with special permission from the Department of Justice, played *The Triumph of the Will* (1935, dir. Leni Riefenstahl). Cinema 16 programmed a wide range of documentaries, ranging from the darkest uses of documentary—Nazi propaganda—to the newest documentaries, both experimental and educational. In so doing, the club promoted the idea that documentaries were worthy of inclusion in film culture.

The fate of documentary film in the United States—as well as the fate of Cinema 16—was linked to the success of imported foreign films. The foreign film market boomed following the war; 1950 to 1966 was the commercial heyday of foreign films in America.[10] Independent companies, including Embassy, Continental, Films of the World, and Times Film, had been importing foreign films since 1946, bringing Italian neorealist films, British New Wave films, and the films of Ingmar Bergman to art house audiences in the United States. By 1957, the market had grown so much that the major studios entered, throwing their weight behind promising European auteurs with production financing deals. At the same time, the venues for showing

---

[9] Program Notes, Spring 1950, in Scott MacDonald, *Cinema 16: Documents toward a History of the Film Society* (Philadelphia: Temple University Press, 2002), 141–43.

[10] Tino Balio, *The Foreign Film Renaissance on American Screens, 1946–1973* (Madison: University of Wisconsin Press, 2010).

foreign films grew greatly in number. By 1962, there were at least forty art houses in Manhattan alone.

The boom in foreign films demonstrated the commercial potential of an untapped market. As a result, revival houses opened, expanding the art house market and displacing cine-clubs like Cinema 16. There were three revival houses in Manhattan in 1961 and eleven by 1971.[11] James Kreul points out that "Cinema 16's demise was not precipitated by the creation of the Film-Makers' Cooperative, but by the development of commercial revival houses such as [Lionel] Rogosin's Bleecker Street Cinema and [Daniel] Talbot's New Yorker Theatre."[12] These revival houses took over the function of Cinema 16, including showing documentary features on occasion. In addition, the people who ran them and other art houses also founded distribution companies that helped stimulate the market for documentary films.

At the same time that art house exhibitors expanded the number of venues in which documentaries could play, a new independent film movement was growing—creating a new context for documentary films. In response to the widespread interest in and admiration of foreign films in the United States, American filmmakers and critics felt a need to promote an alternative to the films associated with the Hollywood studio system. In 1960, several independent filmmakers wrote and signed a manifesto: the Statement of the New American Cinema. These were mainly narrative and avant-garde filmmakers, but documentarians Emile de Antonio and Shirley Clarke were part of the group as well. The New American Cinema movement, nourished by journals like *Film Culture* and the first New York Film Festival in 1963, helped incubate American cinephilia and provided a structure through which new independent filmmakers could gain guidance and exposure. These institutions and conditions paved the way for documentary cinema to thrive in various arenas during the 1960s and 1970s.

While the Direct Cinema documentarians struggled to gain more than a toehold in network television, film critics and cinephiles showed great interest in their work. This recognition helped their films move beyond the commercial world into the cinephilic cultural marketplace, where influential "buffs" praised them and proselytized for their methods. It was, in part, this recognition that aided Robert Drew's associates and protégés to realize that

---

[11] Balio, *Foreign Film Renaissance*, 247–48.
[12] James Kreul, "New York, New Cinema: The Independent Film Community and the Underground Crossover, 1950–1970" (PhD dissertation, University of Wisconsin–Madison, 2004), 220.

their work need not be restricted by network television expectations, that they could gain ground in theaters or at least among college crowds. Though the Direct Cinema filmmakers were not signatories of the First Statement of the New American Cinema or members of the Film-Maker's Cooperative, cinephiles' admiration brought them into contact with the independent and avant-garde filmmakers who were establishing their own institutions. The risks taken by their enterprising peers undoubtedly set an example for those Direct Cinema filmmakers who would self-finance their documentaries and found their own distribution companies later in the decade. It added a huge amount of prestige as well, drawing the documentarians away from the lucrative, controlled, unfashionable network TV market and toward the hipper film festival and campus crowds.

In the summer 1961 issue of *Film Culture*, the editors announced that the makers of *Primary*—Ricky Leacock, Don Pennebaker, Robert Drew, and Albert Maysles—had won the Third Independent Film Award. The editors (perhaps primarily Jonas Mekas) praised the film, as well as *Yanki No!* (1960), in glowing terms, calling it "a revolutionary step and a breaking point in the recording of reality in cinema."[13] They suggest that fiction filmmakers should take cues from Direct Cinema's techniques, and compare the filmmakers' accomplishments with those of past winners: "*Shadows* and *Pull My Daisy* have indicated new cinematic approaches stylistically and formally. *Primary* goes one step further: by exploring new camera, sound and lighting methods, it enables the filmmaker to pierce deeper into the area of new content as well."[14] This appreciation was prescient—later critics would admire Direct Cinema–style documentaries for the same reasons, both their innovative style and techniques, and the way that these techniques transformed the subject matter. By embedding with the subjects—folk singers, mental health institutions, youth gangs—these documentaries would take on more searing urgency, dovetailing with the politically volatile atmosphere.

Film festivals also put Direct Cinema filmmakers in closer contact with the thriving film culture of the New American Cinema movement. Drew Associates' *Crisis: Behind a Presidential Commitment* and *The Chair* screened at the first New York Film Festival, before being broadcast on television.[15] Other documentaries that played the first NYFF were picked up

---

[13] "Third Independent Film Award," *Film Culture* 22–23 (Summer 1961), 11.
[14] "Third Independent Film Award," 11.
[15] ABC broadcast *Crisis: Behind a Presidential Commitment* a month after the NYFF, in October 1963.

by distributors for successful theatrical runs, including Emile de Antonio's first documentary, *Point of Order*. After a short run via self-distribution in early 1964, foreign film importer Walter Reade-Sterling / Continental picked up *Point of Order*, made in conjunction with Dan Talbot of the New Yorker Theater and New Yorker Films. The surprise success of *Point of Order*, which is composed exclusively of black-and-white kinescopes of television footage of the 1954 Army-McCarthy hearings, likely burnished the theatrical potential of Direct Cinema documentaries, for both their makers and potential distribution companies.

In August 1964, the Venice Documentary Film Festival showed both *Crisis* and a short film Drew produced about Kennedy's funeral, *Faces of November*. In August 1964, closer to home, the Gallery of Modern Art in New York highlighted the Direct Cinema movement with a three-week series of films and a symposium. The museum established its "center for the viewing, study and encouragement of new movements in films" in July 1964; the Direct Cinema film series was its first program.[16] The series included *Primary, Showman, Lonely Boy, The Chair, David, Happy Mother's Day, Georg,* and *The Quarters of Paris*, all of which, it was advertised, had not yet been released commercially in the United States. It is significant that an art museum, founded by an heir to the A & P grocery fortune, would host such a celebration of this new style of documentary. Organized by James McBride, who would later play on cinéma vérité conventions in his directorial debut, the faux documentary *David Holtzman's Diary*, the symposium hosted participants Richard Leacock, Jonas Mekas, James Lipscomb (a correspondent for Drew Associates), and Stanley Kaye (director of *Georg*).

Direct Cinema documentaries moved in and out of exhibition sites, from festival to TV to museum series. The struggles with television networks never ceased. When Time, Inc. terminated its contract with Drew Associates, after failing to find an outlet for *The Living Camera*, Drew came to understand that television networks would never welcome his independently produced film journalism.[17] The Drew Associates disbanded.

---

[16] "Gallery of Modern Art to Establish Film Center," *New York Times*, July 23, 1964, 18. The next spring, in April 1965, the Gallery of Modern Art began daily showings of rare and classic films, including an unedited version of *Un Chien Andalou*, films by Jean Epstein and Dimitri Kirsanoff, and a retrospective on Hal Roach. Bosley Crowther, "Modern Art Gallery Sets Daily Showing of Classic Movies," *New York Times*, April 19, 1965, 34. Further film programs included series of films by Busby Berkeley, Arthur Freed, Mervyn LeRoy, Stan Brakhage, and, later, sports documentaries and the Kennedy films made for TV by David Wolper.

[17] As Drew explains, "Critically, the films were winning all kinds of awards and so forth. Breaking new ground. But the reason we made them was to try to establish a form of reporting which would

A few years later, in 1967, the NYFF programmed a significant series of American and Canadian documentary films. This was the first major documentary feature exhibition at the NYFF, and it garnered attention from audiences and critics alike. The success of this series helped a new era of potent social issue documentaries enter the cultural marketplace. It also represented a break with documentaries made earlier in the decade, when American television networks appeared to be a viable source of production financing and airtime. None of the documentaries at the NYFF were supported or had been broadcast by the networks; all were made independently, or under the aegis of the Canadian Broadcasting Corporation or National Educational Television, the precursor to the Public Broadcasting Service.

The NYFF had a major success with American feature documentaries. A Social Cinema in America series was separate from the main program, but by highlighting these documentaries and hosting panels with many of the filmmakers, the NYFF helped to create a recognizable context for them.[18] In the runup to the festival, the *New York Times* dedicated column space to the series. Vincent Canby lavished praise on the films, describing their innovative nature. He wrote, "A preview of the program selections here yesterday revealed that socially and politically committed filmmakers are not only continuing to work with themes that most fiction filmmakers eschew, but that they are also working with an extraordinary new technical freedom permitted by the development of highly sensitive film, light-weight cameras and sound equipment. In all of the most effective films, the real-life characters speak for themselves. The day of the portentous voiceover narration is over."[19]

---

pull audiences and pay for itself. So when Time, Inc failed to sell them and the contract went out, then that was the death of that idea—of trying that idea out. And the films were left—God, they were left to half-assed syndication and half-assed promotion and it was kind of a massacre." "The Reminiscences of Robert Drew." Seven interviews by Barbara Hogenson, October 4, 1979–April 23, 1980 (Oral History Research Office, Butler Library, Columbia University, New York, Mimeographed). Quoted in P. J. O'Connell, *Robert Drew and the Development of Cinema Verité in America* (Carbondale: Southern Illinois University Press), 165.

[18] The films played in the Museum and Library of the Performing Arts, rather than in Philharmonic Hall. Tickets were free. Vincent Canby, "Films of Social Commitment Are Added to Festival," *New York Times*, September 7, 1967, 51.

[19] A number of the films dealt with the political and social questions of the day in a markedly more visceral and hard-hitting way than the journalistic television documentaries of the day. There were films about mental health and the elderly: *Titicut Follies* (dir. Frederick Wiseman), *Warrendale* (dir. Allan King), *Home For Life* (dirs. Gordon Quinn and Gerald Temaner). Others depicted turmoil within the civil rights movement and the problems faced by rural African Americans: *Black Natchez* (dirs. Ed Pincus and David Neuman), *Now* (dir. Santiago Alvarez Roman), *Lay My Burden Down* (dir. Jack Willis), *Malcolm X* (dir. Lee Bethune). Still others analyzed the Vietnam War and antiwar movement: *Sons and Daughters* (dir. Jerry Stoll), *Mills of the Gods* (dir. Beryl Fox), *While Brave Men*

Simply programming the series and pulling together related panels would have been a major step toward establishing a new era in documentary, but reports on audience response raised expectations about the commercial possibilities for socially conscious documentaries. The Social Cinema in America programs were so popular that they "were causing near-riots," according to the *New York Times*.[20] *Variety* reported, "Biggest turnaway crowds were for the Social Cinema series, with 400 being sent home ticketless for the second of two showings of the Canadian doc 'Warrendale,' and about 200 for 'The Titicut Follies' (there might have been more but for the driving rain at the time), and a smaller number for a program of civil rights films ('Black Natchez,' 'Now,' 'Malcolm X')."[21]

Though only a handful of the Social Cinema documentaries went into theatrical release—*Titicut Follies* and *Warrendale*—the series recognized and raised the profile of a significant strain of documentary filmmaking.

Documentaries in Theaters

Shocks of Tourism: Foreign Film Importers and Documentary

At the very moment when Direct Cinema pioneers were struggling for support from broadcast television, foreign film importers were struggling to meet demand. The growing number of independent art house theaters needed product, but there was a diminishing supply of foreign films.[22] So foreign film importers tried something new: distributing documentaries about

---

Die (dirs. Donald C. Bruce and Fulton Lewis III), *The Unique War* (Armed Forces Information Film), *Victory Will Be Ours* (French documentary, other information unknown), *Napalm*. Religion was another subject: *Every Seventh Child* (dir. Jack Willis), *The Holy Ghost People* (dir. Peter Adair). Canby, "Films of Social Commitment," 51.

[20] Vincent Canby, "Film Festival Drawing Diverse Buffs," *New York Times*, September 28, 1967, 58.
[21] The State of Massachusetts attempted to have *Titicut Follies* banned during the festival, a controversy that led to more publicity about and interest in the film. A bomb threat was also called in during the civil rights film program. "Bay State in Move to Bar Prison Film," *New York Times*, September 27, 1967, 42. "Bomb Scares & Debates at Side Events; Demand High for 'Titicut' Pic," *Variety*, October 4, 1967, 15, 18.
[22] Harold Myers stated, "With a couple of notable exceptions, all the highly rated entries had been pre-sold, leaving the indies with little to choose from, other than the pix being screened outside the fest in the trade fair." Harold Myers, "Yank Indies at Cannes Find Pix Mostly Presold," *Variety*, May 23, 1962, 7.

foreign people, places, and cultures using the same marketing strategies as foreign fiction films. Touristic documentaries are designed to shock and amaze audiences, by reveling in exotic landscape, lifestyles, and customs. They do this through the "tourist gaze," a rhetorical framing that foregrounds the cultural, geographical, and physical distance between the documentary subjects and the spectators.[23] Examples include *The Sky above, the Mud Below* (1962, dir. Pierre-Dominique Gaisseau), about a tribe in the jungle of Dutch New Guinea, and *Women of the World* (1963, dirs. Gualtiero Jacopetti, Franco Prosperi, Paolo Cavara), "a colorful, adult travel documentary of people rather than places," both distributed by major importer Embassy Pictures.[24] *European Nights* (1959, dir. Alessandro Blasetti), a performance documentary featuring nightclub acts from several European cities, was first reviewed by *Variety* in Rome in 1959, but only picked up for North American distribution by Burstyn Releasing in 1963, once the supply of foreign films had contracted.

But the most significant, commercially and culturally, was Italian documentary *Mondo Cane* (1963, dir. Gualtiero Jacopetti). *Mondo Cane* played three thousand dates and grossed over $1 million in its first year in release.[25] In the competitive New York City market, it was held over at the Forum for fifteen weeks and at the Little Carnegie for fifteen weeks.[26] The original soundtrack was a best-selling album, and a number of artists recorded versions of the film's theme song, "More." The theme song was nominated for an Academy Award for Best Music (Song). Later, TV stations licensed the film. *Mondo Cane* was so ubiquitous that it brought a new word into the lexicon: "mondo" came to connote any touristic exploitation film.[27]

Times Film Corp. marketed *Mondo Cane* as a titillating film full of spectacle. It also used music and the film's English-language voice-over to market the film. *Mondo Cane* seems exploitative and retrograde to modern

---

[23] Ellen Strain, *Public Places, Private Journeys: Ethnography, Entertainment, and the Tourist Gaze* (Piscataway, NJ: Rutgers University Press, 2003), 16.
[24] *The Sky above, the Mud Below* won the Academy Award for Best Documentary in 1962. Hawk, "Review: La Donna Nel Mondo (*The Women of the World*)," *Variety*, February 27, 1963, 7. Embassy acquired *Women of the World* for $75,000. For a comparison in price between nonfiction and fiction foreign features: in the same year, Embassy bought the American rights to Fellini's *8 1/2* for $400,000. "Embassy's Handle of Product for 1963 Rises to 42, with Reissues," *Variety*, March 13, 1963, 13.
[25] "Times Has 6 for 1964; Sochin Named VP," *Boxoffice*, April 20, 1964, 12.
[26] "Music a Plus for *Mondo Cane*," *Variety*, September 11, 1963, 20.
[27] *Mondo Cane* spawned sequels, as well as other touristic documentaries made by Jacopetti and his associates. See *Africa Addio* (1966, dirs. Gualtiero Jacopetti, Franco Prosperi), *The Wild Eye* (1967, dir. Paolo Cavara).

eyes, but at the time, its content and tone were fun and risqué, unlike the prosaic, didactic documentaries on TV. Times Film Corp. emphasized this aspect of the film in its marketing. The film's posters proclaimed the titillation and novelty on offer: "Overpowering, fascinating—often shocking!" and "Enter a hundred incredible worlds where the camera has never gone before!"

Trade advertisements, too, alluded to the unusual, taboo sites contained within the film. A full-page ad in *Variety*, a few weeks after the film's premiere, touted its record-breaking box office and used a blurb from Bosley Crowther's review that called *Mondo Cane* an "extraordinarily candid factual film."[28] Scrupulous to avoid using the word "documentary," the ad uses instead the term "candid" as a code word for taboo material, notably nudity, which one could not see on television documentaries. This association between *Mondo Cane* and taboo material corresponds to a certain view of foreign films at the time—both foreign film importers and those who opposed their incursion into American theaters nurtured the idea that foreign films were sexually frank and dealt with mature themes. Each side played on this for its own purposes—either to draw audiences to theaters, or to call for censorship and boycott—so this rhetoric was available for the distributor and exhibitors of *Mondo Cane* as well. It certainly fits in with the wider art-film market, as outlined by Barbara Wilinsky, who writes, "This focus on realistic (or adult) themes and subjects (including sexuality) reflects the art films' shift from a focus on the mass audience to a concentration on the more selective (and select) adult audience."[29] Although *Mondo Cane* was clearly a documentary, its distribution resembled that of the provocative foreign fiction film.

As foreign films became scarcer, foreign film importers acquired touristic, exploitation-adjacent documentaries, and art house theaters had unexpected success exhibiting them. Though these films do not fulfill the educational or public-service brief generally associated with documentaries, they were highly visible in theaters at a time when very few documentary films were released theatrically.

---

[28] Ad for *Mondo Cane*, *Variety*, April 24, 1963, 19.
[29] Barbara Wilinsky, *Sure Seaters: The Emergence of Art House Cinema* (Minneapolis: University of Minnesota Press, 2000), 24.

Great-Man History Flops at the Box Office

Hollywood studios' involvement in the documentary feature market also echoed its incursions into the foreign-film market. Witnessing the success that foreign-film importers had in bringing foreign films to American theaters, by the late 1950s, major Hollywood studios began to acquire foreign films and cofinance some foreign productions. Balio points out, "By 1966 the majors dominated the market, having absorbed nearly the entire pantheon of European auteurs with sweet deals offering total production financing, directorial freedom, and marketing muscle."[30] The majors tried releasing some feature documentaries as well, but this experiment was less successful. In 1964, the Hollywood studios once known as the "Little Three," Universal, Columbia, and United Artists, released a spate of documentaries. While Columbia and United Artists acquired their documentaries, Universal did something more unusual: it provided production financing for a documentary. Universal financed the making of *The Guns of August* as part of its New Horizons division, which was meant to develop young talent by providing small budgets for filmmakers who could eventually move into making regular features.[31] Columbia released *The Finest Hours*, a documentary on Winston Churchill, to acclaim from some critics, but disappointment at the box office. While *The Finest Hours* merely resembled television documentaries, the film that United Artists acquired was actually made for television: *Four Days in November*. Produced by major television producer David Wolper, the film covers the assassination of John F. Kennedy. The topic likely appeared to have enough wide appeal to justify a theatrical release, but exhibitors and audiences disagreed: it had only two hundred engagements in its first seven months in release. As the *Variety* report explained, a hit film plays fifteen thousand engagements, and the average film eight thousand: "Admittedly, a documentary takes longer to play off, but 200 dates in seven months is considered ridiculous."[32]

In essence, these studios tried to release TV-style documentaries in theaters, but their efforts were not rewarded. When *Variety* covered these failed attempts in 1965, a studio executive told the reporter, "It just isn't worth the cost of launching them. . . . And you can't blame exhibitors for not booking them when they have a chance to play a *Goldfinger*, *What's*

---

[30] Balio, *Foreign Film Renaissance*, 227.
[31] The division financed three films before ceasing operation. The other films are *Daffy* and *Andy*.
[32] "Dirty Word—'Documentary,'" *Variety*, July 7, 1965, 5.

New Pussycat?, or *Cat Ballou*, instead."[33] Though Hollywood studios had the resources to pour into marketing campaigns, they were practiced at releasing films with wide appeal. Their distribution arms were not geared toward cultivating an audience for individual films the way that independent importers and distribution companies were.

A Banner Year for Documentary: 1967

The year 1967 marked a breakthrough for the market in documentary features. Two self-financed documentaries on youth-focused topics reached high box-office grosses: *The Endless Summer* (1966, dir. Bruce Brown) and *Dont Look Back* (1967, dir. D. A. Pennebaker). Both released by independent distribution companies, the films' success set the terms for the future of documentary distribution—with the right subject matter and skillful handling, documentary films could be commercially viable. While documentaries were often seen as serious and educational, these two films were commercial because of their light subjects. *The Endless Summer* follows two surfers as they travel the world, searching for "the perfect wave." It shows thrilling feats of surfing in exotic locations, so *Endless Summer* delivers touristic attractions like *Mondo Cane*. It also tapped into the current surfing and surf music craze. *Dont Look Back* follows Bob Dylan on his 1965 tour of England. It features Dylan performing on stage at Royal Albert Hall and singing in casual settings with fellow musicians Joan Baez and Donovan. An early observational documentary, *Dont Look Back* is notable for its look behind the scenes at fame. The combination of musical performances and a candid celebrity subject was very appealing.

The Endless Summer was first released via a four-wall arrangement at New York's Kip's Bay Theater in summer 1966. Four-walling means the producers paid to rent the theater and kept all receipts, rather than splitting them with the theater owner. After four weeks there, Cinema V snagged the rights to what trade journals were calling a sleeper hit. Like distributors of other touristic documentaries, Cinema V was founded as a foreign film importer. Because Cinema V unfurled it slowly across the country, *The Endless Summer* had most of its payoff during 1967. It was one of *Variety*'s "Big Rental Films of 1967," earning $2.1 million by the close of the year.[34]

---

[33] "Dirty Word," 5.
[34] "Big Rental Films of 1967," *Variety*, January 3, 1968, 25.

Alongside this phenomenon was *Dont Look Back*. Richard Leacock and D. A. Pennebaker self-financed *Dont Look Back* for $40,000 and formed their own distribution company, Leacock-Pennebaker, to distribute it. When it premiered in May 1967 at the Presidio, a San Francisco art house with 788 seats, no one expected a black-and-white documentary about a folk musician, distributed by a new, independent company, to make waves. However, as *Variety* reported breathlessly, "It immediately matched the hard-ticket *Thoroughly Modern Millie*, which opened the same week at the 1381-seat Orpheum, as the largest grossing picture in town."[35] Not only did *Dont Look Back* do well for a documentary, or any independent film, it kept pace with a lavish studio picture that premiered in a larger theater. In its first weeks, it was "blazing," breaking house records at the Presidio with a gross of $24,000.[36] It opened in New York City in September 1967 and had a repeat performance there. *Variety* reported, "Other newie, *Don't Look Back*, had a fantastic $23,000 initialer at the small 34th Street East; this is a house record except for the first few weeks of the recent *Dirty Dozen* engagement at this artie."[37] *Boxoffice* cited these two films as the start of a trend, writing, "More and more independent releases like this film and *The Endless Summer* are proving box-office attractions."[38] Interestingly, *Boxoffice* highlighted the films' industrial status—"independent"—rather than their mode—documentary.

When *Dont Look Back* started breaking records at the box office, journalists were shocked—high grosses for an independent documentary took them by surprise. The reviewer for *Variety* affirmed that "The Times They Are A-Changin'" "when documentaries about [a poetic folk singer] fill a movie house and gross $42,000 in two weeks."[39] Like many, the reviewer was surprised by *Dont Look Back*'s grosses and saw in them a shift in moviegoing. The idea of a documentary being popular and profitable, especially a black-and-white one shot in 16 mm and distributed independently by the producer's own company, was new. Apart from stylistic innovations and industrial factors, the subject and treatment of *Dont Look Back* was not so unconventional. Just a few years before, *A Hard Day's Night* (1964, dir. Richard

[35] Rick., "Review: *Don't Look Back*," *Variety*, June 14, 1967, 7.
[36] "Picture Grosses: 'Honey Pot' $8,000, Frisco; 'Cross' Crisp 22G; 'Dylan' Hep 24G," *Variety*, May 31, 1967, 9–10.
[37] "Picture Grosses: Post-holiday Blue Nip B'way; 'Emily' Nice $28,000, 'Don't Look' Mighty 23G, 'Clyde' Giant 69G, 4th, 'Night' Hot 80G," *Variety*, September 13, 1967, 11.
[38] "'Don't Look Back,' 'Bonnie, Clyde' Surprise with Big Grosses in NY," *Boxoffice*, September 18, 1967, E-2.
[39] Rick., "Review: *Don't Look Back*," 7.

Lester), a scripted film in which the members of the Beatles play themselves on tour, was one of the biggest hits of the year. Both films were essentially presold properties with built-in audiences: fans of their respective artists' music. Like *A Hard Day's Night*, *Dont Look Back* has a well-known star—Bob Dylan—which many documentaries do not. Dylan's career and all the promotion surrounding it were essentially an advertisement for the film.

Dont Look Back is not only a profile of a cultural icon on the rise, but also about a popular musician. Pop music and youth culture have been significant to the commercialization of documentary film, both in the 1960s and 1970s and in the present. Rockumentaries capture live concerts with thrilling intimacy and aural fidelity. They can also communicate the powerful emotional experience of seeing a live musical performance, through abstract and lyrical film form.[40] In addition to the distinct cinematic potential of musical performance, rockumentaries offer heightened access to stars, biographies of famous figures, and a peek at musical subcultures.

Music documentaries are relatively easy to market because their subjects already have fans. Rockumentaries can be cross-promoted with the musician's record label. In the case of *Dont Look Back*, *Billboard* magazine reported, "Columbia Records, which Dylan records for, is providing theaters with the artist's albums for play in the lobby and outside. Also, Columbia is working on numerous promotion tie-ins for the film."[41] This type of synergy may seem unusual for an independently produced documentary, but it is indicative of the ways that entertainment companies large and small often partner to achieve mutual goals, like record sales and ticket sales. Leacock-Pennebaker was a totally new, unseasoned distribution company, but partnering with Columbia Records helped immensely with the release of *Dont Look Back*. Columbia Records had clout, a network of salespeople on the ground, and ample time and resources for promotion. In many ways, this remains the template for commercially viable documentaries.

Distribution companies at all levels—from small independent distributors to major studios—jumped on the music documentary bandwagon. Peppercorn-Wormser was a new company that principally dealt in sexploitation films and spaghetti westerns. But in 1967, it made a single foray into documentaries, acquiring music documentary *Festival* (1967, dir. Murray

---

[40] Michael Brendan Baker outlines two visual strategies, the journalistic and the impressionistic, in his history of the rockumentary. Michael Brendan Baker, "Rockumentary: Style, Performance, and Sound in a Documentary Genre" (PhD dissertation, McGill University, 2011).

[41] "Dylan Featured in Documentary Film," *Billboard*, September 16, 1967, 4.

Lerner), about the Newport Folk Music Festival, after the film attracted crowds to a late-night screening at the San Francisco Film Festival.[42] A few years later, established independent distributor Cinema V acquired the Maysles' *Gimme Shelter*, which documented the free rock concert at the Altamont Raceway that turned deadly during the Rolling Stones' set. The two music documentaries chronicled below—*Monterey Pop* and *Woodstock*—demonstrate the variable industrial positioning of the rockumentary subgenre, even as it showed remarkable resonance with audiences.

After making *Dont Look Back*, Leacock-Pennebaker found additional success with *Monterey Pop*, featuring performances by The Who, the Mamas and the Papas, Jefferson Airplane, and the Jimi Hendrix Experience. Originally shot for ABC in 1967, the network rejected the film after it was unable to find sponsors.[43] This response underlines the fact that, even though pop music documentaries were very marketable, their subjects were still unwelcome or risky on television. Ironically, ABC's rejection of *Monterey Pop* allowed its producers to reap great rewards at the box office: the filmmakers bought rights to the program from ABC and distributed it on their own. It played at the 1968 Venice Film Festival, and Leacock-Pennebaker released it in theaters in late 1968. In May 1969, *Monterey Pop* was going strong in New York City and had spread to other markets. *Variety* reported, "In its 17th week at the Kips Bay theatre in New York and continuing to pull in excess of $10,000 per at the box office, Leacock Pennebaker's *Monterey Pop* is now booked into 17 of the largest 24 U.S. cities in 20 separate theaters."[44] By pairing Direct Cinema methods with youth-oriented subjects, Leacock-Pennebaker found a way to move their documentary films into the theatrical market and the counterculture. Going to see *Dont Look Back* or *Monterey Pop* in theaters was a way for fans to participate in alternative culture.

Even after the high grosses of *Monterey Pop*, it was a struggle to make what would become the most iconic and highest-grossing music documentary of all: *Woodstock*. No company would provide production funds in exchange

---

[42] The film features performances by folk superstars Joan Baez, Bob Dylan, Peter, Paul & Mary, Judy Collins, and Pete Seeger. *Variety* reported, "*Festival*, Murray Lerner's lyric documentary on the Newport Folk Festival drew the largest crowd, despite the fact it was shown at a special midnight screening after the regular program of Greece's *The Private Right*, directed by Michael Papas, and India's *The Hero*, by Satyajit Ray, both of which drew considerably less." "Upset U.S. Distribs' Emotional Bias; Fest-Panned *War* Opens Big in Frisco," *Variety*, November 8, 1967, 13.

[43] "ABC-TV Reject Making It Now as a Theatrical," *Variety*, January 1, 1969, 29.

[44] "TV-Scratched 'Pop' Goes A-Winging, Tied to Short on Riot Control, Mace," *Variety*, May 28, 1969, 26.

for distribution rights. Only once the importance of the event was apparent did Warner Brothers acquire rights to the film.[45]

Woodstock certainly benefited from the free publicity generated by the actual festival's legendary status, but because it was released by a studio, it also received significant paid publicity. While *Boxoffice* touted the "low cost" of publicity for *Monterey Pop*, like ticket giveaways via college radio stations and appearances by D. A. Pennebaker on local television, Warner Brothers saturated radio stations and newspapers (college, underground, suburban, and major urban dailies) with paid ads for *Woodstock*. It also took pains to differentiate *Woodstock* by actually claiming that it had more documentary value than other music festival films. As *Variety* reported, "Pic is not a 'performance film' in the *Monterey Pop* tradition. About half of *Woodstock* is devoted to actual music performances, the rest centers on the nation's youth and their experiences and behavior during that incredible weekend. It is this approach that is being stressed in the campaign."[46]

Woodstock's business was phenomenal. While other documentaries posted impressive grosses like $7,000 per week in a single theater, *Woodstock* pulled in between $4,000 and $8,700 per day when it was first released.[47] Some New York City theater-owners charged high ticket prices, confident that demand for the film warranted it.[48] By the end of 1970, *Woodstock* was the seventh top-grosser of the year, having earned $7.1 million.[49]

Film Industry Reactions and Predictions

The excitement around surprise box-office hits, the politically potent Social Cinema in America series, and the wave of new distributors

---

[45] Kent E. Carroll, "Youth Swarms, Showmen Shy: N.Y. Talks Young, Unknown Acts," *Variety*, August 20, 1969, 3.

[46] "Bally-High for *Woodstock*; See No Rolling Stones Angle; Clarify Production Relations," *Variety*, March 4, 1970, 7, 24.

[47] "'Woodstock's Gladiator Fanfare Entrance; May Go Night 'n' Day; Also Possibility for Cannes," *Variety*, April 1, 1970, 6.

[48] *Variety* wrote, "Prices for *Woodstock* seats in NY depend on viewing time, with a Fri.-Sat top of $5 for later performances. Theory is apparently that young people pay that much and more for rock concerts and will not resist for *Woodstock*. The top price is believed to be highest ever for non-roadshow in the city—with the sole exception of homosexual beaver houses which put the $5 bite on their patrons." Audiences so wanted to take part in the by-then-legendary music festival that they were willing to buy tickets that cost as much as tickets to view actual "dirty movies." "'Woodstock's Gladiator Fanfare Entrance," 6.

[49] Syd Silverman, "330 Films above $100,000 in US during 1970," *Variety*, May 12, 1971, 34, 37.

led to breathless commentary on the popularity of documentaries and predictions for their future. By September 1967, *Variety* ran the headline "Lightweight Camera 'Verité' Methods New Success in Commercial Play." The article drew attention to the record-breaking grosses of *Dont Look Back* and reported that "industryites are predicting that the next to break out big will be Allan King's 'Warrendale,' [a] Canadian documentary about an offbeat treatment center for emotionally disturbed children."[50] The discourse in such articles demonstrates the industrial conflation between Direct Cinema's stylistic innovations and its unconventional subjects. Though Direct Cinema became an influential style and manner of working, the subjects chosen by directors were more determinative of their market position than was the form. *Warrendale* did not come close to matching the box-office records of *Dont Look Now*.[51] In practice, the only verité documentaries that crossed into the mainstream were those about pop culture.

Despite the lack of recognition from the American film industry, the rise in the number of theatrically released documentaries inspired filmmakers to leave television behind and strike out on their own. In 1968, Bill Greeley, writing for *Variety*, reported that "like the medium's reputable dramatists of a decade ago, video's notable documentarians are fleeing the stifling network confines like undernourished Devil's Island escapees."[52] Greeley considers the early 1960s a bygone golden age of television documentaries. He highlights a dip in the number of television documentaries being made and broadcast, and the two filmmakers named in his article, Doug Leiterman and Art Barron, confess their frustration with network executives delaying and shelving their films. Like many, both Leiterman and Barron were drawn to the freedom promised by the supposedly growing theatrical market for documentaries.

---

[50] "Lightweight Camera 'Verité' Methods New Success in Commercial Play," *Variety*, September 27, 1967, 4.

[51] After premiering at Cannes, where it shared the International Film Critics' Prize with *Blow-Up*, *Warrendale* had a successful run in Canada and played in the Social Cinema in America series. Grove Press acquired *Warrendale* and opened it a year after the NYFF, in September 1968, at the reopening of its art house, the Evergreen.

[52] Bill Greeley, "Docu-Makers Fleeing TV Scene for Well-Trod Road to 'Freedom,'" *Variety*, May 15, 1968, 37.

The Nontheatrical Market: Reaching the College Audience and Forming Cooperatives

In addition to the very visible excitement created by high box-office grosses and festival series, 1967 also saw new distribution companies and experiments in distribution, all of which would emphasize documentary films to some extent. However, most would conclude that theatrically releasing documentaries was a losing game, which led them to concentrate primarily on the nontheatrical market. Distributors built libraries of films, including documentaries, that could earn them slow but steady profits over years, rather than the high-cost hoopla and potential bonanza of a smash success at the box office.

Campus Market and Publishing Model

The power of the youth market, and the possibility of college playoff, was a crucial incentive for distributors to acquire documentaries. Reviews of documentaries often mention the nontheatrical campus market, with critics judging a film "a natural for colleges."[53] In her research on campus film culture, Andrea Comiskey found that "the number of films exhibited on campuses increased significantly throughout the 1960s and, to a lesser extent, during the early 1970s."[54] Film festivals and film culture were two forces acting in tandem to drive the substantial growth in the campus market, and they promoted foreign-language films and documentaries in a volume disproportionate to their commercial presence. According to Comiskey, foreign films were played on campuses more often than any other type, making up 25 to 35 percent of films shown. Documentaries made up between 6.5 and 16 percent of the films played on campuses, being the fourth most common type after foreign language films, classic Hollywood films, and recent Hollywood films. While companies with large catalogs of 16 mm films, like Audio Brandon, continued to service this market, new companies also formed as the market's value became clearer.

---

[53] "*Warrendale*," *Variety*, September 18, 1968, 26. See also Mosk., "Venice Film Festival: *Festival*," *Variety*, September 13, 1967, 6.

[54] Andrea Comiskey, "The Campus Cinematheque: Film Culture at U.S. Universities, 1960–1975," *Post Script—Essays in Film and the Humanities* 30, no. 2 (Winter–Spring 2011), 39.

Pathe-Contemporary was one of the first companies to concentrate on the nontheatrical campus market, using theatrical release as a promotional loss-leader for their films' main profit center. Grove Press and National Talent Service followed suit later in the decade, experimenting with the independent distribution of documentaries and foreign films. While the early foreign-film importers had grown in size and stature, even partnering with Hollywood studios to produce films, these smaller distributors worked at the margins of the industry. They were intertwined with book publishing, and some distribution executives even admitted to using a publishing model to distribute their films—building libraries that could turn a profit over time, rather than focusing on initial theatrical runs to make the bulk of the money.

Publishing company Grove Press had its own New York City art house theater, the Evergreen, when it entered the film distribution business in 1966 by acquiring the Cinema 16 catalog. Subsequently, it acquired several films with literary pedigrees (*Finnegan's Wake*, dir. Mary Ellen Bute), as well as documentaries. Grove's documentary catalog appealed to diverse viewer interests. Its social-problem films appealed to those seeking political engagement, while its sexually explicit films promised titillation. *Variety* headlined its report on the new distributor "Ghetto and Hellhole Films: Grove Aims for Campus & Buffs,"[55] which encompassed both the subjects of the documentaries it acquired and the type of filmgoers it expected to attract. Three of Grove's earliest acquisitions dealt with current social problems: *The Troublemakers* concerns a black community organization in Newark; *The Game* is about teens in gangs in the South Bronx; *Titicut Follies* exposes the frightening conditions at a mental health institution.

Grove also alluded to adult themes in its ads, like the marketing of *Mondo Cane*. In a November 1968 ad in *Variety*, large type reads, "Grove Press presents another four-letter word—'Film.'"[56] Beneath "Film," in parentheses and a smaller type, one reads, "The other one, of course, was 'book.'" This cheeky ad alludes to the curse words that were forbidden on television, and it recalls the advertisements for "frank" foreign films during the past two decades. The difference is that two out of the four films in the ad were documentaries: *Warrendale* and *The Queen*.[57] This points to the

---

[55] Stuart Byron, "Ghetto and Hellhole Films: Grove Aims for Campus & Buffs," *Variety*, October 11, 1967, 5, 24.
[56] Ad, "Grove Press," *Variety*, November 13, 1968, 20.
[57] The other two films in the ad were *Beyond the Law* (dir. Norman Mailer) and *Weekend* (dir. Jean-Luc Godard).

cultural category that documentaries could be slotted into at this point—as shocking exposés meant for adults only, as a glimpse into a deviant subculture. Grove treaded the same water with its successful theatrical release of *Freedom to Love*, an English-language West German documentary about sexual health and liberation. Similar in content to its box-office smash (and censorship bait) *I Am Curious (Yellow)*, it was one of the last films that Grove released theatrically. While Grove had used theatrical release as a publicity tool and loss leader for its nontheatrical business, by 1971, it was feeding its documentaries and fiction films straight to the nontheatrical market.[58]

While more distribution companies acquired documentary features than ever before, many found more success circulating them through the nontheatrical market than the extremely competitive and crowded theatrical market. The growth in campus film societies, and in the number of college students more generally, drove the nontheatrical market.

Experiments in Distribution

At the same time nontheatrical distributors were successfully exploiting the campus market, other groups were experimenting with alternative methods of distribution. Rather than surrendering their work to a commercial distributor, even one focused on the nontheatrical market, a number of documentary filmmakers were intent on distributing their films through more personal channels.

In 1966, Jonas Mekas, Shirley Clarke, and Lionel Rogosin founded the Film-makers' Distribution Center. While its sister organization, the Filmmaker's Cooperative, continues to this day as the primary distribution vehicle for American avant-garde films, Mekas, Clarke, and Rogosin aimed for a more professional, efficient operation to capitalize on theatrical exhibitors' interest in independent and experimental film. The Film-maker's Coop would continue to service nontheatrical venues, while the Film-makers' Distribution Center would concentrate on the theatrical market. Though it was a nonprofit, the Film-makers' Distribution Center operated more like a commercial venture than did the Film-maker's Coop. Kreul writes of these distinctions,

---

[58] "Grove Press Cuts but Not Its Film Sector," *Variety*, May 26, 1971, 4.

While the Cooperative rented films at a fixed flat rate determined by the filmmaker, the Distribution Center had the authority to negotiate guarantees and box office percentage rentals with theatrical venues. And, finally, while it was against Cooperative policy to promote individual films and filmmakers, the Distribution Center could promote individual films and provide publicity materials to theatrical venues.[59]

The Distribution Center's biggest success, by far, was *The Chelsea Girls* (1966, dir. Andy Warhol), but it also distributed documentaries.

Clarke, Mekas, and Distribution Center executive director Louis Brigante curated a group of independent documentaries into what was meant to be an ongoing series called America Today. In late 1966, the documentary showcase had a gala premiere to benefit the Newark Community Union Project, then had a theatrical run at the Film-Maker's Cinematheque. Included in America Today were the following films: *Newsreel: Report from Milbrook* (Jonas Mekas), *Troublemakers* (Robert Machover and Norman Fruchter), *Time of the Locust* (Peter Gessner, about Vietnam), *Now Do You See How We Play?* (Robert Fiore, about an East Harlem teen gang), *Mass* (Bruce Baillie, also known as *Mass for the Dakota Sioux*). While the America Today series was overshadowed by the popularity of *The Chelsea Girls*, Grove Press later acquired *Troublemakers*, and several filmmakers—Fruchter and Gessner—went on to form the overtly political film collective Newsreel. The Distribution Center also released a more formally adventurous documentary made by cofounder Shirley Clarke: *Portrait of Jason*. A vocal critic of cinéma vérité techniques, Clarke designed *Portrait of Jason* as a rebuke of the increasingly popular style of documentaries. *Portrait of Jason* premiered at the 1967 NYFF, then opened at the Distribution Center's new theatrical venue, the New Cinema Playhouse. Despite strong reviews and extensive advertising, the documentary returned disappointing grosses, averaging only $1,300 per week during its first three weeks.[60] The failure of the political documentary series and Clarke's documentary feature hurt the Film-maker's Distribution Center, demonstrating that only Andy Warhol's films had the ability to cross over from film societies and campus showings to commercial theaters. Like the commercial distribution companies above, the Film-maker's Distribution Center had aimed its films, including documentaries, at

---

[59] Kreul, "New York, New Cinema," 384–85.
[60] Kreul, "New York, New Cinema," 485.

the theatrical market, but it ended up only gaining traction in nontheatrical exhibition sites.

Political documentarians in the 1960s and 1970s also experimented with distribution. Determining how to circulate politically oriented films is not only about the best way to reach audiences, but also a decision about which audiences are the most important to reach. Some political filmmakers rely primarily on commercial distributors to circulate their films, while others decide that forming collectives is more efficient and politically potent.

Emile de Antonio, a significant political documentarian of the 1960s and 1970s, worked with commercial distributors to circulate his work. De Antonio distributed his films through foreign-film importer Walter Reade-Sterling (*Point of Order*), short-lived independent distributor Impact Films (*Rush to Judgment*), and the experimental Cinetrees (*In the Year of the Pig*). Completed in 1969, in the thick of both the undeclared war and the growing antiwar movement, *In the Year of the Pig* was de Antonio's most confrontational and topical film up to that point—a collage film that lays bare the political systems and capitalist machine that led to America's involvement in Vietnam. Though de Antonio predicted that the film's primary market would mostly be nontheatrical venues, including campus screenings and political rallies, Cinetrees experimented with theatrical release by making specialized, focused publicity efforts in one city, Boston. Once that experiment was over, yielding limited success, McGraw Hill / Pathe Contemporary acquired the rights to distribute *In the Year of the Pig*.

While de Antonio partnered with commercial distributors of various sizes to distribute his films, other political filmmakers decided to circumvent the established order and form their own production and distribution collectives. Newsreel was one of the most important and visible of these, formed in 1967 by a group of independent filmmakers.[61] In addition to producing its own analytical documentaries, Newsreel acquired films from abroad, like *US Techniques and Genocide in Vietnam* (made in North Vietnam) and distributed other filmmakers' works on a nonexclusive basis.[62]

---

[61] Newsreel started in New York City, then had outposts in Boston, San Francisco, Atlanta, Detroit, Chicago, and Los Angeles. Newsreel (New York) also underwent an enormous change in leadership and membership in 1972, becoming more focused on issues relating to race and class. It changed its name to Third World Newsreel at this time.

[62] For example, Cinda Firestone distributed *Attica* through the commercial distributor Tri-Continental Films, but also made it available through Newsreel. Norberto Lopez made a documentary called *GI Jose* (1974) for *Realidades*, a Spanish-language show on WNET; Newsreel later picked it up and distributed it. Newsreel also distributed the controversial CBS News production *The Selling of the Pentagon* (1971).

When Newsreel was founded, it tried to emulate commercial distribution practices, as Bill Nichols describes:

> As a natural consequence of their previous experience with distribution and of their concern for offering masses of people an alternative to the 6 o'clock news . . . , there were plans to engage in theatrical distribution and to link up with the established 16mm circuits of college and film buff audiences. . . . For the most part, however, Newsreel found access to the established distribution channel clogged or unsuitable and the occasional theatrical screening (at the Elgin, the New Yorker, the Gate and The Film-Maker's Cinematheque) served more a fund-raising function than an ongoing, preferred form of release.[63]

This inability to access ordinary channels of distribution reflects the industry's growing interest in nontheatrical markets, like college campuses, which made it more difficult for small distributors to enter them with any regularity. Rather than concentrate its efforts on distributing work to art houses, where it could reach a great quantity of people and gain favorable reviews in daily newspapers, Newsreel turned directly to political organizers and leaders of social movements. Newsreel aimed to make its films an aggressive, confrontational organizing tool for political leaders. Members of Newsreel would lead discussions following a screening, a task later taken over by the political organizers themselves.

Newsreel's pricing also reflected its focus on political efficacy rather than profit or prestige: "Newsreel sought out and encouraged the audience it wanted to reach with flexible rates that varied from nothing to listed catalogue prices (about $1/minute)."[64] While Newsreel's priority was getting its films to political groups and community organizations, a majority of its rentals went to college groups, even after its seismic shift in focus from white, middle-class issues to those affecting working-class and Third World people in the United States and around the world. According to Nichols, Newsreel had about two thousand bookings in 1974, and reached at least twenty thousand people.[65]

---

[63] Bill Nichols, "Newsreel: Film and Revolution" (master's thesis, University of California, Los Angeles, 1972), 55–56.
[64] Nichols, "Newsreel," 97–98.
[65] Bill Nichols, *Newsreel: Documentary Filmmaking on the American Left* (New York: Arno Press, 1980), 32.

A few years after Newsreel was founded, another political film collective sprang up from the ferment of the women's movement: the still-operating New Day Films. Like Newsreel, New Day used a sliding scale for rentals to women's groups and charged no fees to women's prisons that wanted to show its films. The filmmakers often also lectured or led discussions following film screenings. Otherwise, New Day is different kind of organization that allows for equal measures of autonomy and collectivity. A steering committee, made up of filmmakers, runs the operation and decides on policies. Filmmakers make films on their own, then pool their work in a catalog to market it more efficiently. In the end, though, each filmmaker retains control and actually distributes her work individually, retaining "100 percent of their royalties, minus 20 percent for the co-op's operational costs."[66] While Newsreel strove to be fully democratic and collective at every level, New Day uses cooperation strategically.

The importance of personal contact with audiences and retaining control over one's own work is clear in an anecdote about New Day cofounder Julia Reichert distributing *Growing Up Female*, her first film. "My partner, Jim Klein, and I didn't think about showings in museums or a theatrical release. We saw that film as a tool to help the women's movement grow. My whole thrust was to get it to colleges, high schools, YMCAs, churches. I went on the road with it. I had one print. I went to Cleveland where I had friends in the women's movement, and they arranged showings in people's living rooms."[67] Reichert's account of traveling around the country with a single print of *Growing Up Female* sounds almost evangelical, like a circuit-riding preacher spreading the word to rural communities. It also points to the concept of feminist documentaries as useful media, made to achieve specific ends. These political goals were the reason Reichert and Klein decided to self-distribute, even though professional distribution companies were interested in the film. "We met distributors and heard their offers. We felt as though we would be giving up our work. We would be handing it to others, all men, who did not share our goals."[68]

Instead of relinquishing control of their work, Reichert and Klein founded New Day Films in 1971, along with documentary filmmakers Liane Brandon

---

[66] Cyndi Zale, "Chicago Filmmakers Find Options in Non-theatrical Distribution," *Backstage*, December 12, 1986, 57.
[67] Interview with Julia Reichert, in *Women of Vision: Histories in Feminist Film and Video*, ed. Alexandra Juhasz (Minneapolis: University of Minnesota Press, 1997), 124.
[68] Reichert, interview, 125.

(*Anything You Want to Be*) and Amalie Rothschild (*It Happens to Us*). Over the years, New Day has grown enormously, and its catalog has branched out from feminist films to a range of social-issue documentaries.[69] Like Newsreel, New Day's contracts are not exclusive—filmmakers can sell theatrical or broadcast rights to other companies. Such is the case with New Day's relationship to Kartemquin Films. Established in 1966, Kartemquin first operated as a collective production company, and it self-distributed some of its titles. After the dissolution of the collective and reorganization, the leaders of Kartemquin sought to consolidate its distribution activities. In 1980, they applied to have the film *Taylor Chain: Story of a Union Local* (1981) distributed nontheatrically by New Day, beginning a long-standing, nonexclusive partnership. While later films by Kartemquin have gone into regular theatrical distribution with commercial distribution companies—most notably, *Hoop Dreams* (1994, dir. Steve James) with Fine Line Features—New Day continues to represent Kartemquin's films on the nontheatrical market.

The founding of Newsreel and New Day Films marked the beginning of two nonprofit institutions that would support the circulation of documentary features for many decades. Neither is a commercial distribution company; rather, they offered shared expertise and overhead for mostly nontheatrical distribution. The various strategies they used represent different options for politically oriented filmmakers in an era without many options for circulating independent work.

Conclusion

In the first half of the 1960s, documentaries supplemented the foreign film market. They were marketed to appeal to American audiences for foreign films, hungry for the titillation and tourism of Europe. Little-remembered these days, even disavowed as documentaries, these documentary films were an attractive source of revenue for independent importers. The most historically important documentaries of the first half of the decade, made by Direct Cinema filmmakers, were industrially marginal—they had an unstable home

---

[69] "Today New Day Films is a cooperative collective of over 150 filmmakers and over 200 films that touch on a wide array of social issues including disability rights, feminism, freedom of information, gender equality, globalization, juvenile justice, prisoner rights, queer culture, immigration, sexuality, and the arts, among many others." John Abraham Stover, "The Intersections of Social Activism, Collective Identity, and Artistic Expression in Documentary Filmmaking" (PhD dissertation, Loyola University Chicago, 2012).

on network television and engendered conflict over what was journalism and what was documentary. This core tension between journalistic television and documentary filmmaking would become central again in the 1980s, as independent film advocates fought for support from PBS.

US television networks filled time with inexpensive compilation documentaries, but when the Little Three tried, for various reasons, to launch conventional historical documentaries in theaters, they failed. Their biographical portraits of great men and historical events were too similar to television documentaries. Only when documentaries were distinct enough from television, covering youth-oriented or controversial subjects, did they thrive in theatrical release and the cinephilic cultural marketplace. Documentaries with popular music or performance elements remain the most commercial types of documentary film to this day.

Simultaneously, there was a new market that encouraged distributors to acquire documentary films: the nontheatrical market, specifically the campus market. Commercial distribution companies serviced the campus market and other nontheatrical venues like churches and community groups. The late 1960s and early 1970s were also a growth period for alternative distribution setups, like political film collectives. Fully rejecting the commodity value of documentary and highly committed to using documentaries for public service, the collective approach clashed at times with the approach taken by more entrepreneurial, individual filmmakers. While the nontheatrical, or educational, market persists, its importance for documentary film has been diluted by the advent of home video and the sheer growth in the number of outlets that show documentaries.

2
A Rising Tide

How the Independent Film Movement Boosted Documentaries (1978 to 1989)

The commercial value of documentary films rose significantly between the late 1970s and the late 1980s. Thanks to the maturation of the national Public Broadcasting Service (see Chapter 3) and the rise of the American independent film movement, necessary institutional infrastructure for releasing documentaries stabilized and expanded. The divergent circulation paths of two documentaries that bookend this period—*Word Is Out: Stories of Some of Our Lives* (1978, dir. Mariposa Film Group) and *Roger & Me* (1989, dir. Michael Moore)—convey the scale of the market's growth.

Word Is Out is a documentary woven from interviews with twenty-six gay men and lesbians. In the tender and candid interviews, the participants reflect on their sexual orientation and how it has shaped their lives. The filmmakers took care to represent the variety of gay and lesbian experience in America, with subjects young and old, urban and rural, white and black. The Mariposa Group codirected the film, with Peter Adair often speaking for the group. The makers of *Word Is Out* began their grassroots campaign during production, by holding in-progress screenings. These screenings allowed them to raise production funds, shape the film according to their core audience's input, and market the film far in advance of its actual opening. Once finished, theatrical distributors wanted to acquire *Word Is Out*, but the filmmakers put their political goals ahead of financial ones. The filmmakers wanted to retain nontheatrical rights to the film so that they could hold screenings to benefit local causes in each city it opened, but no distributor wanted to take on the risk of theatrical distribution without also being able to exploit the more certain nontheatrical market.[1] So the filmmakers four-walled the film

---

[1] Another film with political goals, *Seeing Red*, opened the same way. The filmmakers actually had their own nontheatrical distribution company, New Day. So they did not want to sell off all the rights, only the theatrical rights. They ended up self-distributing, with the help of a professional booker.

in a single theater in their hometown of San Francisco in December 1978.[2] It played for fourteen weeks in San Francisco, then moved on to riskier runs in New York and Los Angeles. In April 1979, the filmmakers decided they could not handle the distribution themselves—the process was too slow and labor intensive, and they would not be able to exhaust the market before their upcoming PBS airdate. They sold both theatrical and nontheatrical rights to *Word Is Out* to New Yorker Films, which allowed them to continue holding benefit screenings in each city.[3] The process was fraught, inefficient, and ultimately beyond the scope of an independent producer.

By the end of the 1980s, a documentary about labor issues, directed and fronted by a filmmaker with an outsized personality, was being distributed by a major studio: Warner Bros paid $3 million for the exclusive rights to *Roger & Me*. In *Roger & Me*, director Michael Moore decries General Motors' decision to close factories in his hometown of Flint, Michigan, putting thirty thousand people out of work. Using humor and pop songs, Moore explores how this decision wreaks havoc on the city and its residents. A stark contrast to the somewhat haphazard, ad hoc release of *Word Is Out*, Warner Bros put its strong backing into distributing and publicizing Moore's film, ensuring that it played in mainstream theaters, beyond the urban art house and the university film club. The film made $5 million at the box office. It was broadcast nationally on PBS and sold a record number of copies on home video. While this level of success was anomalous, it did indicate that the ceiling of the documentary market had risen substantially. Importantly, it also served as a bellwether of the increasing tilt away from the public service mentality that informed the special-interest distribution strategy of *Word Is Out* and toward a more conventionally commercial emphasis on reaching a broad, mainstream audience.

In the 1980s, the growth of American independent film culture and institutions provided newfound support for documentary film. New distribution companies were founded to exploit independent films' commercial potential and augment the low number of films coming out of studios. Hollywood studios' strategy of releasing a few tentpole films left theaters with many open playdates in the late 1970s and early 1980s, and new distributors

---

Susan Linfield, "How to Succeed in Distribution without Even Signing," *The Independent*, July–August 1984, 20.

[2] Peter Adair, "Adventures in Distribution," *The Independent*, January 1980, 6.
[3] Adair, "Adventures in Distribution," 7.

filled the void, as foreign film importers had done with the art-house market in the 1960s. These distribution companies showed an interest in documentary film, but they mainly acquired low-risk, marketable documentaries with a music or performance element. At the same time, some practices pioneered by earlier documentary filmmakers continued and took on new strength in the 1980s. While documentarians had experimented with self-distribution and circulation via political collectives in the 1960s and 1970s, filmmakers extended this practice in the 1980s through new exhibitions spaces like Film Forum and innovative distribution companies like First Run Features. Formal experimentation ran through documentaries released by both types of distributors, augmenting the identification of documentary with cinema rather than television.

Documentaries: An Underexplored Part of American Independent Cinema

American independent cinema grew enormously in commercial and cultural clout in the 1980s. There was more financing available for low-budget films, and the nascent home video market was hungry for product.[4] Studios were releasing fewer and fewer films, and distributors could see the potential for strong return on low budgets, in the powerful example of *Return of the Secaucus Seven*, *Smithereens*, and *Stranger Than Paradise*.[5] In response, Hollywood studios opened studio classics divisions to handle foreign art-house and independent films: United Artists founded UA Classics; Columbia and Gaumont founded Triumph Films; Universal founded Universal Classics; Fox founded Twentieth Century Fox International Classics; and Orion founded Orion Classics.[6] Not all of these distributors acquired documentaries, but all participated in the growth of the independent film market, which indirectly grew the possibilities for documentary films. In addition, the decade saw huge growth in the infrastructure that supported and

---

[4] Emanuel Levy, *Cinema of Outsiders: The Rise of American Independent Cinema* (New York: New York University Press, 1999), chap 1. Geoff King, *American Independent Cinema* (London: I.B. Tauris, 2005), 20.

[5] Yannis Tzioumakis, *American Independent Cinema*, 2nd ed. (Edinburgh: Edinburgh University Press, 2017), 209.

[6] For more on the studios' classics divisions, see Yannis Tzioumakis, *Hollywood's Indies: Classics Divisions, Specialty Labels and American Independent Cinema* (Edinburgh: Edinburgh University Press, 2012).

raised the visibility of independent films, like the Sundance Film Festival, the Independent Filmmaker Project, and the Association of Independent Video and Filmmakers. While the first two elements that enabled the growth of American independent cinema—the availability of financing and the burgeoning home video market—did not extend to the documentary field, the growth in new distribution companies and the independent film infrastructure did offer new opportunities to documentary filmmakers.

A number of scholars have investigated the rise of American independent cinema and explicated its contours at particular times in history, but, so far, documentaries have not been fully included in histories of the rise of American independent cinema. Though he covers three hundred films in *Cinema of Outsiders*, Emanuel Levy excludes documentary films, along with other types of movies that he explicitly argues are outside the purview of this era of indie film, like B-movies, straight-to-video movies, genre films, TV-like movies, and costume and historical films.[7] Similarly, documentaries receive only cursory mention in Geoff King's *American Independent Cinema*. Although King admits that documentaries travel along the same lines to theatrical distribution and exhibition as independent films, he justifies excluding them because fewer of them are breakout hits.[8] To King, documentary is important to indie cinema because it influenced the style of many fiction films, not as an element of the indie cinema market itself. But this is a strange exclusion, since so many documentary films were distributed by the same companies in the same manner as the fiction films that Levy and King position as central to the movement.

However, when reading the trade journals at the beginning of the 1980s, one is struck by the prominence of documentaries to the nascent independent film movement. In 1980, a front-page headline in *Variety* proclaimed, "Indie Filmmakers Go Commercial." Stephen Klain, author of the article, points to a crop of eight independent films trying to make it in the mainstream market (Table 2.1). Six out of the eight films are documentaries, and all fit the emerging definition of independent cinema: "regionally produced and tied to an overriding social and/or political consciousness," with "'entertainment value' only a secondary consideration" for the filmmakers.[9] In both subject

---

[7] Levy, *Cinema of Outsiders*, 447.
[8] King, *American Independent Cinema*, 255.
[9] Stephen Klain, "Indie Filmmakers Go Commercial," *Variety*, March 5, 1980, 46.

Table 2.1 Films referenced by Stephen Klain in "Indie Filmmakers Go Commercial"

Title	Director
The War at Home	Glenn Silber, Barry Alexander Brown
Word Is Out	Mariposa Film Group
Best Boy	Ira Wohl
The Trials of Alger Hiss	John Lowenthal
Joe and Maxi	Maxi Cohen, Joel Gold
The Wobblies	Deborah Shaffer, Stewart Bird
Get Rollin[a]	J. Terrance Mitchell
Northern Lights[b]	John Hanson, Rob Nilsson

Source: Stephen Klain, "Indie Filmmakers Go Commercial," *Variety*, March 5, 1980, 46.
[a] Semidocumentary.
[b] Fiction.

matter and market position, documentaries were equal to fiction films in the early days of the independent cinema.

Similarly, in a 1981 *American Film* feature about independent film, entitled "Ordinary People, European-Style," Annette Insdorf identifies both fiction and documentary filmmakers as leaders in this new independent film movement.[10] She first profiles documentarians Ira Wohl (*Best Boy*) and Maxi Cohen and Joel Gold (*Joe and Maxi*) alongside fiction directors John Hanson, Rob Nilsson, and Victor Nunez. Insdorf points out that each of these fiction film directors was offered production deals from major studios, but each rejected the constraints the studios would have placed upon them. This rebellious attitude would become ingrained in the discourse of the emerging independent cinema. Insdorf also used both documentary and fiction films to differentiate this new strain of independent cinema from other filmmakers who could lay claim to being "independent." She writes, "The films of these directors are in fact not commercial in the studio sense, and this distinguishes them from filmmakers like George Romero, Tobe Hooper, John Carpenter, and David Cronenberg, who to one degree or another exist outside the industry orbit, but whose affection for Grand Guignol, violence,

---

[10] Annette Insdorf, "Ordinary People, European-Style, or How to Spot an Independent Feature," *American Film*, September 1981, 57–60.

and sex has attracted commercial money."[11] Not only are these independent films made without the help of studio financing, Insdorf notes, but the alternative nature of their subject matter or style is meant to appeal to audiences by being something *other* than studio films.

Documentaries were central, not peripheral, to American independent cinema at the very moment when commentators were formulating this new and soon-to-be-dominant definition of independence. However, in terms of the theatrical market, documentaries remained firmly marginal throughout the 1980s.

"Grant Pictures" or "Rich Uncle Pictures": Convincing Exhibitors to Play Documentary Films

In the late 1970s and early 1980s, both fiction and documentary independent films faced huge challenges breaking into the commercial market. One reason is that "independent cinema" was an unfamiliar and indistinct concept. As Michael Newman writes, since the late 1980s, "The idea of independent cinema has achieved a level of cultural circulation far greater than in earlier eras, making independence into a brand, a familiar idea that evokes in consumers a range of emotional and symbolic associations."[12] But in the late 1970s and early 1980s, even those in the motion picture industry had misgivings about independently made films. As one commentator counseled in 1981, "Hard-nosed exhibitors often view [independent films] as an indulgence of the rich and spoiled, 'grant pictures' or 'rich uncle pictures,' 'movies which have collected money from everywhere except ticket sales,' as one theater owner puts it."[13] Exhibitors were suspicious of films made outside the normal channels, and they did not trust independent filmmakers to have the bottom line in mind. Even after the much-publicized breakout success of an independent film like *The Return of the Secaucus Seven* (1980, dir. John Sayles), the lack of a fully formed discursive context for independent films, not to mention the lack of sturdy commercial enterprises throwing their

---

[11] Insdorf, "Ordinary People," 58.
[12] Michael Z. Newman, *Indie: An American Film Culture* (New York: Columbia University Press, 2011), 4.
[13] Gerald Peary, "Getting It On, or How to Make Deals and Influence Exhibitors," *American Film*, September 1981, 61–62.

weight behind the films, discouraged most exhibitors from taking chances on independent films.

Documentary filmmakers reported experiencing this kind of attitude when trying to book their films in theaters. Deborah Shaffer, codirector with Stew Bird of *The Wobblies* (1979), relates her experience in self-distribution as follows: "The exhibitors said, 'A documentary? Labor history? You must be kidding.' ... A representative of a theater in New York told [Stew] Bird, 'Come back when you make a movie.' "[14] This disdainful response shows how much skepticism exhibitors had about the box-office potential of independent films, especially documentaries. The task of independent filmmakers and their professional organizations was to show that they had business savvy and that they shared a common goal with exhibitors: for their films to have a successful run at the box office.

But achieving a successful run was made more difficult by the fact that the independent filmmakers and distributors lacked the resources of a studio to advertise their films. Convincing exhibitors to take a chance was one hurdle, which was eased by the lack of studio product in the late 1970s, and the attractive possibility of a breakout success. But educating audiences about the very notion of "independent" cinema was another thing. Not only were the films not inherently or traditionally sellable—no cast of well-known actors, no presold property like a screenplay adapted from a bestseller, little to no genre appeal—advertising was prohibitively expensive. Whether studio film or independent, newspaper and television ads cost the same amount of money. There were no economies of scale to take advantage of. Independent filmmakers and distributors had to figure out how to market their films as cheaply as possible.

Filmmakers put into practice a few strategies to meet these challenges. The first strategy they deployed was to self-distribute their films, drumming up free publicity by appearing in person at screenings/premieres. The success of some of these films led to their being acquired for further exploitation by actual distribution companies. Next, a collective of enterprising filmmakers joined together to form a cooperative distribution company, continuing to use these advocacy strategies on a larger scale, for more films. This cooperative was mission-oriented, like the political film collectives established in the 1970s, but its mission was commercial success and cultural visibility of alternative film. Simultaneously, indies' successes inspired more commercial

---

[14] Peary, "Getting It On," 61.

distributors to acquire independent films for theatrical distribution and use similar release tactics.

Self-distribution was the first step in building a more robust market for documentary feature films. *Variety* first covered the trend in self-distribution in 1976. Addison Verrell relates how John Cassavetes self-distributed *A Woman under the Influence* (1975) to a $6 million domestic gross, and others, like Joan Micklin Silver (*Hester Street*) and documentarians the Maysles (*Grey Gardens*) followed suit.[15] While *Variety* claimed that showing strong grosses in New York City would be enough to guarantee bookings across the country, many independent filmmakers, especially documentarians, took another tack. New York City, while an important market, is also extremely competitive market with very high costs for advertising and theater rental. In response, the makers of *Word Is Out* and *The War at Home* undertook regionally focused self-distribution plans, in advance of their PBS broadcasts. They also used unusual publicity techniques to circumvent the high cost of advertising. This allowed them to achieve both political and financial goals through their distribution process, providing a model for later self-distributing documentarians.

The War at Home is a documentary about the antiwar movement at the University of Wisconsin–Madison. The film shows the campus as a hotbed of activism against the Vietnam War, with clashes between student protestors and police and the bombing of a campus building, Sterling Hall. Codirected by Barry Alexander Brown and Glenn Silber, the film consists of archival footage and interviews with protest participants. The makers of *The War at Home* followed *Word Is Out*'s lead by undertaking a regionally focused self-distribution plan in advance of its PBS broadcast. One of the film's advantages was timing: it followed on the heels of a number of high-profile films about the Vietnam War, like *Apocalypse Now* and *The Deer Hunter*. The film premiered in the makers' hometown (and the subject of the film), Madison, in October 1979. Hometown crowds sold out shows, but the directors knew that opening successfully in other cities would take an enormous amount of work. Community organizing and a major publicity effort helped the film break house records in its first week and be held over for five weeks at the Orson Welles Theater in Boston.

---

[15] Addison Verrell, "So They Distributed Films Themselves: Recent Instances of On-Own 'Trend,'" *Variety*, February 18, 1976, 52.

The makers of *Word Is Out* and *The War at Home* proved their mettle and commitment to selling tickets by taking an active role in self-distributing their films in theaters. Though both films have a strong liberal bent, and the Mariposa Collective used *Word Is Out* to raise money for liberal causes, they were firmly committed to distributing the film to theaters. This is unlike the documentarians working in political film collectives in previous decades, who were more focused on circulating their work to political gatherings or consciousness-raising groups.

Marketing Documentaries as Studios Turn to Exploitation

Self-distribution could yield excellent returns, but only through massive publicity efforts. During the early 1970s, independent exploitation distributors had pioneered a new genre: the family film. They did this by four-walling second-run theaters on a regional basis and concentrating on audiences that seemed to be underserved by studios. It is worth comparing the documentarians' strategy with the commercial independents'. While the documentary filmmakers reached out to community groups, and even held benefits for them, in each city they opened their film, the commercial independents like American National Enterprises and Sunn Classics spent heavily on market research to pinpoint exactly which parts of the country were receptive to their films. They then coordinated targeted television ad buys with short runs at theaters in those areas, squeezing the maximum value out of low-budget, low-production-values films like *The Life and Times of Grizzly Adams* and *Chariot of the Gods*.[16] This practice moved closer to mainstream Hollywood with *Billy Jack*, a family drama and youth revenge picture. It was produced by Warner Bros, but director Tom Laughlin was unhappy with the studio's release effort and won back control of the film in order to re-release it. Justin Wyatt writes about the strategies Laughlin tried. "Rereleased on May 9, 1973, with a generous ad expenditure of $250,000 in Southern California under the four-wall approach to mostly second- and third-run neighborhood theaters, *Billy Jack* grossed $1.02 million in the first week in

---

[16] Gary Edgerton, "Charles E. Sellier, Jr. and Sunn Classic Pictures: Success as a Commercial Independent in the 1970s," *Journal of Popular Film and Television* 10, no. 3 (Fall 1982), 106–18. Sunn Classics continued the tradition of exploitation documentaries or pseudodocumentaries with "phenomena films, or movies that are structured as pseudoscientific investigations into one of nature's mysteries" (109). The most successful of these was *In Search of Noah's Ark* (1977), which grossed $23.7 million.

sixty-two theaters from Santa Barbara to Bakersfield. The gross represented a record box-office return for the region."[17] These grosses caught the attention of studios, which soon shifted the bulk of their advertising budget to television, though they did not practice four-walling. In fact, with the release of *Jaws*, Universal bought national television advertisements, rather than local, and forced exhibitors to chip in to pay for them.

Though independent documentarians did four-wall their films, breaking city by city rather than nationwide, their marketing strategy could not have been more different from that employed by commercial independents and, later, the major studios. Television advertising was prohibitively expensive, and even the cost of newspaper ads could easily overwhelm a filmmaker releasing his film without the resources of a studio. Adair acknowledged that P&A—making prints to circulate and buying advertisements—were fixed costs for all films, and stated, "From what I have learned, the minimum level of these fixed costs is, ironically, the same for little films such as ours as it would be for much larger ones."[18] Since their release strategies could not benefit from any economies of scale, documentarians did what they could to circumvent paid marketing. During the distribution period of *Word Is Out*, Adair says, "The only professional we hired was a publicist—a good decision, I feel, because of the indispensability of their professional relationship with critics and people who can write background articles."[19] Hiring a publicist to work more directly with the media paid off for *Word Is Out*, as well as for *The War at Home*. According to Silber, "We have received extraordinary press. There was yet to be an unfavorable review out of 25 or 30, including *Variety* who more or less said that they thought our film was better than *Apocalypse Now* and *Coming Home*, which is a little bit much."[20] These reviews surely caused exhibitors to give more serious consideration to playing the films, and encouraged audiences to see them.

In addition to good press, the filmmakers showed themselves to be serious about achieving great box-office numbers, demonstrating a common goal with exhibitors. In a vein similar to Universal's forcing theater owners to pay for their national television ad buys, Silber and Brown negotiated with exhibitors to cover some publicity costs. In addition to convincing the Orson

---

[17] Justin Wyatt, "From Roadshowing to Saturation Release: Majors, Independents, and Marketing/Distribution Innovations," in *The New American Cinema*, ed. Jon Lewis (Durham, NC: Duke University Press, 1998), 75.
[18] Adair, "Adventures in Distribution," 8.
[19] Adair, "Adventures in Distribution," 6.
[20] Alan Jacobs, "Profile: Glenn Silber Interviewed," *The Independent*, February 1980, 13.

Welles in Boston to hire community organizers to boost their run, they had exhibitors pay for their travel to meet the press and promote the film. Silber says, "When we show our film out in Portland, Oregon in a few weeks, I am going out there, certainly for the press screenings and to hang around to talk to the community that's supporting our effort. I'm getting the exhibitor to pay for my airfare. It was very easy to convince him that if I went out there and met with the press, we'd get a lot more coverage."[21] These innovative strategies allowed the filmmakers to make an end run around the advertising industry, while showing exhibitors that they were savvy, business-minded filmmakers, not dilettantes making "rich uncle pictures."

In the late 1960s, distribution companies like Pathe-Contemporary, Grove Press, and National Talent Service used theatrical runs as loss leaders for nontheatrical distribution, then turned fully to the nontheatrical market. Filmmakers who self-distributed their documentaries quickly learned this lesson as well: even if their theatrical runs did not net enough money to cover production costs, the work of the publicity machine could be applied to later releases. Adair was encouraged by the limited theatrical release of *Word Is Out*, even as he acknowledged that nontheatrical venues were the primary market for the film.

> By having it in theaters with all the attendant review, publicity and prestige, the main (non-theatrical) market for the film is obviously strengthened. Not only do more potential 16mm users now know about the film, but some are more likely to rent it sight unseen for two reasons: First, they might have read some of the reviews printed nationally; and second, in many of their minds, the film has gained credibility because it was part of the Big Time. In other words, it has lost some of the onus of being a documentary.[22]

Even though other independent filmmakers self-distributed their films, Adair points out two significant differences: the category of documentary is, itself, a stumbling block for theatrical distribution. In general, independent features more closely resemble studio films because of their narrative structure and audience address, which is what allowed independent fiction films to grow in esteem and profitability more quickly and seamlessly than documentaries. Second of all, Adair is aware that the nontheatrical

---

[21] Jacobs, "Profile," 14.
[22] Adair, "Adventures in Distribution," 11.

market is a fairly stable base for documentary films, a low-risk market for documentaries to be sold and rented in. In this way, the Mariposa Group's efforts to distribute the film theatrically, in addition to the national broadcast on PBS, acted as a massive, expensive publicity campaign for the most important phase of release.

These independent documentary filmmakers had two goals when they self-distributed their films: earning back their production costs and proving that alternative films could work in theaters. Their work certainly paid dividends for the cause, by filtering down to exhibitors and other filmmakers. The 1980 *Variety* article trumpeted the effects of these efforts, mentioning "word along the specialized exhibitor grapevine that regional distribution experiments, like the northwestern and midwestern theatre network used by such features as *The War at Home, Word Is Out,* and *Northern Lights,* were paying off at the box office."[23] The greater industry read about these successes, as did the independent film community. In 1980, the Association for Independent Video and Filmmakers' magazine, *The Independent,* published interviews with both Adair and Silber where they discussed their distribution processes in depth.

New Independent Film Institutions Support Documentary

Just as filmmakers worked to market their films effectively, several nonprofit institutions played an important role in raising the profile of documentaries in theaters. The Independent Feature Project (IFP), notably, advocated for independent filmmakers and the inclusion of independent film in theatrical settings. IFP's New American Cinema: A Showcase of Premiere Films was a week-long series of nine independent films, including two documentaries, that was exhibited in theaters in five cities during the summer of 1981.[24] Conceived by IFP's Sandra Schulberg and the American Film Institute's Exhibition Services, and funded in part by the National Endowment for the Arts, the series was "designed to give independent films access to a domestic exhibition/distribution system which has traditionally been resistant to them."[25] IFP hoped to stimulate interest in booking the films, as well as

---

[23] Klain, "Indie Filmmakers Go Commercial," 46.
[24] The two documentaries were *The Day after Trinity* (Jon Else) and *Model* (Frederick Wiseman).
[25] Marian Luntz, "The New American Cinema Showcase," *The Independent,* May 1981, 14.

strengthen the independent film infrastructure by teaching grassroots marketing techniques to local groups. While the effects of IFP's effort are difficult to measure, anecdotally, IFP's example had a powerful effect in opening up commercial theaters to more independent filmmakers and teaching the filmmakers how to handle these opportunities. In 1981, Herb E. Smith, of the Appalachian media arts center Appalshop, had success exhibiting his feature documentary *Handcarved* in a commercial theater in Washington, DC, one of the cities where the Showcase had traveled. He testified, "The Independent Feature Project had just plowed the ground a little bit and we could use some of the recommendations they had for how to work it and all."[26] Not only did the visibility of the Showcase open up more mainstream exhibition possibilities for independent filmmakers, putting on the Showcase allowed the IFP to gather information about distribution and exhibition that it then disseminated to other filmmakers.

While IFP's New American Cinema series traveled around the country, strengthening the regional network of exhibitors interested in independent film, the theater Film Forum helped to till the soil in New York City. New York City is a notoriously competitive market, with high advertising costs and high theater operating costs, making it a risky, expensive place to premiere a film. On the other hand, the significance of the market to the national media means that positive critical response and a successful run in New York City opens up more exhibition possibilities in other cities. As documentarian Julia Reichert learned when self-distributing *Seeing Red*, "Financially, there's very little way to win in New York. . . . Yet the New York grosses are the most important in the country. Other theaters want to know, 'What did you do in New York?'"[27] As Reichert attests, opening in New York is an upfront investment, a gamble on future returns from runs in other cities and, eventually, from the nontheatrical market.

Nonprofit art-house cinema Film Forum eased the difficulties of both self-distribution and the New York City market for numerous documentaries. It was a launching pad, providing a screen to unknown films, where they could be reviewed by major publications, attract a distributor, or prove their appeal to other exhibitors and markets. In 1981, Film Forum's policy was to pay filmmakers 30 percent of the box-office returns or $1,000 for a two-week run, whichever was more. This generous and transparent policy eased the

---

[26] Bernard Timberg and Thomas Arnold, "Voices from the Hinterland: Independent Regional Features—Part 1," *The Independent* November 1981, 13.
[27] Linfield, "How to Succeed," 21.

way for many broke independent filmmakers, who would have usually only seen returns after the theater rental or theater operating costs were covered. It also "gives filmmakers a risk-free way of getting reviews in the *Times*, the *Voice*, and the *Soho News*," noted director Karen Cooper in 1981.[28] An early example of this is the brief, strategic self-distribution of humorous, nuclear-war compilation film *The Atomic Cafe*. Writing in *The Independent* in 1984, Renee Tajima reported, "While negotiating with Libra Cinema 5, Pierce and Kevin Rafferty and Jayne Loader, the producers of *The Atomic Cafe*, opened it for two weeks at the Film Forum in New York, where it became the theater's all-time top grossing film."[29] The filmmakers had attracted a distribution company to handle the film, but they gained the upper hand in their negotiations by showing the excellent business the film could do in the most competitive market. Other filmmakers followed suit. As Susan Linfield reported later in 1984, the documentary *The World of Tomorrow* (1984, dirs. Lance Bird and Tom Johnson) about the 1939 New York World's Fair, was counting on following a similar trajectory as *The Atomic Cafe*. Linfield writes, "The film played for two weeks in Manhattan's downtown Film Forum last March, and [codirector] Bird hopes that *Tomorrow* will follow the path of such films as *When the Mountains Tremble* and *The Atomic Cafe*, which were picked up by distributors following their Film Forum runs."[30] Film Forum performed a unique service to documentarians by launching their films in the hypercompetitive market of New York City.

The market for independent American cinema, especially documentaries, grew through advocacy, at both an individual and an organizational level. These advocacy practices included regional self-distribution and banding together through nonprofit organizations to share risks and information. Filmmakers realized that making good work was not sufficient for achieving visibility; rather, creating and proving the viability of a market for their work was the only way to reach audiences in the long term. Distribution companies were another crucial piece of the puzzle. While most commercial

---

[28] Kathy Davis, "The Return of Film Forum," *American Film*, September 1981, 62. Cooper's personal interest in documentaries is well known, and her influence in the creation of the theatrical market for documentaries cannot be overstated. In 2010, the Museum of Modern Art even organized a retrospective, to celebrate the fortieth anniversary of Film Forum, entitled "Karen Cooper Carte Blanche." It consisted of twenty-one feature documentaries, all of which premiered at Film Forum.

[29] Renee Tajima, "The Theatrical Track from Courtship to Contract," *The Independent*, April 1984, 18–19. Initially self-funded, the filmmakers also gained production funds from Tom Brandon of Brandon Films and the Film Fund. Kathleen Hulser, "Archival Hunt Proves It's a Mad, Mad World," *The Independent*, June 1982, 11, 12, 19.

[30] Linfield, "How to Succeed," 23.

distribution companies were not interested in acquiring documentaries, there were a few stalwarts that had been handling documentaries for years, and a few innovative new companies formed in the early 1980s found ways to exploit the genre.

New Distribution Company: First Run Features

First Run Features was a step beyond self-distribution and nonprofit organizations. First Run did most significant work in building the theatrical market for documentary film in the early days of the American independent cinema movement. It was founded in 1979 as a cooperative venture, by the makers of *The War at Home, Joe & Maxi* (1978, dir. Maxi Cohen), *Northern Lights* (1978, dirs. John Hanson and Rob Nilsson), and *The Wobblies* (1979, dirs. Deborah Shaffer and Stewart Bird). These filmmakers had tried self-distribution, having been part of the group of eight independent films (almost all documentaries) that were "going commercial" in 1980 according to *Variety*.[31] Much like the independent film trade organizations IFP and Association for Independent Video and Filmmakers, the filmmakers who formed First Run Features did so to share information, learn from each other, and manage risk. This consolidation was a way to be more efficient and more visible.

First Run was organized around service deals, wherein it charged a fee to distribute films and left the cost of print and promotion to the filmmaker and exhibitor. This is the opposite of the way that distribution companies would handle a negative pickup, by paying an advance upfront (large if competing with other companies to acquire the film, small if not) and then subtracting the cost of P&A from the grosses. Only after those costs were covered would profits flow back to the producer.

While the filmmakers could choose how much to spend on P&A, they centralized the booking process and hired an expert, Fran Spielman, to run First Run. Spielman had worked for New Yorker Films and Cinema V for many years. She came out of retirement to bring her expertise to First Run Features, bridging the gap between the earlier period of specialty distribution and this new world. Interviewed in 1982, Spielman explained her decision to join First Run Features in 1979: "Not only did I feel what these kids

---

[31] Klain, "Indie Filmmakers Go Commercial," 1, 46.

were doing was important, . . . I also felt that their work deserved a chance in commercial houses. I knew there would be obstacles, but we have a growing track record with exhibitors now and our films have been accepted by them as a workable alternative."[32] Even with these successes, she described her work as "a house-by-house, city-by-city operation," a never-ending process of proselytizing to theater owners. First Run also had a nontheatrical division. In 1982, *Boxoffice* reported that nontheatrical screenings for community groups had not taken away from First Run's theatrical business but had in fact helped it break into theaters.

It is important to note that First Run was not a purely rationalized economic endeavor. It was founded by filmmakers on the faith that there was a better way than isolated self-distribution. And it was run by Fran Spielman with the optimism that their work would pay off and open up new opportunities for independent filmmakers. *Boxoffice* characterized this belief as typical of industry outsiders, writing, "Independent documentary and feature filmmakers have always fought the Battle For An Open Playdate with an optimistic outlook, hoping that their low budget, 'special' films would find their way to first run screens."[33] This may have been ordinary starry-eyed optimism, but the structure of the company proved much more successful than earlier attempts to consolidate indies' distribution efforts, like the Filmmakers' Distribution Center. First Run is still in existence and has distributed numerous notable films, both fiction and documentary (Table 2.2).

First Run's modest success and sheer longevity inspired imitation by a number of other companies, most of which were better funded and resourced. As First Run president and cofounder Barry Alexander Brown noted in 1982,

> We have proved that there is an audience out there looking for our films. Now the majors' classics divisions have picked up on that, so it will be harder from now on to just stumble upon a new gem of a film and distribute it. But this competition gives the independent filmmaker more of a marketplace for his work.[34]

---

[32] David Linck, "First Run Features: Going to Bat for the Small Filmmaker," *Boxoffice*, December 1, 1982, 42.
[33] Linck, "First Run Features," 42.
[34] Linck, "First Run Features," 44.

Table 2.2 Documentaries distributed by First Run Features, 1979–1985

Title	Year	Director
The Wobblies	1979	Deborah Shaffer, Stewart Bird
The Life and Times of Rosie the Riveter	1980	Connie Field
Soldier Girls	1981	Nick Broomfield
Agee	1980	Ross Spears
Stations of the Elevated	1981	Manfred Kirchheimer
Before the Nickelodeon: The Cinema of Edwin S. Porter	1982	Charles Musser
Chicken Ranch	1983	Nick Broomfield, Sandi Sissel
28 Up	1984	Michael Apted
Vietnam: The Secret Agent	1983	Jacki Ochs
Before Stonewall	1984	Greta Schiller, Robert Rosenberg
Sherman's March	1985	Ross McElwee

While First Run did not grow into a mini-major or a competitive independent distributor, it helped lay the groundwork for the commercial exploitation of independent documentaries and fiction films in the 1980s.

New Distribution Companies: Independent and Studio Classics Divisions

Alongside First Run, a number of new distribution companies were formed in the 1980s, and the growth of these companies propelled the growth of the theatrical marketplace for documentary films. The shrinking studio release schedule also affected the market: studios had also been releasing fewer and fewer films throughout the 1970s, reaching a low of seventy-eight films in 1977. By relying on tentpole films, studios left more open dates on exhibitors' calendars, like the market opening that led to the success of *Mondo Cane* and the rockumentaries in the 1960s. While exploitation films had filled these playdates in the early 1970s, the studios had fully integrated the marketing strategies and some genres of exploitation films by the late 1970s, pushing exploitation films out of theaters and into still-developing markets like home video and cable. At the same time, the number of "specialized" distribution companies grew. New independent distributors opened, and studios founded classics divisions to acquire and distribute smaller films.

This growth was spurred on by the surprise success of films like *The Return of the Secaucus Seven* (1980), which grossed $2 million on a $60,000 budget. While fiction films, both American and foreign, were the primary product for these new companies, a few companies also filled out their catalogs with documentaries.

Some of the earliest commercial distribution companies to acquire and distribute documentaries were UA Classics, Cinecom, and Island/Alive. Though they all worked with specialty films—foreign films, American independent films, documentaries—they were organized in a more traditional way than First Run Features. Nevertheless, they had learned from the success of First Run, the earlier distributors like Cinema V and New Yorker, and all the filmmakers who self-distributed. They kept advertising costs low, aiming instead for free publicity by bringing filmmakers to special screenings. They further reduced risk by picking up a particular type of documentary: all three companies primarily acquired documentaries with a music or performance element. In doing so, they tapped into the appeal of watching musical performance on a large screen with powerful speakers. In addition to the cinematic spectacle of musical performance, these documentaries could be marketed through the celebrity of the main subject. While these newer commercial distributors took marketing cues from First Run and the self-distributing documentarians, they mostly acquired the most commercially viable type of documentary: music documentaries.

UA Classics was a short-lived company, in operation for only six years (1980–85), but it successfully released a number of specialty films, including documentaries. Its legacy is most apparent in the independent distribution companies it spawned: UA Classics' former executives went on to found Cinecom (1982–91), Sony Pictures Classics (1992–present), and Fine Line Features (1990–2005). UA Classics paid no advance and split revenue fifty-fifty with filmmakers. UA Classics paid print and advertising costs out of its own pocket, rather than charging those costs to filmmakers as a "distributor's fee," as many commercial distributors did. This incentivized the company to keep its marketing costs extremely low. UA Classics pitched its publicity to a niche audience, replacing expensive television advertising with efforts to get newspaper coverage, like having filmmakers present at screenings. UA Classics' CEO Nathaniel Kwit claimed that the average marketing costs for a theatrical distribution campaign amounted to a shockingly paltry $2,000. Yet, Yannis Tzioumakis writes, "Even if these figures have been exaggerated for publicity purposes and might have been higher in reality, they are nevertheless a far cry from the average marketing and print costs in Hollywood in the early 1980s, which were close to $4 million for the average studio production."[35] UA Classics was an early attempt by Hollywood studios to mimic the small-scale operations and outsize crossover hits of independent distributors.

As the first studio classics division, UA Classics began by distributing European art films, most by well-known auteurs. This falls in line with the strategies of specialty distributors during the 1950s and 1960s. UA Classics distributed *The Last Metro* (1980, dir. Francois Truffaut), *Diva* (1981, dir. Jean-Jacques Beineix), *Veronika Voss* (1982, dir. Rainer Werner Fassbinder), and *Passion* (1982, dir. Jean-Luc Godard). By the end of its lifespan, UA Classics had turned more toward American independent cinema, distributing *Lianna* (1983, dir. John Sayles) and *Streamers* (1983, dir. Robert Altman). At the same time, the division acquired independent documentary films, including *From Mao to Mozart: Isaac Stern in China* (1979, dir. Murray Lerner), *The Weavers: Wasn't That a Time!* (1982, dir. Jim Brown), and *Say Amen Somebody* (1982, dir. George Nierenberg), about gospel music. Each of these films deals with music, with the first two referring to a musical artist in the very title, which significantly eased the difficulty of marketing a documentary feature. The single nonmusic documentary that UA Classics distributed was *Genocide* (1982, dir. Arnold Schwartzman), a documentary about the Holocaust, narrated by Orson Welles and Elizabeth Taylor, that won the Academy Award for Best Documentary in 1983.

While being distributed by a studio classics division was a very desirable outcome for independent documentarians, taking control of distribution out of the filmmaker's hands can also have negative consequences. As *Say Amen Somebody* director George Nierenberg told *The Independent* in 1984, "The film has never played in a Black theater because UA Classics' strength is in art houses."[36] A documentary about gospel music would seem to be a perfect fit for black audiences, but if distributors have little experience with that market, they are going to have a hard time placing a film in it. Director Nierenberg lobbied UA Classics to fulfill his distribution desires, which went beyond commercial success to include "special promotions in Black churches, a benefit for the NAACP, and a concert and screening at the Rikers Island prison facility."[37] Even when films do not have an explicit political mission,

---

[35] Tzioumakis, *Hollywood's Indies*, 29.
[36] Tajima, "Theatrical Track," 20.
[37] Tajima, "Theatrical Track," 20.

documentarians often want to use their films to benefit communities important to them. This desire might appear incompatible with commercial distribution, but some filmmakers were able to negotiate with distributors to achieve specific goals in addition to box-office success and prestige.

Cinecom was formed in 1982 (and bankrupt in 1991) by executives who had left UA Classics.[38] It followed a similar path, distributing both foreign films (including British films like James Ivory's *Room with a View*, 1986, and *Maurice*, 1987) and American independent films by then-proven directors (*Come Back to the Five and Dime, Jimmy Dean, Jimmy Dean* and *Secret Honor* (1982 and 1984, dir. Robert Altman), *El Norte* (1983, dir. Gregory Nava), and *Matewan* (1987, dir. John Sayles). It also mostly distributed documentaries with a performance element, including the Talking Heads' concert documentary *Stop Making Sense* (1984, dir. Jonathan Demme), Laurie Anderson's performance documentary *Home of the Brave* (1986, dir. Laurie Anderson), and Spaulding Gray's monologue performance *Swimming to Cambodia* (1987, dir. Jonathan Demme).

Not all of Cinecom's documentaries were about music, but even those without a performance element had titles and subjects that would have been familiar to exhibitors and potential audiences. One of the first documentaries it acquired was *Burroughs* (1984, dir. Howard Brookner), about author and cult figure William S. Burroughs. Though documentaries are generally difficult to market, Brookner pointed out, *Burroughs* "was easily accessible in its subject matter—you didn't have to explain what it was about, as with a narrative."[39] In addition to the familiar subject, the release of *Burroughs* coincided with Burroughs's seventieth birthday and the release of his new novel. These events generated a wealth of publicity for the film, and Burroughs himself made personal appearances at some screenings to promote it.

Familiar subject matter likely also sold Cinecom on *The Times of Harvey Milk* (1984, Robert Epstein). Milk's assassination had been national news six years before the film's release, and the trial of the assassin was even more recent. In addition, the film appealed to an easily identified and underserved audience: gay and lesbian viewers. Originally picked up by a company called Teleculture, the film rights were acquired by Cinecom after Teleculture

---

[38] Interference from parent company United Artists may have caused the executives to leave.
[39] Linfield, "How to Succeed," 21. Director Brookner reported that exhibitors approached him after the film's New York Film Festival premiere with offers to show the film. Brookner agreed, and he self-distributed *Burroughs* in a few cities before Cinecom acquired it.

abruptly went out of business. *The Times of Harvey Milk* went on to win the Academy Award for Best Documentary.

Island/Alive was also a short-lived enterprise (1983–86) formed during the production of a documentary called *Return Engagement*, about the touring debate between Timothy Leary and G. Gordon Liddy. Fiction filmmaker Alan Rudolph directed the documentary, and Rudolph's producer Carolyn Pfeiffer became the president of Island/Alive. As Pfeiffer put it, "There was a desire to directly generate revenue, by way of a distribution company, from films we would produce."[40] The financing for the company came from two music business executives, Chris Blackwell, record producer, of Island Records and Island Pictures and Shep Gordon, a musician's representative, of Alive Enterprises. Though *Return Engagement* was the impetus for the founding of Island/Alive, its first release was the experimental documentary *Koyaanisqatsi* (1983, dir. Godfrey Reggio). *Koyaanisqatsi* marries surreal cinematography and editing techniques with a propulsive score by composer Philip Glass. The result is a hypnotic meditation on the speed and scale of the modern world.

Director Godfrey Reggio initially self-distributed the film, starting with a single showing at Radio City Music Hall in September 1982. The film then opened at a theater in Los Angeles, where it played for five weeks before moving to another theater. According to the director, the film earned $300,000 during this distribution period, while Island/Alive propelled it to a box-office total over $2 million. Island/Alive's head of distribution, Cary Brokaw, told *Boxoffice*, "Our greatest joy . . . is that we're playing Middle America, which we never expected. It opened in Wichita, did exceptionally well and then followed with a second weekend gross that was even bigger than the first. We're finding that wherever we go the secret is to stage the film as an event. With the right approach we can do well in markets that aren't generally considered sophisticated movie towns."[41] The company used strategies pioneered by filmmakers who self-distributed, by rolling the film out slowly and generating free publicity by making the film an exciting event, often featuring appearances by Reggio and composer Glass. Island/Alive's close connection to Island Records enhanced this strategy, allowing it to coordinate the release of the film's soundtrack with the film's release, on a regional basis. This was similar to the coordination of publicity efforts

---

[40] Jimmy Summers, "Island Alive," *Boxoffice*, August 1, 1984, 12.
[41] Summers, "Island Alive," 12.

between Leacock-Pennebaker and Columbia Records for the release of *Dont Look Back*.

Though these companies did not last long, they helped establish a precedent for the theatrical distribution of documentaries by commercial distribution companies. They adopted and refined the marketing techniques of earlier filmmakers and distributors, and led the way to the bigger documentary hits of the late 1980s.

Tracking Changes in Documentary Marketplace at New Yorker Films: A Case Study

Founded in 1965 by Dan Talbot, owner of the New York City art house New Yorker Theater, New Yorker Films specialized in the distribution of foreign art cinema. Talbot acquired challenging and innovative films, introducing American audiences to films by directors such as Rainer Werner Fassbinder, Ousmane Sembene, Yasujiro Ozu, and Jacques Rivette. With both theatrical and nontheatrical distribution arms, New Yorker Films' catalog played a significant role in establishing the canon of world cinema and circulating auteur theory as the key text for understanding film art. Until the late 1970s, New Yorker Films was also one of the only commercial distributors, along with Cinema V, to regularly distribute documentary feature films.[42]

Examining New Yorker Films' distribution contracts for documentaries between the late 1960s and the mid-1990s offers a window into how the market for documentaries changed. As more distributors acquired documentary features, increased competition affected the distribution deals New Yorker Films made with documentarians. The two areas that change are the extent of rights acquired and the size of the advance paid. New Yorker Films could acquire either all rights to a film, both theatrical and nontheatrical, or nontheatrical rights only. New Yorker acquired only nontheatrical rights when another, more powerful theatrical distributor acquired theatrical rights. The amount of the advance roughly reflects the distributor's estimation of the film's market value and the producer's other distribution prospects. If New Yorker Films paid a small advance or no

---

[42] Cinema V represented *Gimme Shelter* (1970, dir. Albert Maysles), *The Sorrow and the Pity* (1972, dir. Marcel Ophuls), *Marjoe* (1972, dirs. Howard Smith and Sarah Kernochang), and *Harlan County, USA* (1976, dir. Barbara Kopple).

advance at all, one can reasonably conclude that New Yorker Films was not certain of commercial success and no other distributor offered the producer an advance payment.

In the 1970s and early 1980s, New Yorker customarily acquired all rights to documentary features because nontheatrical circulation was just as lucrative as, if not more lucrative than, theatrical release. However, as more theatrical distribution companies acquired feature documentaries, and certain filmmakers gained higher status, New Yorker often split the rights to a film with another company. At the beginning of this period, New Yorker often paid no advance to acquire all rights to a documentary feature. But as competition for documentary features increased, New Yorker paid higher advances for a documentary feature, even if the company acquired only the nontheatrical rights to the film. Tracing these changes in New Yorker Films' practices provides a sharper view of the shifts in the documentary feature marketplace.

New Yorker Films acquired exclusive rights to the following documentary films for a small advance or no advance at all: *Letter from Siberia* (1969), *Millhouse: A White Comedy* (1971), *Angela: A Portrait of a Revolutionary* (1971), *Eadweard Muybridge* (1975), *Word Is Out* (1978), *Koko: A Talking Gorilla* (1979), *I Am What My films Are: A Portrait of Werner Herzog* (1979), *Sans Soleil* (1983, $5,000 advance), *When the Mountains Tremble* (1984), and *Dark Glow of the Mountains* (1984).[43] Some of these films have since entered the pantheon of documentary film. But at the time of their initial release, New Yorker Films was uncertain of their commercial prospects and, being one of the only independent distributors, it had the leverage to pay producers no money upfront.

Commercial success may have been uncertain, but some films returned a fair amount of money to the distributor (and later, the producer, usually via a fifty-fifty split of profits after expenses). Two examples from the early 1980s follow: *When the Mountains Tremble*, a film about political turmoil and civil war in Guatemala, and *Sans Soleil*, an essay film by Chris Marker. Acquired in 1984 for no advance, *When the Mountains Tremble* boasted no ready-made audience or presold idea, except interest in the American invasion of

---

[43] New Yorker Films also acquired the rerelease rights to several documentaries: *Portrait of Jason* (acquired in 1971), *Jazz on a Summer's Day* (acquired in 1974), and a number of films by Emile de Antonio (*America Is Hard to See*, acquired in 1973; and *In the Year of the Pig* and *Painters Painting*, both acquired in 1974).

Guatemala.[44] Universities and film societies booked it quickly, to the tune of $11,000 per two-month period, and the film also made a respectable showing at a number of commercial theaters. Its largest take was over $5,000 in a one-week run at the York Theatre in San Francisco, followed by almost $4,000 in a three-week run at FACETS in Chicago, both during summer 1984.[45]

New Yorker Films paid $5,000 in advance to acquire all rights to *Sans Soleil*.[46] The film showed in a few theaters during 1984 and 1985, but New Yorker booked it mostly in film societies, art museums, and cultural centers like the Japan Society and the Alliance Française. In the first two years of release, theatrical bookings returned over $4,000 to New Yorker, but nontheatrical bookings more than doubled that, returning over $10,000.[47]

The distribution deals for *When the Mountains Tremble* and *Sans Soleil* show how little New Yorker had to pay upfront for feature documentaries in the early 1980s. The films' booking records also point to the strength of the nontheatrical market for feature documentaries, relative to theatrical release.

Yet as early as 1982, New Yorker's distribution deals were already changing because of the increasing number of distribution companies vying for documentary features. A few documentarians were able to sell their film's theatrical rights to other companies and split off the nontheatrical rights to New Yorker Films. *Variety* reported on this trend, "Split of theatrical and nontheatrical rights is considered advantageous to the filmmakers..., whose pic benefits from separate, focused handling by the respective distribs."[48] The reasoning behind this thinking is that a film will have a more successful theatrical run if it is marketed and released by a theatrical distribution company, and a better nontheatrical life if handled by a nontheatrical distribution specialist.

Though New Yorker worked in both the theatrical and nontheatrical market, the new distributors concentrated exclusively on high-risk, high-reward theatrical releasing. This left New Yorker Films to handle the nontheatrical market. For example, Libra Films released *The Atomic Cafe*

---

[44] Distribution Agreement Motion Picture: "When the Mountains Tremble," March 28, 1984, Dan Talbot Papers, Box 154, folder "When the Mountains Tremble, 1993," Rare Book and Manuscript Library, Columbia University Library.

[45] Producers Reports: "When the Mountains Tremble," Dan Talbot Papers, Box 112, folder "When the Mountains Tremble," Rare Book and Manuscript Library, Columbia University Library.

[46] Distribution Agreement Motion Picture: "Sans Soleil," July 5, 1983, Dan Talbot Papers, Box 180, folder "Sans Soleil, 1983–2003," Rare Book and Manuscript Library, Columbia University Library.

[47] Producers Reports: "Sans Soleil," Dan Talbot Papers, Box 103, folder "Sans Soleil," Rare Book and Manuscript Library, Columbia University Library.

[48] "'Atomic Cafe' Rights Libra's Theatrically, Talbot Nontheatrical," *Variety*, April 28, 1982, 5, 46.

theatrically in 1982, while New Yorker Films paid $15,000 for nontheatrical rights.[49] Island Alive Releasing released *Koyaanisqatsi* theatrically in 1985, while New Yorker Films paid $12,500 for nontheatrical rights.[50] In 1991, Triton Pictures released *Hearts of Darkness* theatrically, while New Yorker Films paid $2,500 for the nontheatrical rights.[51] And in 1995, Sony Pictures Classics distributed *Crumb* theatrically, while New Yorker Films paid $10,000 to distribute it nontheatrically.[52]

One reason these feature documentaries attracted distribution companies is that their subjects were presold or tapped into extant audiences, like the rockumentaries of decades past. *Hearts of Darkness*, by Eleanor Coppola—Francis Ford Coppola's wife—covers the infamously dramatic making of *Apocalypse Now*. *Crumb* is a portrait of Robert Crumb, one of the most famous and controversial comic book artists of all time. By taking a new angle on subjects that were likely already familiar to audiences, these documentaries appealed to distributors who saw that marketing them would be easier than marketing a documentary about an unknown or unfamiliar subject.

New Yorker Films' business relationship with documentarian Errol Morris illustrates how changes from larger market shifts intersect with those stemming from individual career growth. New Yorker Films distributed many of Morris's documentaries—both his earliest films *Gates of Heaven* and *Vernon, Florida*, as well as later films *A Brief History of Time*, and *Fast, Cheap, and out of Control*, which followed his breakout *The Thin Blue Line*—but the company's contracts with Morris took very different shape over time. In 1980, New Yorker Films acquired all rights, apart from television, for *Gates of Heaven*. New Yorker Films paid an advance of $3,000 for these rights.[53] The film was booked in both theaters and nontheatrical venues, and these

---

[49] Distribution Agreement Motion Picture: "The Atomic Cafe," May 7, 1982, Dan Talbot Papers, Box 246, folder "Contracts—The Atomic Cafe 1982–2006," Rare Book and Manuscript Library, Columbia University Library.

[50] Distribution Agreement Motion Picture: "Koyaanisqatsi," April 10, 1985, Dan Talbot Papers, Box 179, folder "Koyaanisqatsi 1985–1990," Rare Book and Manuscript Library, Columbia University Library.

[51] Distribution Agreement Motion Picture: "Hearts of Darkness," November 21, 1991, Dan Talbot Papers, Box 178, folder "Hearts of Darkness 1991," Rare Book and Manuscript Library, Columbia University Library.

[52] Distribution Agreement Motion Picture: "Crumb," June 30, 1995, Dan Talbot Papers, Box 246, folder "Contracts—Crumb 1995," Rare Book and Manuscript Library, Columbia University Library.

[53] Distribution Agreement Motion Picture: "Gates of Heaven," October 24, 1980, Dan Talbot Papers, Box 178, folder "Gates of Heaven," Rare Book and Manuscript Library, Columbia University Library.

bookings returned over $40,000 in theaters and $22,000 in other venues in its first two years in release.[54] In 1981, New Yorker Films signed a similar contract for Morris's next film, *Vernon, Florida*, and paid an advance of $4,000.[55] However, this film did not deliver returns as stellar as those of *Gates of Heaven* (less than $3,000 theatrical, less than $6,000 nontheatrical in the first two years).[56]

Morris broke out with *The Thin Blue Line*, which Miramax acquired for $400,000 and shepherded to an impressive $1.2 million theatrical gross. Once this happened, Morris's relationship with New Yorker Films changed: New Yorker would handle only nontheatrical release of his films, and the company would pay higher prices for just those rights than it had for exclusive rights to Morris's features in the past. In 1992, Triton Pictures distributed *A Brief History of Time* in theaters, while New Yorker Films handled the nontheatrical side, paying an advance of $10,000.[57] In 1997, Sony Pictures Classics distributed *Fast, Cheap, and out of Control* in theaters, while New Yorker Films handled nontheatrical bookings, paying an advance of $5,000.[58] As Errol Morris's films proved themselves at the box office, Morris and his producers contracted with newer independent distributors. These distributors presumably offered a larger advance, and likely promised a more aggressive marketing strategy and access to better bookings. The subjects of the films likely also played a part in their perceived market value. For example, *A Brief History of Time* is a portrait of famed astrophysicist Stephen Hawking, and it bears the same title as Hawking's best-selling book.

New Yorker Films' acquisition contracts for documentary films reflected the increasing competition in the documentary market, beginning in the early 1980s. A longtime distributor of documentary features, New Yorker Films continued to acquire documentaries even as new, powerful theatrical distributors began to vie for the same films. This led New Yorker to change its strategy. First, New Yorker ceded theatrical distribution rights to newer, more

---

[54] Producers Reports: "Gates of Heaven," Dan Talbot Papers, Box 142, folder "Gates of Heaven," Rare Book and Manuscript Library, Columbia University Library.

[55] Distribution Agreement Motion Picture: "Vernon, Florida," Dan Talbot Papers, Box 154, folder "Vernon, Florida 1981," Rare Book and Manuscript Library, Columbia University Library.

[56] Producers Reports: "Vernon, Florida," Dan Talbot Papers, Box 103, folder "Vernon, Florida," Rare Book and Manuscript Library, Columbia University Library.

[57] Distribution Agreement Motion Picture: "A Brief History of Time," Dan Talbot Papers, Box 92, folder "A Brief History of Time," Rare Book and Manuscript Library, Columbia University Library.

[58] Distribution Agreement Motion Picture: "Fast, Cheap, and Out of Control," June 23, 1997, Dan Talbot Papers, Box 246, folder "Contracts—Fast, Cheap, and Out of Control 1997," Rare Book and Manuscript Library, Columbia University Library.

powerful companies, instead choosing to handle the nontheatrical market only. Second, New Yorker began to pay more for the distribution rights to documentaries, even when those rights were limited to the nontheatrical market.

As American independent cinema grew in commercial and cultural importance in the 1980s, new distribution companies began to acquire documentary films. No longer was New Yorker Films the only option for distributing documentary features. The fresh interest in documentaries by commercial distributors affected the way that stalwart distributor New Yorker Films contracted with documentary filmmakers (Table 2.3). These shifts evince greater changes in the commercial status of documentary film.

Documentaries Swell in Success as Indies Explode

The late 1970s to late 1980s saw major changes in the visibility and commercial viability of feature documentaries. The growth of the American independent film movement cultivated the market for documentary films with a new network of institutions that provided production and distribution support for independent films and the establishment of new commercial distribution companies interested in independent films. Documentaries were an integral part of the independent film scene at the moment, with "independent" was being redefined and imbued with new cultural meaning. Documentary films achieved enough commercial success in this new environment that they had grown in status and desirability by the end of the decade. Stylistic innovations and connection with the indie film movement positioned documentaries closer to cinema during the decade, creating a separation from television journalism and new cable channels like the Discovery Channel that used formulaic nonfiction series to build a deep archive of low-cost, endlessly re-airable programming.[59]

That said, there were numerous continuities with the previous era. Documentarians continued to self-distribute their films in theaters. At times these efforts were politically tinged, as they often were in the political collectives formed in the 1960s and 1970s. More often, filmmakers pursued self-distribution to prove the commercial viability of their work.

[59] Cynthia Chris, "All Documentary, All the Time? Discovery Communications Inc. and Trends in Cable Television," *Television & New Media* 3, no. 1 (February 2002), 22.

Table 2.3 New Yorker Films contracts for documentary films

Title	Year of contract	Director	Advance paid	Rights
Far from Vietnam	1968	Various	0	All
Letter from Siberia	1969	Chris Marker	0	All
Cuba: Battle of the Ten Million	1971	Chris Marker, Valérie Mayoux	$1,000	All
Portrait of Jason	1971	Shirley Clarke	0	All
Millhouse	1971	Emile de Antonio	0	All
Angela: A Portrait of a Revolutionary	1971	Yolande DuLuart	0	All
David Holtzman's Diary	1973	Jim McBride	0	All
America Is Hard to See	1973	Emile de Antonio	0	All
Birth Film	1973	Susan Kleckner	0	All
In the Year of the Pig	1974	Emile de Antonio		
Jazz on a Summer's Day	1974	Bert Stern	0	All
Birth without Violence	1975	Frederick Leboyer	0	Nontheatrical
Eadweard Muybridge, Zoopraxographer	1975	Thom Andersen, Fay Andersen, Morgan Fisher	0	All
Word Is Out	1978	Mariposa Film Group	0	All
I Am What My Films Are: A Portrait of Werner Herzog	1979	Erwin Keusch, Christian Weisenborn	0	All
Koko: A Talking Gorilla	1979	Barbet Schroeder	0	All
Gates of Heaven	1980	Errol Morris	$3,000	All except broadcast
Vernon, Florida	1981	Errol Morris	$4,000	All except broadcast
The Atomic Cafe	1982	Kevin Rafferty, Jayne Loader, Pierce Rafferty	$15,000	Nontheatrical
Sans Soleil	1983	Chris Marker	$5,000	All
When the Mountains Tremble	1984	Pamela Yates, Newton Thomas Sigel	0	All
Dark Glow of the Mountains	1984	Werner Herzog	0	All
Koyaanisqatsi	1985	Godfrey Reggio	$12,500	Nontheatrical
Shoah	1985	Claude Lanzmann	$50,000	All

Table 2.3 Continued

Title	Year of contract	Director	Advance paid	Rights
Superstar: The Life and Times of Andy Warhol	1991	Chuck Workman	0	Nontheatrical
Hearts of Darkness: A Filmmaker's Apocalypse	1991	Eleanor Coppola, Fax Bahr, George Hickenlooper	$2,500	Nontheatrical
Crumb	1995	Terry Zwigoff	$10,000	Nontheatrical
The Celluloid Closet	1996	Rob Epstein, Jeffrey Friedman	$10,000	Nontheatrical
Fast, Cheap, and Out of Control	1997	Errol Morris	$5,000	Nontheatrical

They also founded a distribution company as a collective venture, coalescing the lessons learned from numerous self-distribution efforts into a formal organization. While there were new commercial distribution companies acquiring documentaries, they followed the same formula established earlier, gravitating to documentaries that featured a musical or performance element, or that had an easily marketable hook.

3
Fighting for a Place on Public Television
Independent Filmmakers Lobby (1978 to 1990)

Before the premiere of *P.O.V.* (1988–present), independent documentarians struggled to place their films on the Public Broadcasting Service. Even when their documentaries played prestigious film festivals and won major awards, filmmakers found it nearly impossible to win a national broadcast on PBS. The advent of *P.O.V.* amended this process significantly, provided a context for films with a distinctive perspective and style. Two examples, *Dark Circle* and *Who Killed Vincent Chin?*, illustrate the importance of *P.O.V.* for bringing independent documentary films to air.

Dark Circle, directed by Ruth Landy, Christopher Beaver, and Judy Irving, highlights the dangers of nuclear waste by focusing on the devastating effects of a leak at Rocky Flats Nuclear Weapons Facility on surrounding families and farms, near Denver, and the building of a nuclear power plant at Diablo Canyon, in the Bay Area. The film premiered at the 1982 New York Film Festival, won the Grand Prize for Documentary at the 1983 Sundance Film Festival, and played in some theaters and on campuses.[1] But getting a national broadcast on PBS was another story. *Dark Circle* was accepted for national broadcast in 1985, but its touchy subject matter and strong advocacy perspective made it problematic to programmers. Both KQED, the San Francisco station, and PBS hesitated to put their logo on the film because of expected blowback. They were worried about accusations of propaganda, since the film eschewed an objective, journalistic tone.[2] Once *P.O.V.* was created, the film finally had a national broadcast on PBS. B. J. Bullert points out that "PBS's acceptance of *Dark Circle* for *P.O.V.*'s 1989 season wasn't as risky a move as it would have been for PBS a few years before the Rocky Flats story had gained national attention. The broadcast took place in a different

---

[1] B. J. Bullert, *Public Television: Politics and the Battle over Documentary Film* (New Brunswick, NJ: Rutgers University Press, 1997), 46.
[2] Bullert, *Public Television*, 48. In the intervening years, *Dark Circle* was shown on WTBS's *Better World Society* series and on Bravo.

media context and within a niche created by PBS specifically for independently produced documentaries with strong points of view."[3] With the filmmakers' perspective and information confirmed by major newspapers and investigations, and a new series to frame it, *Dark Circle* could play on national PBS schedule with less apprehension from station managers and PBS programmers. It was broadcast on August 6, 1989, in the second season of *P.O.V.*[4]

Who Killed Vincent Chin? had a significantly smoother path to national broadcast on *P.O.V.* Made by Christine Choy and Renee Tajima-Pena, the film reveals the racism and anti-Asian sentiment surrounding the murder of a Chinese American engineer by two unemployed autoworkers in Detroit. Coproduced by Detroit station WTVS and the Film News Now Foundation, *Who Killed Vincent Chin?* screened at the Sundance Film Festival and was an opening-night selection at New Directions / New Films. The film was nominated for the Academy Award for Best Documentary Feature in 1989 and won a Peabody Award the same year. With acclaim from significant festivals and awards bodies, the film might have been granted a slot on PBS's schedule. But the existence of *P.O.V.* meant there was an ideal broadcast context already available to *Who Killed Vincent Chin?* It played on *P.O.V.* on July 16, 1989.[5]

For documentary filmmakers—particularly those with strong public service agendas—the relationship between their work and public media is critical. Until the end of the 1980s, however, the processes of securing financial support or reaching public media audiences remained elusive and often contentious for US documentary producers. Frustrated by a lack of opportunities and consideration for their work, independent documentarians lobbied for access to PBS funding and airtime throughout the decade. This campaign gained strength through from the growing community of filmmakers and supporting institutions engendered by the American indie cinema movement. Documentary film advocates were stymied by the conflicts inherent to the American public broadcasting system, including the inconsistent funding of the service and the national-local struggle for control. Those obstacles affected all media-makers working in the public television realm, but there were further, specific struggles for documentarians.

---

[3] Bullert, *Public Television*, 61.
[4] "POV Season 2: *Dark Circle*," PBS, https://www.pbs.org/pov/films/darkcircle/.
[5] "POV Season 2: *Who Killed Vincent Chin?*," PBS, https://www.pbs.org/pov/films/whokilledvincentchin/.

First, local stations feared controversial programs. Unlike television programs that were firmly under the editorial control of PBS and its affiliates, independently produced documentary features were much more likely to tackle controversial subjects in ways that were more challenging or risqué. Second, documentaries features do not abide by the conventional "balanced," objective presentational style of television journalism. Rather, many documentaries are made from a position of overt advocacy or subjectivity on the part of the filmmakers. PBS was unable to integrate documentary cinema into its television programming, reflecting the tension between film and television for documentary.

However, by the end of the 1980s, independent documentarians had succeeded in securing a new program, *P.O.V.*, and a new funding mechanism, the Independent Television Service. These wins were significant for both practical and cultural reasons. In practical terms, they provided financial support to documentary filmmakers: *P.O.V.* pays license fees for films selected for broadcast, and ITVS provides production funding to independent documentarians. *P.O.V.* is a coveted exhibition site for documentary films. Because PBS is a broadcast channel, a *P.O.V.* broadcast has the potential to reach viewers who do not or cannot see documentary films in theaters. This is key to those documentarians who value the public service element of documentary film. Finally, in cultural terms, the national broadcast of documentary films on *P.O.V.*, along with the growing number of documentaries in theaters, reshaped the concept of documentary from journalism and educational tool to entertaining, engaging film.

Association for Independent Video and Filmmakers versus PBS

The organization and financial situation of PBS present certain obstacles for documentary filmmakers. The relationship between the national service and the local stations and regional station consortia is a messy one, and documentary films were often a point of contention. The national service develops a prime-time schedule of programs, which it distributes to local stations in exchange for license fees. Local stations are not compelled to show all the programs or show them at the time indicated, but they must do a certain percentage of "common carriage" to maintain affiliation. Most of the prime-time schedule is made up of long-running series or "strands"—*Antiques Roadshow, Nova, American Masters*. Because of name recognition, familiar format, and consistent scheduling, these series are easy to program and market, especially compared to a one-off film.

A high percentage of PBS's budget comes from station fees, so national programmers have a vested interest in keeping local stations happy. In turn, a high percentage of local stations' budgets is fundraising from "viewers like you"—viewers who pledge money to their local stations. Thus, local stations are highly attuned to what will create loyalty with their viewers. Unlike the BBC, viewers are not required to pay an annual subscription fee to receive PBS.

Other funding for PBS and local stations comes from the federal government and state governments, and it may shift according to who is in power, politically. Advertisements are prohibited, though brief cards from corporate and foundation "sponsors" are shown. The result is that the service's and local stations' funding is unstable.

The organization and unpredictable funding of the PBS system puts it in a precarious position, such that each segment of the institution tends toward conservatism and self-preservation. And yet, during the 1980s, independent filmmakers consistently lobbied for PBS to finance and air independently produced films. Because no commercial network or cable channel supported independent filmmaking, independent filmmakers and their main advocacy group, the Association for Independent Video and Filmmakers, argued that it was PBS's public service remit to support American independent filmmaking. Robert Drew had similarly tried to work with television networks in the 1960s. But where he failed to make a lasting partnership with the networks, independent filmmakers succeeded with PBS.

One reason for that is the community and infrastructure provided by the nascent American independent film movement. The Association of Independent Video and Filmmakers was a very active lobbying group. The association's monthly publication, *The Independent*, published news about public policy, granting agencies, and public broadcasting in nearly every issue. This kept members abreast of new production grants on offer and the latest personnel change at federal agencies and private foundations. It also printed public letters to officials, calls to action, and transcripts of AIVF's meetings with Congress and PBS officials.

Barriers to Accessing Public Television

At the same time as independent filmmakers were figuring out how to get their films into commercial theaters, they were also fighting for a place on public television. This battle included both fiction and documentary filmmakers, but the impact on documentary film was more significant and long-lasting. Independent filmmakers and the AIVF consistently lobbied PBS for access to funding and national broadcasts. The AIVF was deeply involved in this battle, populating the pages of its newsletter, *The Independent*, with transcripts of meetings with PBS officials, position papers that it delivered to Congress, reports on the national public television organization and local public television stations, and comparisons with other nations' television systems.

It may seem strange for filmmakers and their organizations to work so hard to obtain financing and broadcast time from the American public television system. But this relationship was law: the Public Telecommunications Financing Act of 1978 had ordered that a substantial amount of PBS funding go to independent film and television producers, and that it be chosen by a panel of other independent producers. Apart from that, Congress did not include any specific instructions for how this decree should be enacted, or even how much of the programming funds constituted a "substantial" amount. The vagueness of the act led to confusion and a pitched debate between the AIVF, on one side, and PBS and the Corporation for Public Broadcasting, on the other.

It is important to note that there was already a mechanism in place for filmmakers to work with public television. Filmmakers could submit a proposal to win funding for their project through Open Solicitation of the Corporation for Public Broadcasting, at the national level, or through a local station.[6] The film might be granted some production funds, in exchange for rights to the broadcast premiere. Such was the case for *Word Is Out* and *The War at Home*. Both documentaries received some production funds from local stations (WNET and Wisconsin ETV, respectively), and then were broadcast on those stations after their successful theatrical runs. However, PBS and the producing stations did not guarantee broadcast of their funded project. Even when funded films were fed by satellite to local stations for

---

[6] Ellin Stein, "Leaner Times for Documentaries," *New York Times*, June 10, 1984, https://www.nytimes.com/1984/06/10/arts/leaner-times-for-documentarians.html.

broadcast, local stations might decide to schedule them at undesirable times or to preempt them altogether. Independent filmmakers and the AIVF sought more funding for independent work and a regular prime-time spot for their completed work.

However, filmmakers faced many hurdles to accessing funding and wider broadcast. The public television system favors local control, and, like theater owners who considered independent films suspect, local station programmers were very wary of independently produced programs. They were suspicious for a number of reasons: schedule disruption, potential for controversy, and the unwanted flow of financing to independent producers—out of the public television system. Schedule disruption was a real fear for local stations, and it was one reason why they might decline to schedule an independent documentary that PBS had helped fund. The conventional wisdom was that one-off broadcasts of fiction films and documentaries were not conducive to building strong schedules that attracted audiences. In the late 1970s, the public television system was still wrestling with its identity and struggling to survive. Being noncommercial theoretically freed public broadcasters from the tyranny of ratings in making programming decisions. However, both local stations and the national system needed to continually demonstrate their value to audiences and government. Programming continuing series like *Nova* was the simplest solution.

Another reason local stations were wary of independent productions was the potential for controversy, which could anger viewers and lead to state governments threatening to pull funding from precarious stations. Only a decade before, in a significant episode in the history of American public broadcasting, local stations' fear of controversy had actually sunk the National Educational Television Center. NET had operated like a network, supplying public affairs programming to other educational television stations in the 1960s. NET, intent on becoming "the alternative network," had had to attract viewers to its programs with an advertising budget of only $80,000 per year, while the commercial networks were free to spend $1 million on advertising per week. As Carolyn Brooks shows, NET battled against this substantial disadvantage by embracing the free publicity that often accompanied somewhat controversial programs, like "Three Faces of Cuba" (an episode of *Changing World*) and "John Birch Society" (an episode of *Regional Report*).[7]

---

[7] Carolyn N. Brooks, "Documentary Programming and the Emergence of the National Educational Television Center as a Network, 1958–1972" (dissertation, University of Wisconsin–Madison, 1994).

NET differentiated itself by covering topics that commercial broadcasters would not, particularly the plight of African Americans, the treatment of the poor, and the Vietnam War. This made local stations extremely skittish about broadcasting NET's shows. Even though NET's gambit succeeded, leading *Variety* and other media outlets to publicize NET programs more consistently, the local stations won out. In 1967, the Public Broadcasting Act of 1967 created PBS to supplant NET. PBS took over as station manager in 1969, banishing NET to station status. NET became the station WNET and remained a principal producer for PBS, but the new administration of WNET shut out all the producers and filmmakers who had been working for NET for the past decade.[8] The recent history of pre-PBS educational television illustrates some of the hurdles and risks that colored the AIVF's fight for more funding and access to national broadcast.

Finally, the funding and programming of more independently produced films represented a drain on local stations' own power and funding. Any money that went to independent documentarians was interpreted as money that stations did not get for operations or in-system production. In 1979, *The Independent* printed a confidential letter from Bob Thomas, director of the Association of Public Broadcasting Stations of New York, to managers of stations about a meeting of the New York State Electronic Media Organization, where filmmakers were organizing for more access to public television. He writes about the independent filmmakers,

> Their actual purpose is to get their mitts on CPB funds—as much as possible—and their products aired over PTV stations.... Part of the horror of this whole baleful business is that a corporation set up to promote the interests public broadcasting must now by law (and inclination) promote the interests of non-broadcasters.... The bottom line, it seems to me, is to have maximum federal dollars go by law directly to the stations.[9]

Thomas's fear-mongering sentiments set up "non-broadcasters" as the enemy—interlopers who want to take money and power away from the

---

[8] Even though WNET's role in national programming decisions was much diminished, it supported independent filmmaking as a local station, with programs that funded and showcased independent films. Some other stations acquired these series, but broadcast was uncertain and piecemeal because they were not part of the national PBS schedule.

[9] "Confidential: From Bob Thomas," *The Independent*, November 1979, 10.

stations, not as partners whose work could enhance the station's schedule and perceived value.

Local Stations and Documentary Films

Early on, some local stations had found solutions to the problem of independent productions. Local stations could lower their risk by focusing support on an independent documentarian and sticking with him as he became a name brand. They could also support a variety of filmmakers by developing anthology series to showcase independent work.

New York City station WNET supported independent production by funding the production of Frederick Wiseman's films. Following sold-out screenings of *Titicut Follies* at the 1967 New York Film Festival, and the theatrical distribution of the film by Grove Press, WNET commissioned Wiseman to make *High School* in 1968. This was followed by individual commissions from WNET for *Law and Order* (1969), *Hospital* (1970), and *Basic Training* (1971).[10] Then in 1972, WNET signed Wiseman to the first of two successive five-year contracts, which provided production financing for nine more films.[11] Wiseman's productions have also been funded by the Ford Foundation, a MacArthur "genius" grant, the Corporation for Public Broadcasting, and later, the Independent Television Service.

Some have criticized this patronage because Wiseman's observational filmmaking style eschews analysis of current issues and explicit political confrontation. Brian Winston suggests that this made Wiseman's films attractive to the newly formed Corporation for Public Broadcasting. Winston comments, "If the filmmaker could bring the frisson of controversial works without actually causing any real problems that would be ideal."[12] Continued support, either in the form of production funds or airtime, likely comes because of Wiseman's reputation. Wiseman is a known PBS brand, an auteur whose reputation is bound up with the public service broadcaster.

Wiseman self-distributes his films through his company Zipporah Films, as he has since 1971. The stability of this relationship has likely informed his

---

[10] Bryan Winston, "'A Riddle Wrapped in a Mystery inside an Enigma': Wiseman and Public Television," *Studies in Documentary Film* 3, no. 2 (2009), 100.

[11] These are the nine films: *Essene* (1972), *Juvenile Court* (1973), *Primate* (1974), *Welfare* (1975), *Meat* (1976), *Canal Zone* (1977), *Sinai Field Mission* (1978) *Manoeuvre* (1980), and *Model* (1981).

[12] Winston, "A Riddle Wrapped," 100.

decision to self-distribute his work in other markets. Wiseman does not need the resources of a commercial distribution company because his work has a guaranteed broadcast outlet, and box-office revenues do not determine whether he will be able to finance his next film. His deep catalog of documentary films makes it possible to sustain his self-distribution operation. Self-distributing a single film would make overhead costs prohibitively expensive, but spreading the costs over a collection of films makes the venture more viable. Similar logic undergirds distribution via political film collectives.

The relationship between WNET and Wiseman eventually led to national PBS broadcasts and identification of Wiseman as an emblem of independent documentary film on PBS. But this relationship was unique. Other stations supported independent film in ways that spread funds and airtime to more filmmakers but did not sustain their livelihoods. These local stations developed long-running, regular anthology series to showcase independent work, from fiction to documentary to experimental video and film. Writing in *The Independent* in 1979, documentarian and media activist Dee Dee Halleck pointed to these programming exemplars: "*Image Union*, *Frontier*, and *Territory* are regularly scheduled programs of independent work on public television. If you haven't heard of them, it's because you don't live in Chicago, Buffalo or Houston." All were associated with a production center, like a media arts center, and were programmed by a member of the independent film community, not by the station staff members. These programs were AIVF's ideal solution to the problem of independent film on public television, but their advocacy for a national anthology series would not pay off for another decade.

Apart from a few special series, most local stations had abysmal records on relationships with independent producers. The chief programmer at WYES in New Orleans, Julian Cain, describes the financial obstacles to programming independent documentaries. He told *The Independent*, "I can acquire a BBC-produced documentary hosted by a well-known personality for as low as $280 through the Station Programming Cooperative of PBS or through the Interregional Programming Service. . . . My mid-range price for non-blockbuster programming runs between $300 and $500."[13] For filmmakers who spent years, and tens of thousands of dollars, making a documentary, $500 for regional broadcast is a pittance. National broadcast remained

---

[13] Louis Alvarez, "Once in a Blue Moon, Bayou Indies on Local TV," *The Independent*, December 1982, 7–8.

the holy grail for independents not only because of the ability to reach a much larger audience, but also because PBS paid much higher broadcast licensing fees.

Another problem for local stations was union rules, which could prohibit the funding and broadcast of independent productions. "WTTW's labor contract effectively restricts the public from creating programming for Chicago's public TV. The contract states that any program that is produced exclusively for Channel 11 broadcast within 200 miles of the station must be done with the employed union crew of Channel 11."[14] This led Chicago-based documentary collective Kartemquin Films to seek funding from WNET's TV Lab, rather than being able to partner with its local station.

Anthology Series and Expectations of Journalism

In an effort to reconcile the interests of stations and independent filmmakers, PBS introduced several anthology series to collect independent films. Filmmakers would submit their films to a peer panel, made up of both public TV staff and independent filmmakers. These series included *Non-fiction TV* (1978–84, in collaboration with TV Lab's Independent Documentary Fund), *Crisis to Crisis* (1980), and *Matters of Life and Death* (short films, 1981–82).[15] These short-lived series, and the individual documentary films that continued to be programmed, reveal key fault lines that would hobble the AIVF's efforts until later in the 1980s. Station representatives remained concerned about the potential for controversy. With each program, they expressed fears about the show's framing and timing, unconventional formal approach, and its relationship to journalism.

In the case of *Crisis to Crisis*, Program Fund director Lewis Freedman wanted to create an "op-ed" television series that "would supplement the middle-of-the-road broadcast journalism that has little by little taken over the airwaves."[16] Here, the timing of this approach may have jeopardized the program. The Corporation for Public Broadcasting's Program Fund had allocated $1.5 million for the series, and in December 1980, it granted

---

[14] Howard Gladstone, "Outlook for Windy City: Cold Front Moving in Fast," *The Independent*, December 1982, 11–12.

[15] PBS also designed a series called *No Sacred Cows*. Programmers rejected it at the annual Program Fair in 1983, so it was never produced.

[16] Arthur Ungar, "The 'Crisis to Crisis' Series—an 'Op-Ed' Page for PBS," *Christian Science Monitor*, July 23, 1982, http://www.csmonitor.com/1982/0723/072300.html.

production financing to four independent documentaries in its first round. Its first broadcast was *Roses in December* (1982, Ana Carrigan and Bernard Stone), the portrait of an American missionary woman killed in El Salvador, supposedly by members of the Salvadoran National Guard. But by the time of the film's broadcast in 1982, with a new presidential administration in power, *Crisis to Crisis* was already dead. Although the Fund spent a little over $500,000 in its first round, it declined to fund any of the proposals in the next round of the series. Writing in *The Independent*, AIVF president Lawrence Sapadin surmised, "Given the current political climate and the Reagan Administration's undisguised hostility toward CPB, there has been speculation that the Fund found its hard-hitting crisis format too hot to handle."[17] Indeed, the idea of funding and broadcasting op-eds was antithetical to a newly powerful man in Washington: Reagan's appointee to the National Endowment for the Humanities, William J. Bennett. Bennett helped usher in new rules to bar NEH from funding projects that "advocate a particular program of social change or action." As Bennett said in a 1984 interview, "I don't object to point-of-view films. If independent filmmakers have an ax to grind, the First Amendment protects that right—but not their right to use tax dollars to do so."[18]

As the head of one of the most powerful documentary funding agencies, Bennett's views likely led to the end of *Non-fiction TV* as well. The documentary anthology series was an offshoot of the Independent Documentary Fund, created in 1978 with support from the Ford Foundation and the National Endowment for the Arts. Head of TV Lab and the Independent Documentary Fund David Loxton recalled, "There was a period when every documentary we made won every major award."[19] In spite of these successes, the Corporation for Public Broadcasting did not step in to provide continuation funds when the Ford Foundation's support ended in 1983. *Non-fiction TV* broadcast its final season in 1984.

Deviation from traditional documentary form and journalistic norms was another problem that plagued both series and individual documentaries on PBS. Similar problems had dogged Robert Drew and his associates in the early days of Direct Cinema because their work consciously flouted

---

[17] Lawrence Sapadin, "From Crisis to Crisis: Cold Feet at the Program Fund," *The Independent*, May 1981, 8.
[18] Stein, "Leaner Times for Documentaries."
[19] Stein, "Leaner Times for Documentaries."

the conventions of network news reports and documentaries. On a series of short documentaries called *Matters of Life and Death*, the form of its films was an issue. Two of the funded projects, by established filmmakers, were rejected for broadcast because they mixed fact and fiction: *Some of These Stories Are True* (dir. Peter Adair) and *Energy and How to Get It* (dirs. Robert Frank and Gary Leon Hill).[20] While the flexibility of documentary form was a boon to theatrical successes like the humorous compilation-film *The Atomic Café* and dialogue-free, experimental *Koyaanisqatsi*, any television documentary that deviated from conventional form was cause for consternation or cancellation. Documentaries were expected to hew to a relatively neutral style and objective stance, to mimic the standards of journalism.

As PBS vice president of news and public affairs Barry Chase told *American Film* in 1986, "The conventions of TV journalism are a *fait accompli*. . . . I can't change that. The audience expectations are there."[21] These expectations often conflicted with filmmakers' goals. They also set up a strange situation by which PBS funded but then refused to air certain films. One example is *When the Mountains Tremble* (1983, dirs. Newton Thomas Sigel and Pamela Yates), about Guatemalan Indians' opposition to their government. The film clearly favors the side of the Indian guerrillas.[22] Because the documentary's lack of balance does not align with supposed audience expectations about journalism, PBS produced a segment featuring opposing views to follow the film's broadcast. This "wrap-around" segment was meant to neutralize the film's political stance. One of the codirectors of *When the Mountains Tremble* explained the conflict as such: "We wanted it presented as a film. [PBS] wanted it as a public affairs package. They had to say, 'Here's the latest news about Guatemala.' But while our film is a documentary, it's not a news documentary."[23] In 1984, PBS did not have a good way to package or present non-news documentaries. As the decade progressed, the development of documentary series would help clarify the distinction between documentary films and broadcast journalism.

---

[20] Kathleen Hulser, "Truth or Consequences: Fact & Fiction on PTV," *The Independent*, July–August 1982, 4–7.
[21] Debra Goldman, "It's a Rap," *American Film*, September 1986, 17.
[22] In 1984, New Yorker Films paid no advance to acquire the exclusive theatrical and nontheatrical rights to *When the Mountains Tremble*. It premiered at Film Forum in January 1984.
[23] Goldman, "It's a Rap," 18.

Freedom from Controversy: *Frontline*

Rather than continue to fund and air series of independently produced documentaries, CPB's Program Fund turned to a safer solution: *Frontline*. In 1982, the Program Fund granted WGBH $5 million for the series, the largest production grant ever made. Even before the series had a name, its executive producer, David Fanning, told *Broadcasting* that it would not be "'a documentary showcase' but rather an 'exercise in broadcast journalism.'"[24] The deliberate turn away from documentaries with a point of view is even more evident in this part of Fanning's statement: "'The *Frontline* format won't work with people who are more filmmakers than journalists."[25] In addition to this shift away from eclectic documentaries and toward more conventional journalistic forms, the series was not to be programmed through the peer panels that reviewed projects for *Non-fiction TV* and *Crisis to Crisis*. Fanning, formerly the executive producer of WGBH documentary series *World*, would hold all the decision-making power. In order to manage the risk of dealing with sensitive topics and the possible backlash that can accompany investigative journalism, *Frontline* employed a strong executive producer to exercise editorial control. The centralized editorial control of *Frontline* mimicked the network news departments' command over all nonfiction and current events programming, which in the early 1960s had led to internal disagreement over whether or not to broadcast documentaries by independent producers Drew Associates.

While some episodes of *Frontline* were to be produced in-house, others were to be made by independent producers. This would seem to fulfill the congressional mandate of the 1978 act, but the AIVF vehemently opposed the idea that documentaries included in *Frontline* would count as "independent." As former president of WNET James Day explains, filmmakers who worked for *Frontline* were actually "freelance," not independent. "The distinction, [the AIVF] argued, was clear and crucial: independents speak with their own voice, free of outside editorial control, unlike freelancers, whose ideas are subject to the editorial standards of the series they are working for."[26] Of course, during this tumultuous time, having strict editorial standards helped

---

[24] "Public Broadcasting Enters Neglected Documentary Field," *Broadcasting*, January 11, 1982, 55.
[25] Stein, "Leaner Times for Documentaries."
[26] James Day, *The Vanishing Vision: The Inside Story of Public Broadcasting* (Berkeley: University of California Press, 1995), 320.

insulate both the national service and local stations from critics, like NEH chairman William Bennett.

Cable Television and *The Independents*

While *Frontline* became the flagship documentary series on PBS, one cable channel made an unusually strong commitment to independent film: the Learning Channel. Though it did not provide the production funding that so complicated PBS's relationship with independent filmmakers, the Learning Channel created a series intended to be "the premiere national showcase for independent film and video works."[27] It was called *The Independents*, and in its first season, premiering in 1985, it had two parts: *Dis/Patches*, featuring video art, and *Agenda*, featuring documentaries. Independent filmmakers were invited to submit their work. The series was programmed by Gerry O'Grady of Media Study / Buffalo, one of the production centers involved with the local station series *Frontier*, linking it back to public television. But unlike local public television stations, the Learning Channel could afford to pay filmmakers a fair price for the nonexclusive right to show their work: $210 per minute for four showings in three years (just under $19,000 for a ninety-minute feature). The Learning Channel was able to pay filmmakers through funding from the John D. and Catherine T. MacArthur Foundation. The MacArthur Foundation began funding media work in 1983. Its grant to the Learning Channel for *The Independents* was the largest single grant ever given by a private foundation to a media project, for $666,800.

When the Learning Channel began broadcasting *The Independents* in 1985, it was a not-for-profit channel that shared satellite space with other cable channels, broadcasting only between 11:00 a.m. and 4:00 p.m. It had five million subscribers, and in order to grow more subscribers, it had to prove to cable operators that it was worth carrying. *The Independents* was part of their plan to grow. While broad accessibility is an essential part of PBS's mission, the mandate to serve the entire American public detracted from its ability to program more specialized, niche shows. In contrast, the Learning Channel's executive vice president, Robert Shaman, saw the value in independent films for its narrowcasting mission, saying, "The audience for *The*

---

[27] Debra Goldman, "Media Clips: The Learning Channel's Agenda," *The Independent*, May 1985, 4–6.

Independents is a small sliver of our cable universe.... Put all those splinters together and you have a critical mass that makes it attractive."[28] In addition to its mission to gain more subscribers, the Learning Channel had other plans for *The Independents*: selling the packaged series to other broadcasters. Among its first buyers were public television stations WTTW (Chicago) and KTCA (Minneapolis). This move had independent filmmakers reeling: PBS had abdicated its responsibility to independent filmmakers in order to stay safe in a tense political environment, but public television stations in large metropolitan areas still showed a demand for well-curated packages of independent films.

This incident spurred the AIVF to continue applying pressure to PBS to fund and broadcast more independent film. There were open meetings between AIVF members and the heads of PBS. In March 1988, a number of well-regarded independent filmmakers, including documentarians Pamela Yates, Frederick Wiseman, and Marlon Riggs, testified before the House Subcommittee on Telecommunications and Finance about problems that independents had accessing PBS funds and audiences.[29] Transcripts of this testimony were printed in an issue of *The Independent* devoted to advocacy for independents and minority producers in public television. These public debates added urgency to the task of getting a showcase of documentaries on PBS.

The Path to *P.O.V.* and ITVS

While PBS struggled to find a series format to accommodate independent documentary films, it had great success with an anthology of independent fiction features: *American Playhouse*. Presented by a consortium of stations, it provided some production funding and national broadcast to over two hundred independent films between 1982 and 1994. The seal of approval from *American Playhouse* encouraged other organizations and financiers to partner with the filmmakers to fill out their production budgets. It also helped films cross into theaters: about forty *American Playhouse* films were acquired by theatrical distributors and played in theaters before their

---

[28] Debra Goldman, "The Learning Channel, Round Two," *The Independent*, September 1985, 4.
[29] This meeting with the congressional subcommittee preceded the culture wars waged by right-wing activists over Riggs's *Tongues Untied* (1991) receiving a grant from the National Endowment for the Arts and being broadcast on *P.O.V.*

television premieres on PBS.[30] The success of *American Playhouse* also paved the way for *P.O.V.*

The inciting impetus for *P.O.V* originated during a panel discussion at the 1986 US Film Festival (later Sundance Film Festival). Nick Hart-Williams of the UK's Channel Four "reported that Channel 4 has acquired so many independent films and tapes the broadcaster was creating a new anthology series. . . . [*Frontline* executive producer David] Fanning replied that he had often thought there should be something similar on U.S. public television."[31] Clearly, Fanning had never heard of PBS's earlier attempts at documentary anthology series. Word got around to *American Playhouse*'s executive producer David Davis, who had also facilitated the Ford Foundation's grant to WNET's Independent Documentary Fund. He agreed to be executive director of the new documentary series, with Marc Weiss as executive producer. The same consortium of stations that backed Playhouse also backed the series. Cognizant of the suspicion that station staff always have about broadcasting independent film, Weiss proposed the consortium so that, he said, "the stations feel they have a stake in the program."[32] The selection process was also designed to minimize station skittishness and to prevent revolt from the AIVF. Rather than screening applications with a peer panel, like earlier failed series *Crisis to Crisis* and *Matters of Life and Death*, employees of the consortium would make editorial decisions, with input from stations and the independent community.[33] *P.O.V.* was also planned to allow for the possibility of theatrical distribution of the documentaries, prior to their television premiere. Thus, *P.O.V.* was built on the example of *American Playhouse*, outlasting the fiction film series by two decades.

P.O.V. also built on the Learning Channel's *The Independents* series, particularly in its fee to license films. The MacArthur Foundation awarded *P.O.V.* a grant in 1987. As vice president of the MacArthur Foundation's board of directors William Kirby explained to *The Independent*, "We felt the most important influence we could exert was to pay producers and get their works distributed as widely as possible. . . . The question of PBS and its relationship

---

[30] Chelsea McCracken, "Rethinking Television Indies: The Impact of American Playhouse," *Screen* 57, no. 2 (Summer 2016), 219, https://doi.org/10.1093/screen/hjw018.

[31] Debra Goldman, "Media Clips: Package Deal. A New Documentary Series," *The Independent*, December 1986, 5.

[32] Goldman, "Media Clips: Package Deal," 6.

[33] *The Independent* listed some of these members as Lawrence Sapadin, executive director of AIVF, Lillian Jimenez, former program officer of the Film Fund and AIVF chair, and filmmaker Julia Reichert. Goldman, "Media Clips: Package Deal," 6.

to independents is of great concern to us. We feel we may be able to help by inducing PBS, through our own example, to pay more fairly for independent works."[34] Indeed, *P.O.V.* improved upon *The Independents'* compensation to filmmakers: it paid $300 per minute of film, while *The Independents* paid $210 per minute. This level of compensation was much higher than any of the local stations' anthology series had been able to pay, and license fees from *P.O.V.*'s consortium, the American Documentary, Inc., continue to be an important source of revenue for documentarians.

P.O.V. was also a breakthrough because it provided a context for stylistically adventurous and personal documentaries, away from the tight constraints of journalistic documentary. As early as 1986, when the series was first proposed, Weiss expressed his goal that the series "move away from what public television sees as journalism and emphasize instead a strong personal vision."[35] The series was originally entitled *The American Documentary*, but it was changed to avoid confusion with other PBS programs with "American" in the title, and to avoid the widespread negative connotations of the word "documentary." As Weiss joked, "We can't rehabilitate the word if they won't even tune in."[36] Rather, the title "Point of View" connotes the subjective and the personal, two aspects of documentary filmmaking that are distinct from broadcast journalism. The packaging of the program reflects this tilt away from the journalistic as well. In the early seasons of *P.O.V.*, the filmmakers themselves appeared on screen before their films played, in order "to introduce their work and provide a context, explain the motivation for tackling their subject, or give other relevant background information."[37]

Independent producers and the AIVF had long lobbied for a show like *P.O.V.*, and they finally got it. The dividends it paid were not huge box-office receipts, but they were substantial: the prestige of being chosen for the program was akin to winning a prize or getting a critic's seal of approval; a television premiere, with a possible theatrical release beforehand; and a fair payment for the broadcast rights to their work. In addition, their films had national exposure, which translated to a social good that many documentarians aimed for: reaching people who wouldn't or couldn't see documentaries anywhere else.

---

[34] Quynh Thai, "MacArthur Foundation Boosts Media Funding," *The Independent*, July 1988, 4.
[35] Goldman, "Media Clips: Package Deal," 6.
[36] Patricia Thomson, "New Doc Series Gets Ready for Launch," *The Independent*, April 1988, 4.
[37] Thomson, "New Doc Series," 4.

At the same time, in 1988, the Corporation for Public Broadcasting allocated funds for a new production wing for independent filmmakers, focused on underrepresented voices and audiences.[38] The Independent Television Service invests in work as a coproducer, rather than a grantor, but it does not impose a standard format on the documentaries being made. The relationship between the funding arm ITVS and the series *P.O.V.*, and later, *Independent Lens*, is unusual. One would assume that ITVS and *P.O.V.* work hand in glove; instead, they are separate. The series have the right of first refusal to completed ITVS coproductions, so they may choose to program the films, but they are not forced to take them.

Nevertheless, both ITVS and *P.O.V.* were formed at the insistence of independent filmmakers, and they have similar goals. ITVS nurtures formally inventive films made by diverse voices. As Patricia Aufderheide points out, "For example, in the 1990s, while striving to leverage low-cost new video technologies and spread limited budgets, ITVS became effectively an incubator of the subgenre of personal memoir documentary, from *A Healthy Baby Girl* (1997) to *When Billy Broke His Head . . . and Other Tales of Wonder* (1995) to the teen-to-teen personal storytelling of the eight-part series *The Ride* (1994). By 1993, a sixth of the submissions to ITVS were personal memoir. The form rapidly spread to commercial media."[39] As this example reveals, ITVS's production funds supported and legitimized documentarians experimenting with new types of nonfiction storytelling.

Success: Independent Documentarians Win Airtime and Funding from PBS

Over the course of the late 1970s and 1980s, the independent film community pushed PBS to increase monetary investment and airtime in documentary films. Filmmakers and their allies argued that PBS had failed to implement the Public Telecommunications Finance Act of 1978, which ordered that a substantial amount of funding go to independent producers. However, local stations stood staunchly against the disbursement of funding or airtime to independent films, especially independent documentaries. Even when local stations did take the initiative to showcase independent work, they were

---

[38] Patricia Aufderheide, "Documentary Filmmaking and US Public TV's Independent Television Service, 1989–2017," *Journal of Film and Video* 71, no. 4 (2021), 4.

[39] Aufderheide, "Documentary Filmmaking," 8.

unable to actually support the high cost of film production. The national service would have to package independent work for the whole system in order to compensate filmmakers fairly. PBS was able to do this with fiction films first, on *American Playhouse*, but it faltered on documentaries. This reluctance stemmed from programmers' and local stations managers' desire to retain editorial and financial control over programming, rather than hand it over to unaffiliated filmmakers. They also feared that independently made documentaries would stir up controversy by flouting audience expectations of journalism, even when dealing with politically explosive subjects. Finally, after years of pressure from independent filmmakers and the AIVF, in 1988 PBS instituted a sustainable solution: *P.O.V.* Through many seasons of national broadcast, *P.O.V.* encouraged the diversity of styles and stances in documentary cinema, setting it apart from the conventions of journalism. In licensing their work to *P.O.V.*, filmmakers retain editorial control. It has provided consistent financial support to the documentary film community for decades and normalized the concept of non-news documentaries. *P.O.V.*, and later addition *Independent Lens*, balance the core tension between film and television in documentary.

P.O.V. developed in tandem with documentary films' popularity growing as part of the American independent cinema movement, as discussed in Chapter 2. It also coincided with the explosion of nonfiction programming on the Discovery Channel, founded in 1985. Cable television's embrace of nonfiction programming led some cable channels to experiment with producing and licensing documentary film in the 1990s. That development is discussed in Chapter 4.

P.O.V. and its later companion series *Independent Lens* have become key institutions for supporting and circulating independent documentary films in the United States. However, an event in 1990 lives larger in the popular imagination: the release of documentary miniseries *The Civil War* (1990, dir. Ken Burns). Broadcast on consecutive weeknights—a scheduling practice known as "stripping"—*The Civil War* attracted approximately fourteen million viewers each night.[40] Just two years after *P.O.V.* secured a place for independent documentary features on PBS's national broadcast, *The Civil War* was hailed as a "major ratings victory." It propelled director Ken Burns into the spotlight, where he became an enduring emblem of PBS.

---

[40] Richard Gold, "PBS Turns Swords into Shares," *Broadcasting*, October 1, 1990, 38.

The success of *The Civil War* secured continued production funding from both public media and corporate sponsors for Burns's future projects. With stable financing, Burns followed an efficient mode of production at his company Florentine Films / American Documentaries. He worked on multiple projects at once, overseeing coproducers for each project.[41] Burns's next releases were the feature-length *Empire of the Air* and the nineteen-hour miniseries *Baseball*. The success of these works propagated a very traditional documentary style: an objective stance, historical subject matter, voice-over narration, expert talking heads, and staid visuals. It also reinforced the link between television and documentary, even as studio classics divisions and independent distributors were bringing more and more documentaries to theaters. While PBS is more widely cited for its support of Burns's conventional television miniseries, its support for independent documentary films has been a pillar of the industry for over thirty years.

---

[41] Gary Edgerton, *Ken Burns' America* (New York: Palgrave, 2001), 87.

4

Television or Cinema?

Redefining Documentary for Prestige and Profit (1990 to 1999)

By the early 1990s, more and more distribution companies wanted to acquire documentaries, inspired by the box-office performance of films like *Roger & Me* (1989, dir. Michael Moore)—$5 million—and *Madonna: Truth or Dare* (1991, dir. Alek Keshishian)—$15 million. At the same time, the independent distributors and studio classics divisions that had banked on indie film in the 1980s were becoming more powerful in the 1990s. As they acquired more documentary films, they also pushed for recognition of their documentaries, seeking to demarcate them from the doc films supported by television (PBS, HBO). This led to two consequences: (1) a gap widened between those small indie distributors that distributed the largest number of documentaries using art-house strategies and those that distributed the biggest documentaries, and (2) HBO, which had been producing documentaries since the 1980s, shifted its strategy in order to stay in the awards game. The Sundance Film Festival's documentary program also reflected this shift, with broadcast-length documentaries giving way to feature-length documentaries by the early 2000s.

Throughout the 1990s, more than a dozen documentaries earned over $1 million in theatrical release, including *Hoop Dreams* (1994, dir. Steve James), *Crumb* (1995, dir. Terry Zwigoff, $3 million), *When We Were Kings* (1996, dir. Leon Gast, $2.7 million), and *Buena Vista Social Club* (1999, dir. Wim Wenders).[1] One of these highly successful documentaries is *Paris Is Burning* (1991, dir. Jennie Livingston). The distribution of and industrial discourse around *Paris Is Burning* show that, even with very visible documentary hits in the 1990s and powerful distributors picking up documentary films, earlier paradigms remained in place. In particular, self-distribution

---

[1] Mike Goodridge, "Top 10 Documentaries at Box Office, 1991–2000," *Screen International*, June 23, 2000, 43.

How Documentaries Went Mainstream. Nora Stone, Oxford University Press. © Oxford University Press 2023.
DOI: 10.1093/oso/9780197557297.003.0005

continued to play a role in documentary film circulation, especially with help from Film Forum. And though the powerful distributors aimed to demarcate theatrical feature documentaries from television documentaries, they continued to be intertwined. In this moment, the tension between film and television rose to the surface.

Paris Is Burning is an observational account of New York City drag ball culture and a character study of the queens in the scene. In sequences from the ball competitions, drag queens dance, walk the runway, and display their glamorous costuming. These are dazzling spectacles of talent, set to popular music, within a vibrant community space. Other sequences in *Paris Is Burning* explore the offstage lives of ball contestants. In intimate interviews, the queens, mostly black and Latinx, discuss their upbringing, livelihoods, and the "houses" they belong to. *Paris Is Burning* has become a classic of American documentary because of its combination of spectacle, humanity, and exploration of a significant queer subculture. *Paris Is Burning* first played at gay-themed film festivals in 1990 and then at the Sundance Film Festival in January 1991. Sundance was already known for distributors' bidding wars over independent fiction films and a handful of documentary films. But, despite winning the Documentary Grand Jury Prize, *Paris Is Burning* was not acquired by a theatrical distributor. Instead, two months after Sundance, in March 1991, Livingston self-distributed *Paris Is Burning*. The theatrical run began at Film Forum. In this way, Livingston followed the example of the many documentarians who had self-distributed their films and used Film Forum as a launching pad in the past.

At Film Forum, *Paris Is Burning* took off—it grossed an incredible $500,000 during its four-month run at the theater. During that time, Prestige Films picked up the film for theatrical distribution, following the pattern set in the previous decade. But Prestige did not operate like the distributors that worked with documentaries in the 1970s and 1980s; it was a division of Miramax, the notoriously ambitious, controversy-mongering film company. In August 1991, Prestige expanded *Paris Is Burning* into twenty markets, and announced plans to branch out from there to seventy-five screens. The film eventually grossed $4 million, making it one of the top-five grossing documentaries of the 1990s. Even though *Paris Is Burning* initially moved through the market like the self-distributed documentaries of the past, its wild success at Film Forum and acquisition by a powerful distributor catapulted the film into uncharted territory. If a documentary about black and Latino drag queens could earn $4 million at the box office, documentary film's commercial potential seemed greater than ever before.

The recognition of this potential seeded a drive to redefine which films could be nominated for the Academy Award for Best Documentary Feature. A symbol of prestige that often translated into better market position, filmmakers and distributors pushed to change the nominating standards to demarcate theatrical documentaries from television documentaries. *Paris Is Burning*, *35 Up*, *Hearts of Darkness: A Filmmaker's Apocalypse*, *A Brief History of Time*, *Madonna: Truth or Dare*, *Blue Planet*, *At the Max*, and *Empire of the Air* were highly regarded, successful, theatrically distributed documentaries left without Oscar nominations in 1992 alone. Other recent documentaries ignored by the Academy included *The Thin Blue Line*, *Roger & Me*, and *28 Up*. A number of the directors of these documentaries, including Jennie Livingston, Michael Apted, and Ken Burns, accused the Academy of "promoting unknown docus [rather] than honoring the finest examples of the genre."[2] Simultaneously, Miramax executives circulated a letter to Academy president Bruce Davis and the press, pushing for changes to the documentary category of the Academy Awards. Miramax cochairmen Bob and Harvey Weinstein and executive vice president Russell Schwartz suggested renaming the category "nonfiction" to remove the negative associations of the word "documentary."[3] Most pointed was their desire for the Academy to de-emphasize documentary films made for television. They wrote, "Are not the Oscars meant for theatrical films? . . . The rules are loose here, and should be further defined."[4]

Of course, even documentaries distributed theatrically are often financed partly by television. *Paris Is Burning* was, in fact, funded by PBS affiliate WNYC and the BBC, in addition to foundation grants.[5] The real goal was to tip the scales toward the powerful independent distributors and studio classics divisions that had only recently began acquiring and releasing documentary films. They demanded credit and Oscars for their investment, and they wanted to police the borders of the category. In particular, the goal was to disqualify documentaries made for HBO, which played at film festivals

---

[2] Charles Fleming, "Oscar Mocks Boffo Docs," *Variety*, March 2, 1992, 41.
[3] The Miramaxers suggested that the nominating committee be expanded from sixty to two hundred members.
[4] Joseph McBride, "Miramax Urges Docu Rule Revamp," *Variety*, March 16, 1992, 5.
[5] Lucas Hilderbrand, *Paris Is Burning* (Vancouver: Arsenal Pulp Press, 2013), 14.

and on HBO, and often won Oscars. In a bid to own the prestige of award-winning documentary films and protect their bottom line, ascendent indie cinema distributors tried to box out cable television.

This public campaign increased pressure on the Academy, and in June 1995 it announced new rules for the documentary feature category. To qualify for nominations, documentary films would be required to play in theaters for at least one week.[6] By requiring that documentary films be released theatrically, despite the historically difficult prospects of doing so, the Academy's mandate shifted power to the well-resourced theatrical distribution companies able to afford the high costs of a theatrical campaign *before* the Academy Awards. As filmmaker Robert Epstein wrote in 1992, "The current hassle [over Academy Award nominations] may not be so much art versus commerce as much as whose art, whose commerce?"[7] Powerful independent distribution companies and studio classics divisions demanded awards for the documentary films they propelled to box-office success, and they got their wish.

This upheaval signaled shifting industrial and generic boundaries. Film distributors' changing business practices and HBO's programming strategies helped bring about a shift in the status of documentary in the American media landscape. Documentary films were becoming increasingly important to the commercial film industry. They were also widely recognized as cinematic, rather than purely journalistic and informational. They had acquired the sheen of quality and import via association with American indies and public broadcasting, differentiating them from the nonfiction television programming pitched as family entertainment.

---

[6] *Documentary* magazine outlined the most consequential changes:
> In 1996 and thereafter, a documentary film will no longer qualify for Academy Award consideration by participating in a film festival. The Documentary Screening Committee will only consider those films that have had theatrical exhibition of at least seven days during the qualifying period. Documentarians will have the option of screening their films either in Manhattan or in Los Angeles County for a qualifying run."

"Academy Awards Rules Revised," *Documentary*, April 1996, https://www.documentary.org/feature/academy-awards-rules-revised. Changes to the nominating procedure that went into effect immediately in 1995 included Feature Documentary Screening Committee split into two groups, Los Angeles and New York. Each group screens half the submissions and narrows to group of finalists, then the other group watches the finalists. Then they decide on the five nominees. Change in scoring system, now a scale of 6 to 10, rather than 4 to 10; 6 to 10 is what the Academy does in other categories.

[7] Robert Epstein, "Latest Academy Stir-Fry: Documentary Pictures," *Los Angeles Times*, March 12, 1992, F3, F8, F9.

Documentaries in Theaters: Indiewood and the Second Wave of Studio Classics Divisions

In the 1990s, competition in the independent film arena became fiercer. Once Hollywood saw that independent films could appeal to large audiences—examples like *She's Gotta Have It* (1986, dir. Spike Lee, $7 million domestic) *sex, lies, and videotape* (1989, dir. Steven Soderbergh, $24 million domestic), *Pulp Fiction* (1994, dir. Quentin Tarantino, $108 million domestic)—they moved into the market. Studios bought many independent distribution companies, and they founded their own specialty divisions as well. Suddenly, more companies than ever were acquiring and releasing independent films, including documentaries, in theaters, and they had more money to market their releases than ever before. This fundamental shift in the structure of the industry shifted the status of the documentary film. As the decade went on, a chasm opened between the most dedicated, consistent distributors of documentaries—very small, independent companies—and those distributors that, with the vast resources of global conglomerates, plucked the most marketable documentaries from film festival slates and propelled them to high visibility, if not stunning box-office grosses. The result was a stratification of the theatrical market for documentary films: a few films earned most of the critical acclaim, screen time, and audience attention, while the majority of documentaries struggled to hold onto screens and expand beyond a few urban markets. Nevertheless, the visibility and acclaim of the few top documentaries led to more interest in and acceptance of the genre as a theatrical film product. The changing of Academy Award nominating rules formalized the shift in the status of documentary that had started slowly in the 1960s, with the tentative move by Robert Drew and his associates D. A. Pennebaker and Ricky Leacock from television journalism to independent film.

This period saw growth in the number of distributors handling documentaries and in the number of documentaries being released theatrically. However, this growth resulted in higher churn and steeper competition than the specialty market had ever experienced before. This caused a split between those companies releasing documentaries for a core audience and those releasing documentaries in hopes of attracting a general audience. Independent film adviser Peter Broderick defines a core audience as that linked by identity (religion, ethnicity, sexual orientation) or interest in a subject matter, while a general audience is broader and need not have specific ties to a film's subject or message.[8]

A few companies, like Zeitgeist Films and Seventh Art Releasing, theatrically distributed the greatest number of documentary films during the 1990s. Their small annual slates were mostly documentaries. They acquired a variety of documentaries, often by new filmmakers, and rolled them out slowly and methodically, city by city. This process, a traditional art-house release strategy, allowed them to carefully target their marketing to a core audience and take advantage of the free publicity generated in each release area, rather than spending freely to attract a general audience. They also held onto the nontheatrical and educational rights to the documentaries because they recognized the potentially long life the films could have after theatrical release, just as self-distributing filmmakers and specialty distributors had learned in previous eras. Nevertheless, theatrical release was never just a loss leader for these distributors: by keeping marketing costs low and rolling out films carefully, ticket sales could generate solid income.

The most powerful and well-resourced distribution companies had a different strategy for releasing documentaries. Major independent Miramax and studio specialty divisions like Fox Searchlight and Sony Pictures Classics, founded as distributors, had started producing their own fiction features by the end of the 1990s.[9] They offset the high risk of producing their own films and spending astronomical sums acquiring high-profile festival films by acquiring lower-priced documentaries. These large distribution companies also mitigated risk by acquiring documentaries made by well-known filmmakers or about major celebrities. These documentaries were designed and marketed to reach a general audience, rather than a core audience. Though these distributors released relatively few documentaries, their documentary releases generally reached higher box-office numbers and were more visible than those released by small, independent outfits. These companies also spent so much on marketing a few documentaries that they pushed for the Academy to emphasize initial exhibition context as the deciding factor for Oscar nomination contention. However, none made

---

[8] Peter Broderick, "Maximizing Distribution," originally published in *DGA Magazine*, January 2004. Republished on http://www.peterbroderick.com/writing/page20/maximizingdistribution.html.

[9] Yannis Tzioumakis, *Hollywood's Indies: Classics Divisions, Specialty Labels, and American Independent Cinema* (Edinburgh: Edinburgh University Press, 2012).

documentary films the centerpiece of their companies because their returns were not high enough to support their large corporate apparatuses.

This led to a paradox: the most consistent distributors of documentary films were not the most visible. They are often left out of accounts of documentary film in the 1990s because writers tend to focus on the highest-grossing films, rather than tracing the contours of the whole theatrical releasing landscape. Describing individual theatrical distributors and the strategies they used to release documentaries will reveal the wide gulf between small independent distributors and powerful studio specialty divisions.

Indiewood: Specialty Labels Provide Value in the 1990s

The disparity between distributors of documentaries is an effect of the popularization of indie cinema and the radical reconglomeration of the film industry in the late 1980s. Media industry and consumer electronics companies acquired media production companies in order to feed the home entertainment pipelines they owned: they needed content for their cable channels and video companies. As Yannis Tzioumakis describes, "This 'reconglomeration' came into full force in 1989–90 with Sony's takeover of Columbia (1989), the Time Warner merger (1989), the takeover of MCA Universal by Matsushita (1990) and Disney's aggressive expansion to other media segments following the 1990 announcement of the 'Disney Decade,' a corporate plan to reinvent and expand Disney on a global scale in the 1990s."[10] This industry-wide reorganization came at the exact moment when American independent cinema was growing in popularity and acclaim, reaching new audiences and looking like a perfect growth area. Following this high-level reorganization, studios bought or formed specialty labels in quick succession. In 1993, Disney acquired Miramax and Turner Broadcasting bought New Line Cinema (including its specialty label Fine Line Features). Most of the studio classics divisions formed in the 1980s were short-lived, but this new wave would have more staying power: Sony Pictures Classics, formed in 1992, and Fox Searchlight, formed in 1994, are still in business. Gramercy, distributor of PolyGram productions, was founded in 1992 as Universal's art-house label; it was rolled up with October Films in 1999, forming USA Films, which later

---

[10] Yannis Tzioumakis, *American Independent Cinema*, 2nd ed. (Edinburgh: Edinburgh University Press, 2017), 262.

became Focus Features. Paramount Classics / Vantage was founded slightly later, in 1997.

All the major conglomerates wanted to acquire or create their own specialty labels. In the 1990s, the value of specialty labels was unquestioned. First of all, specialty labels allowed conglomerates to bring different kinds of product to the same market—they could place action films *and* indie dramas in theaters. Second, specialty labels fed the conglomerates' cable and video delivery systems. They won prestigious awards like Oscars, and they delivered excellent box-office returns to their parent companies. By the middle of the 1990s, the major conglomerates controlled over 96 percent of box-office returns. Tzioumakis points out that "the specialty film distributors that have been associated heavily with the American independent film sector (Miramax, New line, Gramercy, Fine Line, Sony Pictures Classics and Fox Searchlight) accounted for 11.78 per cent of the theatrical market, representing both a very healthy picture for the sector and a significant contributor to their conglomerate parents' bottom line."[11] These highly successful and profitable specialty film distributors pushed the popularization of American independent cinema in the 1990s, leading to the rise of "indiewood" filmmaking. Documentary films were one part of this rise.

The Core of Theatrically Released Documentaries in 1990s

Small independent distributors handled a greater number of documentaries and had a more eclectic lineup of documentaries than the growing number of specialty film distributors. One example of this is Zeitgeist Films. Founded in 1988, the distribution company is still in operation. It has released many well-known documentary titles, including *Manufacturing Consent*, *The Gleaners and I*, *The Corporation*, *Into Great Silence*, *Up the Yangtze*, *Trouble the Water*, and *Bill Cunningham New York*. Zeitgeist focuses on distributing a small slate of films and mainly markets to a core audience, though there are occasionally bigger successes that reach a general audience.

Nancy Gerstman and Emily Russo founded Zeitgeist Films after having learned the business of film distribution at First Run Features and Interama, respectively. The first documentary they acquired, *Let's Get Lost* (1988, dir. Bruce Weber), garnered an Academy Award nomination for Best

---

[11] Tzioumakis, *American Independent Cinema*, 264.

Documentary. Though the founders did not plan for their catalog to be mostly documentaries and foreign films, Zeitgeist hasn't distributed an American fiction film since it released *Poison* (1991, dir. Todd Haynes) to great acclaim, controversy, and a box-office gross of $800,000. As Gerstman told *Variety* in 1995, "It's easier for us to find films by younger, newer filmmakers, whose movies might not be commercial enough for larger distribution, but who can still get the kind of press that larger distributors would go for.... We helped open the door for larger companies to see that there was revenue to be made from these smaller films."[12] Once the door was open, the larger companies were willing to circumvent the marketplace and start investing in promising talent, leaving fewer and fewer independent fiction films available for acquisition. Indeed, after *Poison*, Sony Pictures Classics financed Haynes's follow-up, *Safe* (1995).

Nevertheless, documentaries were much more than a consolation prize for Zeitgeist. Documentaries can be up to a half of the company's annual slate of five to six films, and Zeitgeist's principals have found ways to market them very successfully. Zeitgeist's marketing strategy is targeted—try to reach a core audience of people who are interested the subject of a documentary, rather than blanketing a general audience with ads. This attitude is reflected in Russo's statement from 1999: "Sometimes documentaries can be easier to release than features.... They have very specific built-in audiences, and you just need to find that audience."[13] According to Gerstman, the first part of reaching that audience is researching the documentary's subject area thoroughly, to figure out who will be interested in it. Then Zeitgeist makes calls to groups that care about the subject and delivers materials to them. The company also creates posters, trailers, and postcards, and does wild posting in urban areas. Finally, Zeitgeist works with radio stations and travel agents to create ticket contests, a form of free publicity.[14]

Zeitgeist bases its acquisition decisions on the quality of a film and on the possible audiences it can market to. For example, Gerstman relates the process of marketing *The Corporation* (2004, dirs. Mark Achbar and Jennifer Abbott), a documentary that asks, If the Fourteenth Amendment regards corporations as individuals, what type of person would a corporation be? She says, "When you come to *The Corporation*, there are like fifty subject areas

---

[12] Laurence Lerman, "Smaller Indies Find Tough Going," *Variety*, September 18–24, 1995, 22.
[13] Holly Willis, "Docus Struggle in Theatrical Runs," *Variety*, April 5–11, 1999, M74.
[14] Nancy Gerstman in conversation with the author, November 2016.

that it can go to in a school. Therefore, in terms of marketing it, it was a really interesting film to market. There weren't any other films like it. We worked really hard with everyone from anarchists to economics majors."[15] This work paid off in the form of $2 million in box office receipts, and sales of one hundred thousand DVDs and one thousand educational DVDs.[16] Zeitgeist distributed other politically oriented documentaries like *Manufacturing Consent* (1993, dirs. Mark Achbar and Peter Wintonick), a documentary on Noam Chomsky; *Ballot Number 9* (1995, dir. Heather Lyn MacDonald), about the fight to stop a proposed anti-LGBT law in Oregon; and *A Place Called Chiapas* (1998, dir. Nettie Wild), about an uprising in Mexico in response to the passage of the North American Free Trade Agreement. Other subject areas Zeitgeist has mined include LGBTQ issues, with films like *Silverlake Life: The View from Here* (1993, dir. Peter Friedman), *Coming Out Under Fire* (1994, Arthur Dong), *Paris Was a Woman* (1996, dir. Greta Schiller), and *The Brandon Teena Story* (1999, dirs. Susan Muska and Greta Olafsdottir). Zeitgeist has also released more personal portrait documentaries like the female road-trip movie *Anthem* (1997, dirs. Shainee Gabel and Kristin Hahn), the playful, essayistic *The Gleaners and I* (2000, dir. Agnes Varda), and *Bill Cunningham New York* (2010, dir. Richard Press) about the fashion street photographer.

Zeitgeist remains focused on theatrical release because it has been its most consistent area of success. Gerstman and Russo also acknowledge the importance of educational sales and television licenses, but television channels' changing priorities can affect the company's business. Gerstman recalls, "When the Sundance Channel was buying films, we had wonderful sales. Then they started their own original programming and it really dried up."[17] By staying small and focused, Zeitgeist has outlasted many of the larger companies that briefly distributed documentaries in the 1990s.

Many new film distributors took risks by participating in bidding wars for hot films and marketing them to general audiences, hoping to generate a windfall profit. Zeitgeist's principals take on a different type of risk: they acquire unusual, formally inventive, politically potent documentary films, often made by early-career or unknown documentarians. Their risk is in the type of films, rather than in speculative acquisition practices and high advertising costs.

---

[15] Nancy Gerstman in conversation with the author, December 2017.
[16] Nancy Gerstman in conversation with the author, December 2017.
[17] Nancy Gerstman in conversation with the author, November 2016.

In Contrast: General Documentary Releases

While Zeitgeist marketed documentary acquisitions to a core audience, studio specialty divisions pitched documentaries to a general audience. *When We Were Kings* is a documentary about the "Rumble in the Jungle," the legendary 1974 prizefight between Muhammed Ali and George Foreman. It was produced by David Sonnenfeld, a major music manager who packaged the film with an all-star soundtrack. Thus, *When We Were Kings* fits squarely in the realm of commercially viable documentaries about celebrities, with the added appeal of popular music. The film inspired a bidding war at Sundance in 1996, which ended when Gramercy, a well-funded company controlled by Universal and Polygram, paid an advance of $3 million. Gramercy released the film in limited release during the 1996 fall season, then put it in general release in early 1997. Leading up to the film's general release, Mercury Records' label DAS heavily promoted the soundtrack album, featuring James Brown, B. B. King, and Bill Withers, along with contemporary artists The Fugees, Bryan McKnight, and Diana King. MTV broadcast a concert celebrating the film and its soundtrack just days before the general release.[18] The film won the Academy Award for Best Documentary Feature. Despite this major marketing push and the Oscar, *When We Were Kings* earned only $2.5 million at the box office—less than the advance paid at Sundance.

This was the fate of many documentaries acquired and released by specialty labels and large indie distributors in the 1990s. While $2.5 million would be a great windfall for Zeitgeist or Seventh Art, it was not enough of a return on investment for these larger companies. While more studio specialty labels and well-resourced independent distributors dipped into the theatrical distribution of documentaries in the 1990s, none made documentaries a central part of their businesses. They experimented with releasing documentaries because acquiring them was less risky than the other move they were making: producing and financing fiction films. They used synergy to release soundtrack albums and released the documentaries on their own video labels, which were stocked at normal rental stores. This led to a handful of documentaries being widely known and lauded. This helped to raise the ceiling for the success of documentary films and led to more interest in the genre from both industry insiders and audiences. However, even

---

[18] Jim Bessman, "Mercury Ready to Rumble with Ali Film's Soundtrack," *Billboard*, January 18, 1997, 9, 15.

with expensive marketing campaigns and partnerships with record labels, the payoff for documentaries was not consistent.

Several companies distributed only a single documentary during the decade. In spite of the relatively successful and high-profile releases of *When We Were Kings* and *Hoop Dreams*, respectively, Gramercy and Fine Line released no other documentaries in the 1990s. Even when documentary films earned accolades and strong box-office returns, the rewards were often not worth the expense for the specialty divisions of conglomerates. There were also a number of new, bullish companies that drove their resources into acquiring and releasing a few documentaries during the decade. The short-lived Triton had two high-profile documentary releases, *Hearts of Darkness: A Filmmaker's Apocalypse* and *A Brief History of Time*, before its foreign investors pulled out and effectively ended the company. Triton Pictures picked up *A Brief History of Time*, based on Stephen Hawking's best-selling book and directed by Errol Morris, and played it in more than one hundred theaters. It eventually grossed $2.3 million.[19] October Films was short-lived, but successful: before being acquired by Universal in 1999, it released three documentaries by well-known directors: D. A. Pennebaker (*The War Room*), Michael Apted (*Moving the Mountain*), and Jim Jarmusch (*Year of the Horse*). *The War Room* grossed $850,000 at the box office. October also spent $40,000 on an Academy Awards push, but *The War Room* did not win the award.[20] Later in the decade, as the specialty labels became more and more like ministudios, producing their own expensive, star-driven features, new companies popped up to take over the ground they had ceded. Artisan and Lions Gate were two extremely well-funded, bullish independent companies that aggressively acquired festival films, including documentaries, and coproduced features immediately upon their founding.[21]

Many of the documentaries that studio classics divisions and larger independent distributors acquired were made by well-known filmmakers, some of whom had been working for decades. For example, well-funded distributors handled all the films released in the 1990s by longtime documentarians D. A. Pennebaker and Errol Morris. These filmmakers' name recognition

---

[19] Goodridge, "Top 10 Documentaries," 43.
[20] The film was nominated, but it lost the Oscar to *I Am a Promise: The Children of Stanton Elementary School* (dirs. Susan and Alan Raymond) a documentary made for HBO.
[21] Lionsgate acquired *Mr. Death: The Rise and Fall of Fred A. Leuchter, Jr* (1999, dir. Errol Morris), *The Eyes of Tammy Faye* (2000, dirs. Fenton Bailey and Randy Barbato), *Beyond the Mat* (2000, dir. Barry W. Blaustein), *Fahrenheit 9/11* (2004, dir. Michael Moore), *Grizzly Man* (2005, dir. Werner Herzog).

and experience making and promoting films meant their films were less risky investments. A few of their films also had recognizable figures in them, like Bill Clinton (*The War Room*) and Stephen Hawking (*A Brief History of Time*), which made these documentaries an easier sell to exhibitors and audiences.

Among the large, conglomerated film companies, Miramax and Sony Pictures Classics were the most consistent distributors of documentaries throughout the 1990s. They both had large annual slates of films, often between twenty and forty. They aggressively acquired films at Sundance and other festivals, and began financing and coproducing films as more companies fought to acquire films through negative pickup.

Sony Pictures Classics was also committed to documentaries. It released a number of them during the 1990s, both from established filmmakers like Errol Morris (*Fast, Cheap, and out of Control*, 1997) and Robert Epstein (*The Celluloid Closet*, 1996) and from newer filmmakers like Chris Smith and Sarah Price (*American Movie*, 1999) and Terry Zwigoff (*Crumb*, 1995). Sony Pictures Classics generally did not acquire political or historical documentaries. Rather, most of its films are character studies of unusual people, like *Crumb*, *American Movie*, and *Fast, Cheap, and out of Control*.

Like the other specialty divisions that released documentaries, Sony Pictures Classics was interested in selling documentaries to general audiences, rather than a core group that would be naturally interested in a film by virtue of its subject matter. *The Celluloid Closet* is a good example of this strategy. It premiered in September 1995 at the Venice Film Festival, where *Variety* gave it a glowing review. Reviewer David Rooney called it "immensely entertaining" and predicted that it "stands to bust out of niche markets into significantly broader commercial territory."[22] After splendid reviews and strong ticket sales at the New York Film Festival, Sony Pictures Classics picked it up in October 1995. It then played at the Sundance and Berlin Film Festivals, which helped drum up publicity.[23] The film finally opened in limited release March 15, 1996. It played on thirty-eight screens at its peak, and grossed $1.4 million.

By the end of the decade, new companies entered the specialty market and tried their hand at releasing documentaries. From its founding in 1997, Artisan Entertainment did it all: develop, produce, market, and distribute

[22] David Rooney, "Review: *The Celluloid Closet*," *Variety*, September 11–17, 1995, 106–7.
[23] Because *The Celluloid Closet* was coproduced by HBO, Sony Pictures Classics allowed the channel to show it once before the film's release. David Noh, "Opening the Closet," *Film Journal International*, March 1, 1996, 24, 199.

films, both wide-release genre fare like *The Blair Witch Project* (1999, dirs. Daniel Myrick and Eduardo Sánchez) and art-house films like *Pi* (1998, dir. Darren Aronofsky).[24] One of Artisan's early releases was the music documentary *Buena Vista Social Club* (1999, dir. Wim Wenders), which earned a sensational $7 million at the box office and was nominated for an Academy Award. Artisan Entertainment also acquired StartUp.com (dir. Chris Hegedus) prior to its festival run, in August 2000. As announced in *Variety*, the company planned to premiere the documentary at the Sundance Film Festival in 2001 and release it theatrically soon thereafter. Specialty labels began using a festival runs as a marketing campaign for already-acquired fiction films as a strategy in the mid-1990s. By the end of the 1990s, they were employing this strategy for documentary films as well.

Though the most consistent documentary distributors were small, independent companies, there are always large, ambitious distributors that try out documentaries, pushing some to great grosses and high visibility. As the large companies begin to produce their own films and move away from acquiring documentaries, new companies enter to fill the void. This is a pattern that continues in the twenty-first century. Commercialization of documentary films was an uneven process, pushed haltingly by gambling big companies with their one or two shots, and with consistent support from very small independent distributors that build their business on documentaries.

HBO Documentary: Skating the Knife's Edge between Film and Television

By the mid-1980s, broadcast networks had almost ceased producing documentaries, with only fifty-one hours of documentary programming in 1977 and even fewer, thirty-one hours, in 1987.[25] But on cable television, nonfiction programming thrived. The founding of the Discovery Channel in 1985 and the rapid growth of its parent, Discovery Communications, made documentary programming ubiquitous on television. While Discovery did make some forays into the theatrical market, by and large, Discovery and other cable channels the Learning Channel, the Arts & Entertainment

---

[24] Lissa Gibbs, "Distributor F.A.Q.: Artisan Entertainment," *The Independent*, January–February 1999, 41–43.
[25] Michael Curtin, *Redeeming the Wasteland: Television Documentary and Cold War Politics* (New Brunswick, NJ: Rutgers University Press, 1995), 246.

Network, and Lifetime primarily produced low-cost, episodic nonfiction television. This meant they stayed out of the hunt for prestige that caused theatrical distributors to try to draw sharp distinctions between television documentaries and film documentaries.[26]

HBO had different programming strategies and goals. HBO started funding and programming documentary-style television early in the 1980s. Its television series *America Undercover* was a consistent source of production financing for independent producers, during a time when PBS was undergoing turbulent changes in funding structures and programming strategies and when commercial networks were reducing their news department staffs. HBO-funded documentaries also earned major accolades, like nominations for the Academy Award for Best Documentary Film, and a win for *Down and Out in America* (1986, dir. Lee Grant). However, partly in response to the growing theatrical market for documentaries and changes in Academy Award qualifying rules, HBO shifted its strategy in the 1990s. HBO began to finance and acquire more feature-length documentaries, thus attaching its brand to the newly visible and profitable genre of popular documentaries. HBO also began working with more well-known filmmakers like Spike Lee.

HBO Documentaries as Original Programming

HBO was founded as a pay-cable channel to showcase the latest mainstream American films. However, as a result of a rocky relationship with the studios supplying these films, HBO began to develop original programming in the early 1980s to lessen its dependence upon studio films.[27]

Original programming was a way to fill schedule hours for a lower cost than acquiring blockbusters. At first, HBO's original programming included boxing matches, stand-up comedy specials, and documentaries, or what executives preferred to call "nonfiction television." Along the way, HBO

---

[26] Discovery bought the Learning Channel in 1991. Bill Edelstein, "Producers Hitch Stars to Docus," *Variety*, April 3–9, 1995, 9–10.

[27] During the first half of the 1980s, Hollywood studios actively resisted the home video market. Executives worried that selling copies of their films would significantly decrease the value of their libraries. This allowed independent distributors to thrive, but it also meant that HBO was an important outlet for studios' recent releases to be seen after their theatrical run. Michele Hilmes, "Pay Television: Breaking the Broadcast Bottleneck," in *Hollywood in the Age of Television*, ed. Tino Balio (Boston: Unwin Hyman, 1990); Stanley H. Slom, "HBO: How Fuchs—and HBO—Rose to the Top," *Variety*, July 27, 1992, 36, 71.

developed into a kind of low-budget film and television studio, producing programs that echoed both public television series and direct-to-video exploitation films. HBO also adopted marketing techniques from studio classics divisions and independent distributors, using limited theatrical releases and awards-qualifying runs in key markets to highlight its most prestigious/serious documentaries.

One of the first documentaries produced for HBO was *She's Nobody's Baby: American Women in the Twentieth Century*, a one-hour program produced by *Ms. Magazine* in 1981. For its broadcast of the show, HBO won the first Peabody Award for a pay-cable channel. Then in 1984, HBO took a bigger step into the documentary market with its nonfiction series *America Undercover*. *America Undercover* strained the boundaries of the term "series" for a number of reasons. It had no driving theme or central philosophy. Its episodes were made by independent producers, who were funded by HBO and whose work was overseen by HBO executives. For many years, *America Undercover* did not have a consistent timeslot on HBO's schedule. Most episodes of *America Undercover* were one hour long, but some were one and a half hours, and some were multipart events. HBO's branding of the show was fluid—sometimes it was marketed as a series, other times the fact that a film was produced for the series was downplayed. This series ended around 2006 when HBO began marketing its documentaries individually.

America Undercover encompassed films on a mix of topics, both socially relevant and openly salacious. The series' first season consisted of six episodes: "Murder: No Apparent Motive," about serial murders, "Stoned: Kids on Drugs," "When Women Kill," "One Man's Fight for Life," "Being Homosexual," and "Getting Even: When Victims Fight Back." These episode titles get at the series' most typical subjects: violent crime, illicit drugs, and sexuality. The series has also covered sober topics like poverty in the United States, abortion, the AIDS epidemic, and rape. In the 1990s, HBO increased the strands under *America Undercover*'s banner with *Real Sex* (1990) and *Taxicab Confessions* (1995). The addition of *Real Sex* and *Taxicab Confessions* added an explicitly tawdry aspect to *America Undercover*, and usually garnered the series' highest ratings, though the two strands made up only 10 percent of HBO's nonfiction output.[28]

HBO's method for producing documentaries differs from that in place at commercial networks and within American public broadcasting. The three

---

[28] "Staying Real," *Broadcasting & Cable*, November 4, 2002, 15A.

commercial television networks placed their news divisions firmly in charge of reporting and producing nonfiction. As a general rule, the networks do not commission independent productions or accept submissions from outside producers of documentaries or nonfiction pieces.[29] Editorial control is centralized within the news departments because network documentaries are usually journalistic. Drew Associates' documentaries were a significant exception to this rule, but their observational nature provided cover by distinguishing them from the news departments' journalistic pieces. HBO also exercised editorial control over individual episodes of *America Undercover*, but it did so by hiring and collaborating with independent producers, rather than maintaining a news department. While PBS holds calls for individual projects to be financed and curates collections of finished films in its anthology series like *P.O.V.*, HBO reached out to filmmakers and pitched subject matter for them. The filmmakers would then create a detailed prospectus, including a list of interview subjects, and present it to HBO for approval. HBO executives viewed dailies and were involved in the editing process with the filmmaker. HBO provided production budgets between $200,000 and $300,000 in the 1980s; by 1997, budgets hovered around $600,000.[30] This is similar to PBS's process for its themed series, like *American Experience* and *American Masters*, and its investigative journalism series, *Frontline*, in which there is substantial collaboration between the PBS executive producers and the independent producers making the episodes.

In the early days of *America Undercover*, HBO did not acquire completed documentaries; rather, executives took a firm hand in producing the work they wanted to air. While PBS was dedicated to funding projects through meritocratic processes like open solicitation, HBO espoused no such commitment. Rather, HBO chose independent producers based on "who the person is, what's the angle, and his or her experience," explained longtime executive producer Sheila Nevins.[31] Choosing independent producers based on their professional experience and portfolio of work is a safe and rational way of operating. It lowers the risk that HBO would finance work that did not meet its standards, but it also raised the barrier of entry to newer producers with fresh ideas. This led HBO to hire many documentarians and

---

[29] Significant exceptions include Robert Drew's work and the historical clip shows like *Project XX*.
[30] Stephen Farber, "HBO Documentaries Fill 3 Networks' Breach," *New York Times*, June 27, 1984, C26; John Dempsey, "HBO Docu Dilemma: Ted vs True Grit?," *Variety*, February 10–16, 1997, 27, 29.
[31] Larry Jaffee, "Plugged In Producers: A Guide to Working with Cable Networks," *The Independent*, June 1991, 25.

journalists who had proven themselves through work on the networks and on PBS. For example, the first episode of *America Undercover* was made by Imre Horvath, a former producer for CBS's *60 Minutes*. Over the years, many filmmakers who had worked with PBS worked with HBO as well. These include Jon Alpert and Maryann DeLeo, Renee Tajima and Christine Choy, and Rob Epstein. HBO also kept talent in its stable, contracting filmmakers to make multiple works for them. HBO even took on projects that otherwise would have fit into PBS's schedule, like Susan and Alan Raymond's follow-up to their groundbreaking PBS verité series *An American Family*.[32]

Another aspect of *America Undercover* that differs from network news–produced nonfiction and independent documentaries on PBS is its scheduling. For the series' first eighteen years on air, it was programmed at irregular intervals, on different days at different times. HBO did not operate according to network scheduling logic, mainly because its primary programming is feature-length films, which vary in length.

What Is an HBO Documentary?

From the very beginning of *America Undercover*, HBO executives worked to position the series as entertaining and cinematic, pushing away conventional definitions of documentary. In an article introducing the series, Bridget Potter, senior vice president of original programming, explicitly stated that HBO's documentaries are not news documentaries. "We are not trying to make or report the news, such as the networks frequently have done with their documentary reports. We simply are trying to enlighten, which is another form of entertainment."[33] In addition to aligning *America Undercover* with entertainment, rather than information, journalism, or the public forum, Potter pointed to the difference in subject matter between "traditional" documentaries and *America Undercover*. Potter said, "To most people, documentaries mean programs about Indonesia and talking-head discussions. . . . ABC News next month will air a three-hour program on education in America. Now that's a documentary. But with nonfiction tv, it's fascinating to see people's lives unfold."[34] Here Potter also alluded to the

---
[32] Recently, HBO even took over the long-running PBS Kids' series *Sesame Street*. It covers production costs for the show in exchange for the right to premiere the new episodes on HBO. The episodes are then syndicated back to the series' original home, PBS.
[33] Clarke Taylor, "HBO Sees Harvest in Documentaries," *Los Angeles Times*, April 20, 1984, H12.
[34] "HBO Following the Docu Trail via 'America Undercover' Fare," *Variety*, August 15, 1984, 72, 76.

narrative aspect of *America Undercover*'s documentaries, seeing lives "unfold" generally being more entertaining than the analysis of educational systems. Nevins put it plainly: HBO documentaries must be "a high profile, high gloss concept."[35] In other words, the subject matter should be broadly and immediately appealing, and the finished product should look expensive and inviting. Specifically, as people associated with this work observed, such documentaries should look like a feature film.

Personnel hired to make episodes for the series echoed Potter's statements, and even praised HBO for its focus on visually driven nonfiction films. Malcolm Clark, executive producer of the first-season episode "Being Homosexual," declared that HBO was "putting filmmaking values back into documentaries. At HBO they stress the visual, while network documentaries are often nothing but radio with a light on."[36] One way that HBO stressed the visual was by allowing the use of reenactments, a technique that was all but taboo in documentary practice in the mid-1980s. For example, in the first season's first episode, "Murder: No Apparent Motive," the filmmakers staged a scene of a woman being abducted. In response to this, ABC News head Richard Richter told the *New York Times*, "I am frankly appalled by some of the techniques they use on HBO. They have used dramatizations within a documentary. That's the kind of tampering with the documentary form that set a dangerous precedent."[37] Here the entertainment value of recreated footage clashed with more traditional journalistic values held dear by networks.

America Undercover films were not only visually "high gloss," they also used sensationalist narrative strategies and content choices. Because HBO held editorial control, executives worked directly with filmmakers to make these decisions, usually in the name of entertainment. In the very first season of *America Undercover*, some filmmakers alleged that HBO executives encouraged them to add in elements to jazz up the films. Clark, executive producer of "Being Homosexual," told a reporter, "HBO wanted more people who had an ax to grind, so there would be more conflict."[38] Another person who worked on an episode about cocaine abuse among ordinary Americans alleged that HBO coerced the producers into adding a segment on cocaine use among celebrities. Cis Wilson, associate director of documentaries at

---

[35] Jaffee, "Plugged In Producers," 25.
[36] Farber, "HBO Documentaries," C26.
[37] Farber, "HBO Documentaries," C26.
[38] Farber, "HBO Documentaries," C26.

HBO, did not deny that she gave these editorial notes. She claimed that "Being Homosexual" was "a little too soft" without segments on the difficulties of being gay in America. She also defended the move to focus on celebrities' drug use by appealing to the value of context, as well as entertainment value. "We wanted to remind people of the jet set that has received most of the publicity. That way you have context for the rest of the show. And frankly, we needed something to make the film move."[39] HBO's *America Undercover* married prurient subject matter with sensationalist filmmaking techniques and narrative strategies, going against the grain of both network news reporting and independent documentaries on PBS.

Producing for HBO

Most independent producers were happy with their experience working with HBO, not least because the process was smooth and the production budgets were generous. Filmmaker Renee Tajima said, "It was clear we were hired hands, freelance workers hired to make the program for HBO . . . we sit down, we fight, we discuss, we throw things out. [HBO] knows how to work with filmmakers. If you want to develop a good relationship, there's a degree of professional respect. If we weren't happy, we'd take our names off it."[40] While independence and the retention of editorial control are often cited as crucial values for people working with PBS, it is clear that many filmmakers were glad to have the opportunity to make work on a stable financial basis and with competent collaborators like the executives at HBO.

This satisfaction is also reflected in the fact that many filmmakers teamed up with HBO again and again during the 1980s and 1990s. HBO signed some to contracts to make multiple documentaries. For example, Jon Alpert started making the film *One Year in a Life of Crime* (1989) while a correspondent on NBC's *Today* show. But the network was interested only in short segments, not in a feature-length documentary, so Alpert brought the completed film to HBO. HBO bought it, then contracted Alpert and his associate Maryann DeLeo to make a number of films for *America Undercover*, including *Rape: Cries from the Heartland* (1991), *High on Crack Street: Lives Lost in Lowell* (1995), *A Cinderella Season: The Lady Vols Fight Back* (1998),

---

[39] Farber, "HBO Documentaries," C26.
[40] Jaffee, "Plugged In Producers," 25.

Latin Kings: A Street Gang Story (2003, dir. Alpert), and *Dope Sick Love* (2004, dir. Felice Conte, EP Jon Alpert). HBO also commissioned Maysles Film to make multiple films for the series: *Abortion: Desperate Choices* (1992), *Letting Go: A Hospice Journey* (1996), and *LaLee's Kin: The Legacy of Cotton* (2001), all directed by Albert Maysles, Deborah Dickson, and Susan Froemke. The latter film was nominated for an Academy Award for Best Documentary Feature.

Nurturing relationships with documentarians paid off in prestige. HBO first garnered an Academy Award nominated for best documentary feature for *Soldier in Hiding* (1985, prod. Japhet Asher), just a year after the premiere of *America Undercover*. HBO's first win came for the 1986 film, *Down and Out in America*. It was directed by actress Lee Grant, who made a handful of documentaries for HBO. Bill Guttentag made many films for *America Undercover*, and earned two Oscar nominations for HBO: *Crack USA: County under Siege* (1989) and *Death on the Job* (1991). Partnering with Susan and Alan Raymond, HBO earned an Academy Award nomination for *Doing Time: Life inside the Big House* (1991) and a win for *I Am a Promise: The Children of Stanton Elementary School* (1993). Documentaries produced for HBO were a consistent presence at film festivals and in the running for Academy Awards, a situation that other filmmakers and Miramax executives protested in early 1992.

HBO Shifts Documentary Strategy to Emphasize Film over Television

Though those protests in 1992 did not lead to immediate change, the Academy did respond with rule changes in 1995. According to the new regulations, documentaries would need to be theatrically released in order to qualify for the Academy Awards; film festival screenings would not count. Around the same time as the announcement of the rule change, and partly in response to it, HBO shifted its strategy around documentary programming. First, HBO pivoted toward investing in more feature-length documentary films, which would allow it to continue vying for Academy Awards. It also began paying for qualifying runs—limited theatrical releases—of some documentaries to meet awards requirements. Second, HBO increased the amount of documentary programming it produced. In 1996, HBO nearly doubled nonfiction production, increasing its investment from thirteen to twenty-four documentaries per year.[41] This was part of a larger strategy to create more original programming. And while original fiction films cost HBO about $7 million to produce, by the mid-1990s, hourlong documentaries cost HBO about $600,000.[42] Documentaries were a cost-effective way for HBO to expand its slate of original programming, and they brought an additional bonus: prestige and buzz.

In 2001, HBO gave *America Undercover* a stable place on the schedule, and a prized one at that: Sunday night, following megahit series *The Sopranos*.[43] By that time, the balance of HBO documentaries had shifted to include more acquisitions than in the early days. *Broadcasting & Cable* reported, "[HBO] finances about 60 percent of the films it airs, acquires another 20 percent and co-finances the rest."[44] To illustrate HBO's strategy during the mid- to late 1990s, I will turn to a few of its higher-profile feature documentaries.

Investing in talent also helped HBO pivot to the theatrical realm. Though Carolyn Anderson writes that HBO began releasing its documentaries in theaters in 2002, with the founding of HBO Theatrical Films Releasing, the company actually made forays into theatrical releasing earlier, working with already-established film distributors and filmmakers self-distributing their work.[45] Robert Epstein directed *Common Threads: Stories from the Quilt* (1990), which won an Academy Award for HBO. Then, during the course of making his next film, *The Celluloid Closet*, with codirector Jeffrey Friedman, Epstein convinced HBO to invest. *The Celluloid Closet* played at major festivals, including the 1995 Venice Film Festival, 1995 New York Film Festival, and 1996 Sundance Film Festival, and it attracted the attention of a theatrical distributor. Sony Pictures Classics acquired the film during the New York Film Festival. *The Celluloid Closet* screened on HBO once, in March 1996, and then Sony Pictures Classics released it theatrically.[46] It earned $1.4 million in theaters.

HBO also worked with directors Joe Berlinger and Bruce Sinofsky on a film to be released in theaters, through self-distribution. The filmmakers had self-distributed their first film, *Brother's Keeper*, in 1992, racking up $1.2 million.

---

[41] Rich Brown, "Original Cable Programming: HBO," *Broadcasting & Cable*, February 19, 1996, 36.
[42] Dempsey, "HBO Docu Dilemma," 29.
[43] Bob Fisher, "*America Undercover* Reaches its Prime (Time) of Life), *Documentary*, April 1, 2001, https://documentary.org/feature/america-undercover-reaches-its-prime-time-life.
[44] "Staying Real," *Broadcasting & Cable*, November 4, 2002, 15A.
[45] Carolyn Anderson, "Theatricals," in *The Essential HBO Reader*, ed. Gary Edgerton and Jeffrey Jones (Lexington: University of Kentucky Press, 2008).
[46] Noh, "Opening the Closet," 24, 199.

HBO fully funded their second film, *Paradise Lost: The Child Murders at Robin Hood Hills*, for $750,000. It premiered on HBO in June 1996, then earned $250,000 at the box office via self-distribution. Though the box-office earnings were not spectacular, the television ratings were. *Variety* reported, "On the night of its first HBO showing, *Paradise Lost*, which deals with the aftermath of the murder of three 8-year-old boys in Arkansas, chalked up to a 10.9 rating and 17 share in HBO households, winning the night against Big Four programming in those homes."[47] Excellent ratings and a theatrical release certainly helped build HBO's brand, even if the documentary was more pulp than prestige fare. By 1997, HBO had signed Berlinger and Sinofsky to make three more documentaries for the channel.

Finally, HBO made a significant partnership with filmmaker Spike Lee in the mid-1990s. It financed his documentary *4 Little Girls* about the 1963 Birmingham, Alabama, church bombing that killed four girls and helped catalyze the civil rights movement. In what would become a standard practice to circumvent the Academy's nominating rules, HBO paid for a theatrical release of *4 Little Girls*. It opened at Film Forum in July 1997 and played in three more theaters over the summer and fall, grossing a little over $200,000 total.[48] While the film did not secure an Oscar nomination, the qualifying run raised the profile of both *4 Little Girls* and HBO. HBO continued to partner with Lee on some of his documentary works, including *Jim Brown: All American* (2002) and his two-part series on the effect of Hurricane Katrina on New Orleans, *When the Levees Broke: A Requiem in Four Acts* (2006) and *If God Is Willing and da Creek Don't Rise* (2010). Lee's documentaries gained substantial acclaim, with *When the Levees Broke* screening at the 2006 Venice Film Festival, the 2008 Whitney Biennial, and winning Emmy Awards, Peabody Awards, and NAACP Image Awards. All of these honors reflected well on HBO, even if the glory was centered upon Lee.

In the end, enhancing HBO's brand was the ultimate reason for its investment in documentaries: ratings mattered less because there were no advertisers to please. Instead, subscribers must believe that HBO is worth paying for, and documentaries were part of the holistic picture. This is why Sheila Nevins called a 2002 documentary on the global AIDS epidemic a "low watch but high visibility show."[49] By earning accolades and awards, it would

---

[47] Dempsey, "HBO Docu Dilemma," 29.
[48] Todd McCarthy, "*4 Little Girls*," *Variety*, July 21–27, 1997, 38. Box-office take from *The Numbers* online: https://www.the-numbers.com/movie/4-Little-Girls#tab=summary.
[49] "Staying Real," *Broadcasting & Cable*, November 4, 2002, 15A.

burnish the HBO brand, even if it did not earn ratings to match episodes of *Real Sex* or *Taxicab Confessions*.

It was in the 1990s that HBO became a major player in the field of documentary film. While HBO had been producing and commissioning documentary programming since the early 1980s, its strategy changed in the 1990s. Partly as a response to changes in the Academy Award nominating rules, HBO began to invest in more feature-length documentaries, rather than one-hour films. It also doubled production of documentaries in 1996, as part of an overall strategy to enhance its original programming. Most of HBO's documentaries were intended only for cablecast, but others were produced for possible theatrical distribution as well. These films went to theaters in myriad ways—through acquisition by theatrical distributors, through self-distribution by filmmakers, and through HBO paying for award-qualifying theatrical runs. HBO would employ this final strategy more and more in the late 1990s and into the 2000s, in order to place its documentaries within the conversation about film, rather than television. For its growing commitment to documentary, HBO reaped many rewards: high ratings, critical acclaim, and numerous prizes from both film and television societies.

Indie TV: Ancillary Outlet, Then Producer, for Documentary Films

While HBO shifted strategy to make more documentaries for theatrical release and award qualification, another cable channel adopted a similar strategy. The Independent Film Channel was founded in the mid-1990s to capitalize on the mainstreaming of independent film culture.[50] Its programming was primarily feature films, including documentaries, which the channel licensed from over a dozen distribution companies.[51] IFC also produced original nonfiction programming for the channel, at a cost between $70,000 and $200,000 per hour, similar to the cost of nonfiction series on basic cable channels like Discovery and HGTV. Then, IFC began financing and coproducing documentary films to be released in theaters.

---

[50] For more on the Independent Film Channel and the Sundance Channel, see Robert Eberwein, "The IFC and Sundance: Channeling Independence," in *Contemporary American Independent Film*, ed. Chris Holmlund and Justin Wyatt (London: Routledge, 2005), 265–81.

[51] Jim McConville, "IFC on the Movie," *Broadcasting & Cable*, February 26, 1996, 48, 44; Jim McConville, "More Subs for IFC," *Broadcasting & Cable*, April 29, 1996, 90.

These films were budgeted around $1 million, much higher than the nonfiction television programs.[52] They did this through a division named IFC Productions. IFC Productions produced documentaries for possible theatrical release through its distribution company IFC Films.

IFC Productions' push to produce original films relied primarily on funding films by well-known directors, including lauded documentarians. IFC Productions' first film was *Gray's Anatomy* (1997, Steven Soderbergh), a Spaulding Gray performance documentary. IFC Productions also funded documentaries by two documentary auteurs, Errol Morris and Werner Herzog. *Mr. Death: The Rise and Fall of Fred A. Leuchter, Jr* (1999, dir. Errol Morris) was distributed by Lions Gate, and *My Best Fiend* (1999, dir. Werner Herzog) was distributed by New Yorker Films. In addition, IFC Productions provided partial funding and support for independent fiction films including *Men with Guns* (1997, dir. John Sayles), *Boys Don't Cry* (1999, dir. Kimberly Pierce), and *Girlfight* (2000, dir. Karyn Kusama).

The fruits of this venture were a growing library of films, and the possibility of prestige and profit. This library of films would lessen IFC's dependence on the distribution companies from whom IFC bought the rights to show films. This is similar to HBO's push to create original fiction and documentary films, along with other original programming. Unlike most of HBO's productions, however, IFC was intent on pushing the films through the entire film distribution cycle before showing them on its own channel. IFC president Kathleen Dore said, "We won't be seeing these films until after five to six years for the most part—after pay per view, after HBO and after broadcast windows. We are really looking forward to having them available to us at some point down the road."[53] This move was also a response to what executives perceived as an opening in the market. In 1997, IFC senior vice president of programming and production Jonathan Sehring explained, "There is really a funding gap right now in terms of independent and quasi-independent distribution. . . . The Miramaxes and New Lines of the world have gotten so large they have all but abandoned getting involved in ultra-low-budget projects."[54] While larger companies were distributing and marketing documentary films and other independent films, they were not producing them regularly. Finally, these executives likely also understood

---

[52] Donna Petrozzello, "New Networks: Doing More with Less," *Broadcasting & Cable*, October 20, 1997, 42; McConville, "IFC on the Movie," 48, 44.
[53] Joe Schlosser, "IFC Will Fund Independent Films," *Broadcasting & Cable*, March 10, 1997, 68.
[54] Schlosser, "IFC Will Fund," 68.

that guiding a film through the distribution cycle was necessary to qualify it for film awards, according to the new qualifying rules for the Academy Award for Best Feature Documentary.

With IFC producing and distributing films and HBO working with distribution companies to release its films in theaters, the borders between independent film and cable television were fully breached. Cable companies' incursions into film companies' territory added pressure to an already tumultuous time of transformation in the independent film sector.

Runtimes as Indicator of Target Market

While television remained intertwined with documentary into the 1990s, the theatrical release potential of documentaries increased. Distributors seeking low-budget indie films often acquired documentaries as well. Film festivals, particularly the Sundance Film Festival, were a major showcase for these films. Analyzing Sundance's documentary programming over the decades offers another angle on the changing status and commercial center of documentary film. Tallying a film's runtime is one way to determine intended exhibition market. A documentary shorter than seventy minutes is likely intended for broadcast and/or the educational market, while a documentary longer than seventy minutes is feature length and has theatrical potential. Some documentaries produced for television, or acquired by television stations and cable companies, were eighty or ninety minutes long. But documentaries that were sixty minutes or fewer were easier to sell and easier for programmers to schedule.

While the number of documentaries at Sundance increased steadily from 1986 to 2006, so did the total number of films screened.[55] The percentage of documentaries as compared to the overall program went up and down, but it was the same in 2006 as in 1986: 18 percent. So the proportion of documentaries to the total number did not change significantly. However, the format of the documentaries at Sundance did shift over the same period. In 1986, 47 percent of documentaries at Sundance were feature length. In 1991, 53 percent were feature length. The trend toward feature documentaries continued: in 1996, 84 percent of documentaries were features. The balance

---

[55] Number of films and runtimes tallied from Sundance Institute Digital Archive, "Sundance Film Festival," https://history.sundance.org/programs/Sundance%20Film%20Festival.

Table 4.1 Documentaries at the Sundance Film Festival, 1986–2001

Year	Total films screened	Docs screened	Percentage of films that were docs	Feature-length docs screened	Percentage of docs that were feature length
1986	83	15	18	7	47
1991	129	17	13	9	53
1996	184	25	13	21	84
2001	220	27	12	17	63

evened slightly in 2001, with 63 percent of documentaries running seventy minutes or longer (Table 4.1).

This change in the format of the documentaries at Sundance shows two trends: filmmakers responding to the new possibilities for documentaries, and the Sundance Film Festival becoming more enmeshed with the film industry. More filmmakers recognized that the theatrical market for documentaries was growing, so more made feature-length documentaries, rather than aiming for broadcast. At the same time, the Sundance Film Festival recognized that it had the power to bolster the theatrical market for documentaries, so it programmed an increasing number of feature-length documentaries.

Conclusion

The mainstream film industry's interest and investment in American independent film extended somewhat to documentary features, with more documentaries released in theaters than ever before. Studios and well-resourced independent companies added one or two documentaries to their large annual slate of films, but smaller independent companies actually handled the majority of documentary theatrical releases in the 1990s. These different types of distribution companies had different patterns of documentary acquisition, marketing, and release. While the smaller independent firms took risks on documentaries by first-time or unknown filmmakers and marketed them to a specific niche, the specialty labels battled for the splashiest documentaries on familiar topics or made by market-tested directors.

At the same time, premium cable channel HBO had been cultivating its brand, and gaining low-cost programming, by producing documentary films and integrating them in film culture. While HBO had been producing a documentary series since the mid-1980s, it shifted its strategy in the 1990s to ramp up production on documentaries and concentrate more on documentary films that could be released theatrically. The basic cable channel Independent Film Channel followed HBO's example by producing documentaries and independent fiction films specifically for theatrical release, under the banner IFC Productions. Theatrical release, and the attendant marketing and publicity, lend legitimacy and increase awareness of a film.

The combined interest from cable channels and theatrical distributors continued the documentary's shift in status from television journalism to independent film. Network news divisions were no longer a dominant source of documentary, and many of the norms of television journalism were pushed aside in favor of other approaches to the creative treatment of actuality. With this shift came new stakeholders, and conflict between them: studio classics division executives demanded recognition for the documentaries they distributed, and cable television executives adjusted their strategies in response. And through documentary film's participation in the American indie movement, documentarians gained a new ancillary market: basic cable channels.

5
The Docbuster Era (2000 to 2007)

In the early 2000s, one documentary after another earned phenomenal box-office grosses, breaking records and rising to new heights of popular consciousness in the United States. Box-office figures from the biggest successes from two major years, 2003 and 2004, point to the heightened market for documentaries. MGM/UA released *Bowling for Columbine* (Michael Moore) in late 2002, and in 2003 it became the highest-grossing documentary in history, with a record $21.5 million at the box office. It also won the Academy Award in early spring 2003, twinning profitability with prestige. In the summer months, three documentaries succeeded commercially at the same time: *Winged Migration*, *Spellbound*, and *Capturing the Friedmans*, eventually reaching grosses of $11.6 million, $5.7 million, and $3.1 million, respectively. Other top-earning documentaries from 2003 alone include *Tupac Resurrection* ($7.7 million), *To Be and to Have* (*Être et avoir*, $7.6 million worldwide), *The Fog of War* ($4.1 million), *The Real Cancun* ($3.8 million), *Step into Liquid* ($3.6 million), *My Architect* ($2.8 million), and *DysFunkTional Family* ($2.5 million). The next year, 2004, a number of documentaries captured big box-office numbers, including *Super Size Me* ($11.5 million), *What the #$'! Do We Know* ($10.9 million), *Touching the Void* ($4.5 million), *The Corporation* ($3.4 million), and *Born into Brothels* ($3.4 million). But these respectable returns pale in comparison to the behemoth that was *Fahrenheit 9/11*. It earned a whopping $119 million domestically, a record unsurpassed by any documentary since.[1]

The subjects of these films varied widely, encompassing gun control, migratory birds, penguins, climate change, dance competitions, a family rocked by allegations of child abuse, fashion design, and corporate fraud. Tone, structure, and style also ran the gamut, from comedic to poetic, narrative to argument-based, using direct address, a collage aesthetic, reenactments, interviews, and home movies. Despite these differences, writers have often

---

[1] All box-office figures from The Numbers, https://www.the-numbers.com/movies/genre/Documentary.

generalized about the films' appeal when offering explanations for the documentary boom. In a new iteration of the core tension between documentary film and television, many writers and pundits claimed that the newly popular reality TV genre made viewers more accustomed to nonfiction media, and thus more likely to buy tickets to documentaries. Others claimed that conglomerate-owned television news programming was the bad object driving audiences toward documentaries.[2] This critique of the commercial nature of TV news implies that documentary film is not commercial, concerned with public service rather than ratings or ticket sales.

These responses, echoed in both *Variety* and *Cineaste*, suggest that audiences have the freedom to choose the media that suits them, and that they automatically vote for that media through ticket sales. This argument is tempting because it fulfills the popular trope of the eventual full democratization of media, in which consumers can access all media that interests them (and distributors can profit) indefinitely through the power of digital technology. Chuck Tryon has convincingly critiqued this teleological and utopian vision of media democratization, as powerfully instantiated in Chris Anderson's *The Long Tail: Why the Future of Business Is Selling Less of More*. Tryon contends that Anderson's argument "downplays the role of theatrical distribution and other classical 'gatekeeping' mechanisms in shaping the reception and marketing of movies."[3] This is precisely the case for much writing that tries to account for the documentary market during this period.

As much as the early 2000s ushered in an exciting time of heightened visibility and availability for documentary films, this period was more a time of evolution than revolution. The growing visibility of documentary films during this period is the result of a highly developed and stable commercial market, not an expression of consumer freedom and media democratization. By the early 2000s, every level of the documentary market had grown, so there were a greater variety of financing sources, a number of distributors that released documentaries theatrically, and a robust ancillary market that could capture revenue after the peak publicity engendered by a theatrical release.

During this time, theatrical distributors and other gatekeepers did not wane in importance; rather, new distribution companies and new marketing

---

[2] David Rooney, "What's Up, Docs? Auds Love Reality," *Variety*, June 23–29, 2003, 16; "The Political Documentary in America Today," *Cineaste*, Summer 2005, 29–36.

[3] Chuck Tryon, *Reinventing Cinema: Movies in the Age of Media Convergence* (Piscataway, NJ: Rutgers University Press, 2014), 96.

methods brought more documentaries to theaters than ever before. One sort of gatekeeper grew in number during this period as well: the film festival. There was overall growth in the number of film festivals, and specifically, the number of exclusively documentary festivals. Festivals also became increasingly imbricated with the film industry. By awarding grants for production and running labs to mentor documentarians, film festivals bolstered the infrastructure that allowed for the documentary feature market to regularize and stabilize.

Because theatrical release raises the profile of films through advertising, publicity, and reviews, the larger number of documentary features in theaters led to a stronger ancillary market for documentaries. Cable television and DVDs were the sturdiest downstream markets for documentary films. Discovery and A&E followed HBO's model for building documentaries into their businesses and catalogs, as prestige products and as gateways to the theatrical market. At the same time, DVD became a significant ancillary market for documentary features. With so many companies committed to financing and acquiring documentary features, the market became more competitive.

Theatrical Distribution of Documentaries in the Early 2000s

While the previous decade had finally cemented the documentary film as a theatrical product rather than a type of television journalism, the early 2000s saw documentary films earn unprecedented revenue in theaters. At certain times in the 2000s, there were multiple documentaries playing to large, general audiences, some at multiplexes rather than the traditional art house. In the previous decade, a few companies released the most visible documentaries, often marketed to a more general audience, while certain smaller distributors actually distributed a larger quantity of documentary films in theaters and targeted niche audiences. In this decade, the situation became complicated due to wider shifts in the specialty film business. While independent fiction films seemed to hit a wall in terms of profitability, there was room to grow in the documentary market, and more companies than ever began releasing documentaries in theaters. Writing in *Filmmaker Magazine* about the watershed year of 2003, Mary Glucksman pointed out this sea change. She stated, "In fact, only six indie fiction features—three horror pics and three female-helmed films—released in 2003 scored double-digit box office.... Documentaries, meanwhile, performed in record numbers, with four distributors earning considerably more [from their documentary releases] than the narrative features on their slates."[4] The idea that documentaries could outpace fiction films for multiple companies was new, and it encouraged more distributors to acquire and release documentaries.

The split between distributors marketing documentaries to general audiences and those marketing to niche audiences, as identified in the last chapter, becomes more complex in the "docbuster" era. Two companies, Lionsgate and Sony Pictures Classics, distributed both very high-grossing documentaries—*Fahrenheit 9/11* and *Sicko* for the former, *Winged Migration* for the latter—in addition to a long list of eclectic documentaries that did not cross over to general audiences. Apart from Lionsgate and Sony Pictures Classics, the highest-grossing documentaries during this time were released by companies that otherwise released few documentary films, similar to the previous decade. MGM/UA (*Bowling for Columbine*), Paramount Classics / Vantage (*An Inconvenient Truth*), and Warner Independent (*March of the Penguins*) acquired a few high-profile documentaries, but these were special cases; they mostly pursued in-house production of fiction films with high production values, becoming more and more like their parent companies.

At the same time as a few documentaries earned truly record-breaking returns at the box office, new companies Magnolia, ThinkFilm, IFC Films, and Roadside Attractions released many documentary films, filling the gap left by specialty divisions and former independents that had moved closer to mainstream studio productions and release patterns. They also partnered with institutions like HBO, which nurtured another facet of the documentary market. The documentary features these companies released earned consistently strong, midrange grosses. Finally, long-running independent distributors New Yorker Films, Zeitgeist Films, and Shadow Distribution continued to release documentary features, with more succeeding at higher levels than before. For example, Shadow's release of *The Wild Parrots of Telegraph Hill* earned a truly incredible $3 million.

With few exceptions, documentaries retained the trappings of an independent release, even as deep-pocketed specialty divisions acted more and more like studios in terms of their narrative film releases. Within the wider world of specialty film, documentaries stood out because distributors acquired them, rather than produced them. And they mostly released them

---

[4] Mary Glucksman, "The Numbers Game," *Filmmaker*, Winter 2004, 78.

slowly via a limited release and then opened them wider if it appeared they would be successful. This release strategy was a continuation of the strategies used to release documentaries in the past.[5]

New elements emphasized in how distribution companies marketed documentaries. First is the appeal to the family sector. By booking the stars on talk shows and targeting PTA listservs with marketing emails, distributors appealed to parents, making the case that both adults and children would enjoy a documentary. This strategy was key to documentary films crossing over to the mainstream. Auteur appeal was another novel strategy for marketing documentaries during this time. There are few documentarians who are household names, but one of them is both director and star of his own films: Michael Moore. Moore's recognizability and notoriety made his films easier to promote. Sergio Rizzo describes Michael Moore as a commercial auteur. He writes,

> Like other commercial auteurs, Moore's celebrity as an auteur "produces and promotes texts that invariably exceed the movie itself, both before and after its release." . . . these texts work to prepackage the film, as in "a Michael Moore movie," helping it to address its segment of the viewing audience across various distribution methods: movie theater, cable, home video, and Internet.[6]

Moore's participation in leftist political discourse helps to promote his films as they move through various release windows. Interestingly, his celebrity works in two ways: his name promises a certain type of film, and it also promises the presence of the director-star himself.

Controversy was another significant marketing appeal for documentary features during this time. Distributors had marketed documentaries like *Mondo Cane* and *Warrendale* on the basis of their lurid content, but they capitalized on provocation to a new degree during this time period. Distributors ably used controversy to generate organic publicity on

---

[5] The norm for specialty divisions was to open their films wide, on at least one thousand screens. By 2007, the average cost for producing a specialty film was $49.2 million, with marketing costs averaging $25.7 million. Motion Picture Association of America, "Entertainment Industry Market Statistics," 2007.

[6] Sergio Rizzo, "The Left's Biggest Star: Michael Moore as Commercial Auteur," in *Michael Moore: Filmmaker, Newsmaker, Cultural Icon*, ed. Matthew H. Bernstein (Ann Arbor: University of Michigan Press, 2010), 30. The same could be said of Morgan Spurlock, director of *Super Size Me*, *Where In the World Is Osama Bin-Laden*, and *The Greatest Movie Ever Sold*.

mass-communication outlets as varied as network talk shows, national newspapers, and political websites. *Capturing the Friedmans* was marketed this way, and it had the added allure of ambiguity: *Capturing the Friedmans* was promoted as a film to-be-talked-about. Political provocation was another facet of controversy-as-promotion. *Fahrenheit 9/11* was marketed on the basis of its politically sensitive content, and the circumstances of its release contributed a double layer of controversy.

Analysis of the release circumstances of four documentaries, including their acquisition, marketing and publicity strategies, and dissemination, reveals continuities between the "docbuster" period and earlier eras. Released by different companies and dealing with vastly different topics, these films—*Spellbound*, *March of the Penguins*, *Capturing the Friedmans*, and *Fahrenheit 9/11*—were all popular documentary hits. Yet, apart from *Fahrenheit 9/11*, all reached their impressive grosses through slow rollouts, appealing to niche audiences more than to general audiences, and relying on organic publicity more than paid advertising. Thus, *Fahrenheit 9/11*'s release pattern and marketing strategies should be seen as extremely exceptional, even for this era. The other three films' histories are more exemplary of the way that independent companies and studio classics divisions distributed documentaries during the "documentary boom" of the early 2000s.

Spellbound (dir. Jeffrey Blitz) is a funny and heartwarming documentary about kids preparing to compete in the 1999 National Spelling Bee. *Spellbound*'s appeal lies in its characters: each tween competitor has a distinct personality and backstory. The film follows a conventional crisis narrative—it all leads up to the National Spelling Bee. HBO acquired *Spellbound*, then partnered with ThinkFilm to release the film in theaters in April 2003. *Spellbound* began its theatrical run with an exclusive engagement at Film Forum, with screenings sold out for three weeks. In June, two months after its initial release, ThinkFilm predicted a final gross for *Spellbound* of $3 million.[7] The film eventually scored $5.7 million at the box office. Though ThinkFilm was a new company, it drew on existing documentary institutions like Film Forum and HBO to launch *Spellbound*.

Festival play and free preview screenings built positive word of mouth, at a lower cost than paid advertisements in newspapers or on television. ThinkFilm executive Mark Urman reflected, "For every person who saw 'Spellbound' for free [at a film festival or preview screening] . . . it was as

---

[7] Rooney, "What's Up, Docs," 7.

good as seven inches of ads in the New York Times."[8] Timing the release of *Spellbound* with the 2003 National Spelling Bee meant that ThinkFilm built in angles that were easy for the media to cover. *Variety* reported that ThinkFilm had plans to buy TV ads, but they were able to book the stars of the film—child spelling bee contestants—on talk shows instead. "Twice they shelved TV ad campaigns after the kids in the film were asked to appear on *Oprah* and *The Today Show*, giving the pic better and more targeted coverage than money can buy."[9] These appearances on national talk shows meant that word of *Spellbound* reached a wide swath of American adults, including the parents of children. This strategy served as a valuable model for documentaries that could appeal to families, like *March of the Penguins* and *Mad Hot Ballroom*. In addition to national media publicity, ThinkFilm also targeted specific groups through niche marketing. Its grassroots campaign emailed educators and parents on listservs and worked with family- and education-oriented groups like the PTA and local libraries.

The theatrical campaign for *March of the Penguins* was similarly pitched to families and drew on associations with a trusted institution, the National Geographic Society. It was also rolled out slowly, though it expanded to more screens and grossed much more than *Spellbound*. *March of the Penguins* (dir. Luc Jacquet) follows a year in the life of a colony of emperor penguins, as they mate and endure the brutal Antarctic climate. Framed as a survival story, the film's main appeal is watching the hilarious and graceful penguins hunt, play, and protect their fluffy offspring. The story takes place against the spectacular landscape of Antarctica, fulfilling the touristic desire to see alien and awe-inspiring scenery.

Produced in France for $2.4 million, *March of the Penguins* was acquired by Warner Independent Pictures and National Geographic Feature Films for $1 million for North American release. To appeal to the American market, executives made significant changes to the original film. They wrote expository, voice-of-god narration voiced by Morgan Freeman to replace the original French narration, which is from the penguins' perspective.[10] They also had a new orchestral score composed, to replace the original electronic score.

---

[8] Anthony Kaufman, "Marketing Case Study: 'Spellbound,'" *Variety*, August 18, 2003, variety.com/2003/scene/markets-festivals/marketing-case-study-spellbound-1117891028.

[9] Tamsen Tillson, "Sales Strong for Unique Nonfiction," *Variety*, September 27–October 3, 2004, 16.

[10] Doreen Carvajal, "Compared with Their Filmmakers, the Penguins Have It Easy," *New York Times*, September 28, 2005, nytimes.com/2005/09/28/movies/compared-with-their-filmmakers-the-penguins-have-it-easy.html.

National Geographic Feature Films executive Adam Leipzig describes how and why they acquired the film and invested in changing it for the North American market.

> There was nothing else in the movie marketplace remotely like the penguins. They were the ultimate product differentiator. . . . there hadn't been a hugely successful nature documentary before. But there had been *Winged Migration*, and other nature films that attracted smaller audiences. We had evidence there was an audience for the film—we just didn't know how big it would be.[11]

Because of the uncertainty in how *March of the Penguins* would appeal, Warner Independent and National Geographic first opened it on a few screens in New York and Los Angeles, without a large, expensive marketing push. As Leipzig describes, "Only when that niche audience came out for the movie, and kept coming, did we gradually expand, eventually to 2,500 screens. . . . We went niche. Then the niche grew into astounding success."[12] By initially targeting niche audiences, the distributors could judge whether or not interest was high enough to push it to general audiences. *March of the Penguins* eventually earned $77 million in theaters (fifteen times as much as *Spellbound*), making it the second highest-grossing documentary ever. It also won the Academy Award for Best Documentary Feature.

This approach worked extraordinarily well. Attracting both adults and children meant these documentaries were four-quadrant films, a mark of broad audience appeal that studios aim for in their tentpole films.[13] An exhibitor, Greg Laemmle, president of Laemmle Theatres, made this point clear. Referring to *March of the Penguins*, he said, "You've got that rarest of commodities—an art-house film that also appeals to families. Just as we saw with *Spellbound* and *Winged Migration*, you've got something where people are coming with kids and people who have no kids are coming."[14] The crossover appeal of *March of the Penguins* was not just from niche to general audiences, but a demographic crossover as well. Documentary films are

---

[11] Adam Leipzig, "10 Lessons 'March of the Penguins' Taught Me about Success and the ROI of Risk," *Cultural Weekly*, June 27, 2013, culturalweekly.com/10-lessons-march-of-the-penguins-taught-me-about-success-and-the-roi-of-risk.

[12] Leipzig, "10 Lessons."

[13] The four quadrants are males under twenty-five, females under twenty-five, males over twenty-five, and females over twenty-five.

[14] Roshan McArthur, "Super Fluffy Animals," *Guardian*, July 15, 2005, G2, 7.

painted as serious and often politically engaged, which implies an adult audience, but the success of these documentaries is due in great part to their appeal to children and their parents.

One niche group in particular found *March of the Penguins* to be ideal family fare: conservative Christians. Though the distributors did not specifically target this niche with marketing, conservative Christians publicized *March of the Penguins* in their community media outlets. Christian publications highlighted the film, ministers published viewing guides on their websites, and church groups took trips to the theater to see the film. The film appealed because there is no mention of "political" issues like evolution and climate change, and because it evinces a pro-family stance. Writing in the Christian-oriented *World Magazine*, Andrew Coffin interpreted the procreation story in *March of the Penguins* as evidence of intelligent design and suggested that parents reinforce this idea with the children they accompany to the film. "That any one of these eggs survives is a remarkable feat—and, some might suppose, a strong case for intelligent design. . . . It's sad that acknowledgment of a creator is absent in the examination of such strange and wonderful animals. But it's also a gap easily filled by family discussion after the film."[15] The fact that *March of the Penguins* centers on a nuclear family of penguins appealed to conservative media figures in a more general way, beyond the idea of intelligent design. Both the editor of the *National Review*, Rich Lowry, and conservative radio host Michael Medved praised the film for emphasizing the penguins' dedication to their families. Lowry told a gathering of young Republicans that "penguins are the really ideal example of monogamy," while Medved expressed to an interviewer that *March of the Penguins* is "the motion picture this summer that most passionately affirms traditional norms like monogamy, sacrifice and child rearing."[16] The passion that the American Christian niche felt for *March of the Penguins* demonstrates that when unexpected groups support a film and mold an interpretation of it for their members, they can greatly expand the audience for it.

While *Spellbound* and *March of the Penguins* were heavily marketed to parents and families, in addition to niche audiences, *Capturing the Friedmans*

---

[15] Conservative columnist George Will countered, "If an Intelligent Designer designed nature, why did it decide to make breeding so tedious for those penguins?" Jonathan Miller, "March of the Conservatives: Penguin Film as Political Fodder," *New York Times*, September 13, 2005, nytimes.com/2005/09/13/science/march-of-the-conservatives-penguin-film-as-political-fodder.html.

[16] Miller, "March of the Conservatives."

and *Fahrenheit 9/11* were sold, principally, on the controversial nature of their subject matter. *Capturing the Friedmans* is a true-crime documentary about a father and son convicted of child pornography and sexual abuse. The events take place in a quiet, verdant suburb, making the crimes even more shocking. *Capturing the Friedmans* taps into audiences' deep appetite for true-crime stories. In addition, the film's ambivalent stance encourages viewers to act as jurors weighing the evidence against the main characters, sparking debates over their guilt or innocence.[17] *Capturing the Friedmans* juxtaposes home movies of the Friedman family with contemporary interviews, playing with ambiguity and memory like a family-centered *The Thin Blue Line*.

Similar to *Spellbound* and *March of the Penguins*, festival play, word of mouth, and publicity helped sell *Capturing the Friedmans*, which was acquired by HBO in advance of its festival play. The film premiered at the Sundance Film Festival to acclaim, but it was not immediately acquired by a theatrical distributors. A few months later, Magnolia Pictures, a new distributor, bought the theatrical rights to the film. The film began its theatrical run at three New York City theaters. It set a box-office record for documentary at the Angelika Film Center. Magnolia rolled out the film slowly, playing in a maximum of seventy-eight theaters at a time.

The film's scandalous story, real-life mystery, and discourse of ambiguity allowed Magnolia to follow a similar marketing strategy as ThinkFilm did for *Spellbound*. "We didn't have to spend much on advertising because it was so publicity-driven," [Magnolia's Eamonn] Bowles says. "I thought the subject matter was going to be more difficult to get past, but the film hit a chord, and it got incredible word of mouth. People hung out for hours discussing it—I've never seen audiences get engaged like that.[18]" Once again, television appearances and newspaper articles pushed the film without the distributor having to invest in paid advertising. According to *Filmmaker Magazine*, the *New York Times* wrote nine articles about *Capturing the Friedmans*, covering every angle "from the legal section to the op-ed page."[19] Director Jarecki also appeared on the *Today Show* and *Charlie Rose*. *Capturing the Friedmans* became a box-office success and cultural phenomenon by taking

---

[17] For more on the true-crime documentary genre, see Kristen Fuhs, "The Legal Trial and/in Documentary Film," *Cultural Studies* 28, nos. 5–6 (September 3, 2014), 781–808, https://doi.org/10.1080/09502386.2014.886484, and Tanya Horeck, *Justice on Demand: True Crime in the Digital Streaming Era* (Detroit: Wayne State University Press, 2019).

[18] Glucksman, "The Numbers Game," 79.

[19] Glucksman, "The Numbers Game," 79.

an equivocating stance on a lurid story. This open-ended narrative approach invited audience discussion and high-profile media speculation.

Fahrenheit 9/11's stance is not equivocating or ambiguous. It is a denunciation of the media's role in the election of President George W. Bush, its fear-mongering in the wake of the September 11 terrorist attacks, and its cheerleading for the war on terror. The film is also an indictment of Bush's ineptitude, ulterior motives for invading Afghanistan and Iraq, and connections to the bin Laden family. Most of all, *Fahrenheit 9/11* is an argument against reelecting Bush in the 2004 presidential election. This argument comes in the form of a comedic, fast-paced film with clever montages and a big-personality narrator, director Michael Moore himself. Moore was already a celebrity at this point, having been the narrator of the Oscar-winning *Bowling for Columbine* (2002) and a visible liberal activist.

Fahrenheit 9/11 is the rare documentary to be produced by a large studio with an equally large budget. Moore's celebrity, along with his two television programs, encouraged Disney/Miramax to provide production financing for *Fahrenheit 9/11*. In return for fronting the $6 million budget, Disney/Miramax got the right to distribute the film domestically.[20] Bought by Disney in 1993, Miramax had moved from a distribution company to a producer as well, using the resources of the studio to invest in higher-budgeted and higher-profile films, winning awards along the way. However, parent company Disney blocked Miramax's release of *Fahrenheit 9/11*, causing a controversy laced with accusations of censorship.[21] Harvey and Bob Weinstein, founders of Miramax, fanned the flames of controversy as they formed a separate company, the Fellowship Adventure Group, to purchase *Fahrenheit 9/11* back from Disney.

Fahrenheit 9/11 played the Cannes Film Festival in May 2004, in the midst of this firestorm. The film's premiere coincided with France's and other American allies' very negative views of the United States and the Bush administration's unilateral invasion of Iraq. Painted as a victim of censorship and a cri de coeur against Bush, *Fahrenheit 9/11* won the Palme d'Or. Lionsgate and IFC acquired the theatrical rights to the film at Cannes. The controversy provided a flash point for publicizing the film, and also became

---

[20] Disney advised Moore's agent not to allow Miramax to invest in the project because the film could alienate families that does not agree with its politics.

[21] Jim Rutenberg, "Disney Is Blocking Distribution of Film That Criticizes Bush," *New York Times*, May 5, 2004, https://www.nytimes.com/2004/05/05/us/disney-is-blocking-distribution-of-film-that-criticizes-bush.html.

a main theme for the paid advertising. Posters featuring Michael Moore standing next to President George W. Bush were printed with the tagline, "Controversy? What controversy?" These posters, and much of the film's publicity and marketing, linked the film's distribution controversy with its fiery message against the current presidential administration.

Fahrenheit 9/11's controversial subject matter and brush with censorship increased its appeal for many, convincing audiences that attending the film was a way to participate in high-stakes politics. As Tom Sherak of Revolution Studios commented on the film's huge opening, "If you make it feel like it has urgency, people will have to go."[22] As powerful as this urgency was in pushing ticket sales, it was matched by a powerful and confident release strategy. Lionsgate's risky decision to open *Fahrenheit 9/11* wide actually allowed the marketing to pay off. *Fahrenheit 9/11* opened in 868 theaters on June 23, 2004, earning $21.8 million and rising to number one at the box office.[23] That first weekend's earnings alone made the film the top-grossing documentary of all time. *Fahrenheit 9/11* eventually playing in more than two thousand theaters and grossed $119 million in North America. The film's domestic box-office take was the seventeenth highest of all films released in 2004.

While writers were keen to group together popular documentaries to highlight the surprising "docbuster" trend, the individual circumstances of release are largely determinative of their box-office grosses. The early 2000s saw more powerful distribution companies release documentaries and exploit trends like family appeal and controversial subject matter. While the quantity of documentaries released increased, the typical release pattern did not change radically. Though the early 2000s saw numerous documentaries cross over to the mainstream, the vast majority were still initially released like art-house and small indie films: on very few screens, relying on critical acclaim and early grosses to determine the next steps of release. This distinguishes documentaries from most other specialty films released at the time, which were being released wide right from the start. Older institutions like Film Forum continued to help launch documentary films into theatrical release, while HBO increased its aggressive acquisition of documentary broadcast rights.

---

[22] Sharon Waxman, "The Political 'Fahrenheit' Sets Record at Box Office," *New York Times*, June 28, 2004, nytimes.com/2004/06/28/movies/the-political-fahrenheit-sets-record-at-box-office.html.

[23] Waxman, "Political 'Fahrenheit' Sets Record."

Film Festivals: Quasi-Industrial Players

Film festivals have always been important to the documentary market. As events that showcase films for their artistic and political significance rather than commercial prospects, film festivals were a natural home for documentaries, which have usually been separate from the commercial arena of cinema. Marijke de Valck characterizes festivals as "sites of passage" because they are obligatory stops along a film's journey through the market. She writes, "Festivals are sites of passage at which 'art cinema,' 'world cinema,' and 'auteur cinema' find audiences and through which they might attract sufficient attention for further release."[24] For many years, the prospects for further theatrical release were slim for most documentary features. Nevertheless, the exposure and cultural prestige conferred through festival screenings could help a documentary feature be nominated for an Academy Award, be acquired by a nontheatrical distributor, or be licensed by a broadcaster.

In the late 1990s and 2000s, a number of new festivals dedicated to documentary films were founded. There was also an explosion in the sheer number of film festivals around the world. Some major film festivals also increased their purview during this time period, at the moment when the market for documentary features expanded and stabilized. These major festivals developed programs to fund documentary projects and mentor filmmakers throughout the process. By acting as quasi studios, film festivals were more firmly integrated in the documentary feature market. Film festivals' traditional role as curators and exhibitors also supported the documentary feature market: festival programmers' decisions on what to screen influenced the hungry buyers of documentaries (theatrical distributors, cable companies, and, later, streaming services).

The 2000s and 2010s saw major growth in the number of film festivals. According to Stephen Follows, as of 2013 there were around three thousand film festivals in the world, and 75 percent of all film festivals were created between 2003 and 2013. In 1995, the number of film festivals increased by 1.1 percent, the first time there was growth greater than 1 percent. This growth rate jumped to 2.7 percent in 2000. In 2003, there was a 4.3 percent

---

[24] Marijke de Valck, *Film Festivals: From European Geopolitics to Global Cinephilia* (Amsterdam: Amsterdam University Press, 2007), 106.

growth in the number of film festivals. In 2005, 2006, and 2007, the growth rate jumped up to and hovered above 8 percent.[25]

During this growth period, there was also a blossoming of film festivals dedicated to documentary films. For many years, there were only a few documentary-specific film festivals, with one founded each decade in a different European country: Visions du Reel, in Switzerland (founded 1969); Cinema du Reel, France (founded 1978); and International Documentary Filmfestival Amsterdam (IDFA), the Netherlands (founded 1988). The first American documentary-specific festival is Hot Springs Documentary Festival, Arkansas (founded 1992). Hot Docs Film Festival, Canada, and Sheffield International Documentary Film Festival, United Kingdom, followed swiftly thereafter, in 1994. The growth in the number of documentary film festivals began in the late 1990s and the first half of the 2000s. In the United States, these included Full Frame Documentary Film Festival (1998), SF Docfest (2001), MoMA's documentary fortnight (2001), Big Sky Documentary Film Festival (2003), AFI Docs (2003), True/False Film Festival (2004), Camden International Film Festival (2005), and Atlanta DocuFest (2005). A number of international documentary film festivals were formed around the same time, including DOXA (Canada) in 1998, CPH: Dox (Denmark) in 2003, Doclisboa (Portugal) in 2003, and London International Doc Fest (United Kingdom) in 2007. Having more documentary festivals is significant because they demonstrate, on a large scale, that audiences exist for documentaries. Film festivals generate press in local and regional outlets, engaging audiences by drawing connections between documentaries and proximate community concerns. Even when they do not have an official film market, they facilitate the documentary industry by being a meeting place for nonfiction film professionals.

The growth in documentary film festivals is significant, but there was also a change in the scope of some major film festivals' operations that effectively strengthened the infrastructure of the documentary market. In the past, film festivals had pointed out trends in documentary and been consistent supporters of independent documentary filmmaking. The Social Cinema in America sidebar at the 1967 New York Film Festival drew attention to the cinéma vérité movement, and showed that there was an audience eager for socially conscious, observational documentaries. The Sundance Film

---

[25] Stephen Follows, "How Many Film Festivals Are There in the World?," *Stephen Follows, Film Data and Education*, August 19, 2013, https://stephenfollows.com/many-film-festivals-are-in-the-world/.

Festival showed documentary features from its inception, then founded its documentary competition in 1982. Sundance became a major showcase for documentaries during the indie cinema renaissance of the 1980s and 1990s, with many theatrical distributors acquiring documentary features after their Sundance screenings.

But in the late 1990s and early 2000s, many major film festivals took on new responsibilities, becoming nonprofit granting agencies and education centers. De Valck argues,

> An important trend of the late 1990s is that film festivals turn en masse to the industry's facilitating services. They organize film markets, industry meetings, producers' networks, training for script development and production, and all kinds of seminars. With these kinds of initiatives, festivals try to make useful contributions to the development of the transnational film market.[26]

This was true for both fiction and documentary films, and the change took place at general festivals and documentary-exclusive festivals.

For example, in 2001, the Sundance Institute took over administration of the Soros Documentary Fund from the Open Society Foundation. The Soros Documentary Fund had been awarding production grants totaling $1.5 million annually, which the Sundance Institute continued with its Sundance Documentary Fund.[27] This was Sundance's first step toward being a nonprofit agency for documentary features.[28] Following that, the Sundance Institute moved into education and training for documentary filmmakers. Founded in 2002, the Documentary Film Program offered "creative and strategic support in addition to providing grants for nonfiction filmmakers."[29] The next year, the Documentary Film Program continued its professionalization program with a Composers Lab and an Edit and Storytelling Lab.[30]

---

[26] De Valck, *Film Festivals*, 109. Dina Iordanova points out that, during the early to mid-2000s, some of the largest festivals also built "talent campuses"—Berlin and Busan—and others have gone beyond granting supplementary production funds to actually commissioning films—among them New Crowned Hope Festival in Vienna, Austria. Dina Iordanova, "The Film Festival as an Industry Node," *Media Industries Journal* 1, no. 3 (January 1, 2015), https://doi.org/10.3998/mij.15031809.0001.302.

[27] Susan Zeller, "Soros Fund Moves to Sundance," *RealScreen*, January 1, 2002, http://realscreen.com/2002/01/01/soros-20020101/.

[28] The Sundance Institute offered its first Feature Film lab in 1981.

[29] "Sundance Institute Timeline," https://www.sundance.org/timeline.

[30] "Sundance Institute Timeline," https://www.sundance.org/timeline.

Hot Docs, a documentary-exclusive film festival in Toronto, similarly developed programs to tighten its connections with the film industry during this time.[31] In 2000, Hot Docs began the Toronto Documentary Forum (later called Hot Docs Forum), a setting in which filmmakers pitch documentary projects to international financiers.[32] The next year, the festival founded its market, the Doc Shop, which runs concurrently with the film festival. It also introduced other "market initiatives" like Rendez-vous, which formalized one-on-one meetings between filmmakers and producers/distributors.[33]

Programs like these involved film festivals in earlier phases of the filmmaking cycle. Rather than the film festival being only a "site of passage," it became a pivotal element of preproduction for selected documentary features. Festivals were a key element that sustained the documentary market as documentary features became more prevalent in theaters. Because market stabilization requires the regular production and release of product, these film festival programs strengthened the documentary market's infrastructure.

In addition to running labs, hosting pitch events, and doling out grants, film festivals' traditional role—programming and curation—also increased in importance. With the documentary feature market expanding, and the increased ease of making documentaries with digital cameras and editing platforms, film festivals screen submissions and put their stamp of approval on films. This means that broadcasters and distributors do not have to sift through everything themselves; instead, they rely on festivals to bring the best of the best to their attention. Through their preproduction mentoring and market-focused programs, festivals identify potentially successful projects at earlier and earlier stages, and can connect documentarians with theatrical distributors and broadcasters.

In one example, the Sundance Film Festival's documentary programming reveals festival programmers' understanding of the increased commercial potential of releasing documentaries in theaters. In 2001, 63 percent of the

---

[31] Hot Docs was founded in 1994.
[32] Betsy McLane, "Hot Docs and the Toronto Documentary Forum," *Documentary*, October 1, 2000, https://www.documentary.org/feature/hot-docs-and-toronto-documentary-forum.
[33] Ezra Winton has convincingly argued that, as it pursued industrial connections and mainstream audiences for documentaries, Hot Docs lost both its critical edge and its contact with the Canadian film community making radical committed documentaries. He describes this change as Hot Docs going from being "locally-responsive, advocacy-oriented and artist-run festival to an internationally-responsive, market-oriented, commercial festival." Ezra Winton, "Good for the Heart and Soul, Good for Business: The Cultural Politics of Documentary at the Hot Docs Film Festival" (PhD diss., Carleton University, 2014), 11, https://doi.org/10.22215/etd/2014-10051.

Table 5.1 Documentaries at the Sundance Film Festival, 1996–2006

Year	Total films screened	Docs screened	Percentage of films that were docs	Feature-length docs screened	Percentage of docs that were feature length
1996	184	25	13	21	84
2001	220	27	12	17	63
2006	224	43	18	42	98

documentaries screened at Sundance were feature length.[34] Following the runaway success of the "docbusters," in 2006, 98 percent of the documentaries screened at Sundance were feature length (Table 5.1). This demonstrates both filmmakers and festival programmers responding to the shift in the market for documentary films. The major film festivals are quasi-industrial players, even as they often brand themselves as separate from the mainstream film industry.

In addition to starting programs to facilitate the production and distribution of documentary films, major festivals began giving documentary features more recognition than they had in the past. At the time of their premieres, *Bowling for Columbine* and *Fahrenheit 9/11* were two of the only documentaries to ever play in competition at Cannes. In 2004, surfing documentary *Riding Giants* was the opening night film at the Sundance Film Festival. This marked the first ever time a documentary opened the festival. In offering pride of place to feature documentaries, these major film festivals tacitly acknowledged their increasing audience draw and cultural relevance.

During this period, film festivals increased in number, as did documentary-specific film festivals. A number of powerful film festivals also expanded their reach with granting, mentoring, and pitching programs. These programs nourished the documentary film market by facilitating the production and distribution of high-quality documentary films. As the major film festivals became more deeply imbricated in the film industry, they fostered a stronger connection between the documentary world and the film industry.

---

[34] Runtimes tallied from Sundance Institute Digital Archive, Sundance Film Festival, https://history.sundance.org/programs/Sundance%20Film%20Festival.

Following HBO's Lead: Cable Channels Use Documentaries to Break into the Theatrical Market

As documentaries came to be accepted as theatrical fare, cable companies began to invest earlier and more often in documentary films. HBO led the charge, partnering with theatrical distributors, but other companies joined as well. Discovery, A&E, and HDNet produced and acquired documentary features with the intent of releasing them theatrically. The growing number of cable companies interested in documentary films strengthened the market and encouraged filmmakers to make features for theatrical distribution.

While HBO had begun to partner with theatrical distributors and four-wall theaters for qualifying runs for its documentaries as early as the 1990s, such partnerships became a systematic strategy in the 2000s. In 2003, *TelevisionWeek* reported that, of the forty documentaries airing on HBO and Cinemax each year, the plan was to do theatrical releases for six or seven of them.[35] One reason HBO and Cinemax implemented this plan was to mollify documentarians who wanted their films release in theaters. As Sheila Nevins said in 2003, "If a producer wants [a theatrical release] and you deprive him of that, you might be making HBO not the best place for documentaries, and it needs to be.... It's our job to keep the producers happy."[36] She also pointed out the benefits that could flow from HBO working with documentarians and distributors to get the films theatrically released.

> [We want] to be part of the theatrical promotional campaign so we can be sure we are thought about properly and are part of the ultimate marriage of the filmmaker and the distribution plan. I want to get signage. I want HBO's moniker to appear in reviews. I want acknowledgement between theatrical and TV distribution that this is part of the wonderful world of exposure and that this can be compatible.[37]

Nevins acknowledges that, for HBO, the theatrical release of one of its documentaries is quite literally a marketing campaign for the film's eventual broadcast, and for the brand as a whole. "TV numbers are so vast compared to movie theater numbers," says Nevins, "there'll be a lot of people who won't have seen but will have heard of it. If it had gone direct to TV, and this is

---

[35] Daisy Whitney, "HBO Tests In-Theater Releases," *TelevisionWeek*, May 26, 2003, 12.
[36] Whitney, "HBO Tests In-Theater Releases," 12.
[37] Whitney, "HBO Tests In-Theater Releases," 12.

certainly true with *Spellbound*, we would not have been able to have marketed it sufficiently to arouse interest in it."[38] To accomplish this, HBO worked with major independent theatrical distributors. In 2003 alone, HBO partnered with ThinkFilm for *Spellbound* and *Bus 174*, Magnolia Films for *Capturing the Friedmans*, and New Yorker Films for *My Architect*.

At the same time that HBO was working on this strategy for theatrically releasing documentaries that it acquired, it also began releasing some of its fiction films theatrically. In the process, HBO was subject to the specialty market's turmoil. With a glut of films being released, HBO found that its documentaries actually performed better in theaters than its fiction films. HBO Films had produced *Real Women Have Curves* (2002, dir. Patricia Cardoso), which Newmarket Films released to a good gross of $7.7 million. But the production company's other fiction features rarely grossed over $1 million. *Elephant* (2003, dir. Gus Van Sant), *American Splendor* (2003, dirs. Shari Springer Berman, Robert Pulcini) and *The Notorious Betty Page* (2005, dir. Mary Harron) were critically acclaimed, but did not attract large audiences.[39]

As HBO solidified its commitment to documentary features and experimented with the theatrical release of fiction films, its strategies inspired imitators. During the early and mid-2000s, other cable companies began to invest in documentary films that they could eventually program on their channels. Though better known for their nonfiction series and reality television programs, these cable conglomerates followed HBO's lead to scavenge for prestige by producing and acquiring documentary films. They also tacitly acknowledged the competitive market for broadcast rights to documentaries by getting involved with these films early in their lives, rather than after their theatrical release.

Discovery had tried to release documentaries theatrically in the 1990s, but the box-office performance of *The Leopard Son* was not adequate, and the company turned to making documentaries for the large-format market. Discovery again took the plunge into feature documentaries in 2003 with production company Discovery Docs. It partnered with CameraPlanet, which planned to release the films theatrically in at least five cities before

---

[38] Kathy A. McDonald, "Nonfiction as Entertainment," *Variety*, August 25–31, 2003, A24.

[39] HBO Films first partnered with Fine Line Features to release its films. But Fine Line closed in 2004, leaving HBO without a guaranteed theatrical distributor. Interestingly, at this point, in 2004, HBO could have bought Newmarket Films, but decided not to expand into theatrical distribution itself. Rather, HBO and Newmarket Films kept their fiction features in the Time Warner fold by releasing them through Picturehouse.

airing on the Discovery Channel. In carving this path, Discovery aimed to produce films with the best-known documentarians, gaining the right of first refusal for projects proposed by Barbara Kopple, Michael Apted, Nanette Burstein, and Chris Hegedus and D. A. Pennebaker. Executives acknowledged that theatrically releasing their films would please the filmmakers and benefit Discovery through the exposure of a theatrical run. Their first release was a film on the *Brown v. Board of Education* court case called *With All Deliberate Speed* (2004, dir. Peter Gilbert, released by CameraPlanet), followed by *Grizzly Man* (2004, dir. Werner Herzog, released by Lionsgate) about a bear fanatic who was killed by bears. While *The Leopard Son* had been pitched as a family film, Discovery Docs took a different tack in the 2000s. *With All Deliberate Speed* is a historical documentary, and *Grizzly Man* is a portrait of an unusual character. Neither is pitched at children. *With All Deliberate Speed* did not perform particularly well at the box office, but *Grizzly Man* earned an impressive $3.1 million.

In 2005, A&E followed suit and opened a division, A&E Indie Films, to produce and acquire broadcast rights to feature documentaries. Its first in-house production was *Jesus Camp*, which Magnolia Films picked up and released in September 2006. It grossed over $800,000 and was nominated for an Academy Award. A&E Indie Films also acquired the broadcast rights to a documentary with a lot of buzz before its premiere at Sundance in 2007: *My Kid Could Paint That*. Released in theaters by Sony Pictures Classics, it earned $200,000. Neither film was a breakout hit at the box office, but they laid the groundwork for A&E Indie Films.

A&E opened the Indie Films division to rejuvenate the A&E brand, which was, by the early 2000s, associated with the series *Biography* and a lot of reality TV. President of A&E Robert DiBitetto admitted as much: "I don't think anybody viewed IndieFilms as a huge contributor to earnings.... But within the overall company plan, there was an excitement about what these films could bring to us, in terms of credibility and filmmaker relationships. We talked about it elevating the brand, and it gave us an opportunity to get us off the TV pages and have a different set of viewers and writers and eyes on it."[40] DiBitetto states plainly that the hoped-for rise in a brand's prestige is intimately linked to its release of theatrical films, even though the company's profits are rooted in cable television. The longer cycle of a feature film release, including an initial festival run, also means that there is more time to build

---

[40] Gordon Cox, "A Decade of Distinction," *Variety*, April 12, 2016, 31–32.

awareness and publicize the film. As Molly Thompson, senior vice president of A&E Indie Films, said in 2016, "Television films come and go.... Whereas if you're in the press for a whole year, the way we were last year for *Cartel Land*, it can really make a film special."[41]

In addition to raising the film's profile, a theatrical release matters to many filmmakers. Just as HBO and Discovery Docs cater to filmmakers, so too does A&E Indie Films. Documentarians get the final cut, and, thanks to the conglomerate's substantial cash flow, they are paid well. As *Variety* reported in 2016, a decade after the company's founding, "It's the kind of atmosphere that inspires loyalty. Amir Bar-Lev, for instance, has made three films with A&E IndieFilms: *My Kid Could Paint That*, *The Tillman Story*, and *Happy Valley*, the last about the Penn State football scandal. He says he's continually impressed by how much freedom the division gives him, and how much appetite for challenging content there is."[42]

While Discovery's and A&E's main business remained in cable television, the two companies followed HBO's example and invested in documentary features. By producing or acquiring them prior to a festival run, the companies benefited in multiple ways. They associated their brand with a theatrically released film during its long journey through festivals, theaters, awards season, video on demand, and home video. And at the end, they owned the broadcast rights to the film, as well.

Docbusters on DVD: Home Video as New Ancillary Market

The "docbuster" era is largely defined by the most visible measure of success: box-office grosses. However, profitable theatrical release does not provide the full picture of the highly developed and stable market for documentary films. Fiction films earn most of their profits from ancillary sales—via direct-to-consumer means like video on demand and other home video, and via the licensing of broadcast rights in multiple windows (premium cable, basic cable, network TV). The documentary market also benefited from ancillary sales, in order to capture the value of a film after it has been through theatrical distribution. Nontheatrical and educational distribution

---

[41] Cox, "A Decade of Distinction," 32.
[42] Cox, "A Decade of Distinction," 32.

had long been the main ancillary market for documentaries, even as fiction and entertainment media shifted from 16 mm to video. But the home-video market for documentaries was underdeveloped until the invention and diffusion of the DVD.

The DVD market exploded at the same moment as the "documentary boom" happened. This coincidence grew into a mutually reinforcing relationship between DVD companies and the theatrical documentary market. DVD labels and rental companies concentrated their growth on documentary features, to an extent no VHS label or rental company had. The growing prestige and popularity of feature documentaries in the 1990s encouraged DVD companies to invest in and connect their brands with documentary films in the early 2000s. This was a similar gambit as HBO's association with documentary films, which offered prestige and differentiation from other cable companies. The healthy DVD market for documentary features inspired confidence from theatrical distributors that their acquisitions would pay off after the theatrical release period.

According to Alisa Perren, the rapid increase in DVD sales and rentals, beginning in 1999, affected the indie film business, and thus the documentary business. One reason major studios kept their specialty divisions in business was because of the ancillary value promised by distributing their library titles via new technology. She writes, "Libraries gained value in part due to the expansion of the DVD business, and due to the widespread belief that there was substantial money to be earned once broadband became widely diffused and content could be more easily delivered over the Internet."[43] DVDs were cheap to manufacture, and they offered significant improvements on VHS: much higher fidelity copies of films and enough data space to be packaged with extras. Executives anticipated that customers would purchase new copies of their films, even if they had the VHS of them, because of these qualities. These qualities were assumed to be especially prized by customers buying classic, foreign, or documentary films.

The two most important companies in the realm of documentary films on home video were Docurama and Netflix. Their business models were very different, yet each had significant effects on the business of documentary film. The businesses partnered with each other as well as with other producers and distributors of documentaries. They also inspired imitators,

---

[43] Alisa Perren, *Indie, Inc.: Miramax and the Transformation of Hollywood in the 1990s* (Austin: University of Texas Press, 2012), 220.

who saw that customers responded to the products and services they offered. The existence of these two companies signals the maturity of the documentary market in the early twenty-first century, just as much as the more visible, high box-office grosses of "docbusters" do.

Founded in 1999 as an outgrowth of New Video, Docurama was the first home-video label to release documentaries exclusively. Eschewing a position alongside longtime retailers of educational and documentary films, or a non-profit mandate, Docurama cofounder Steve Savage proclaimed the coming popularity of documentaries: "They're the next wave. . . . The signs are everywhere."[44] Savage noted the growing presence of documentaries on cable, at film festivals, and in theaters. He turned out to be correct, and Docurama's slate of releases grew each year, from eight in 1999, to twenty in 2003, to thirty-six in 2004. He said, "You didn't use the 'd' word a few years ago if [documentaries] was the genre you were distributing. . . . It has gone from being the 'd' word to the buzz word. 2004 will be much hotter than 2003. Our catalog and new titles are on fire."[45]

Docurama's catalog contained a range of documentaries, both new releases and older films. Many were highly lauded films about serious topics, like the 2001 Academy Award winner *Murder on a Sunday Morning* (dir. Jean-Xavier de Lestrade) about a black youth accused of murdering a white tourist; the 2001 Academy Award–nominated *Children Underground* (dir. Edet Belzberg), about five homeless children in Bucharest; and Sundance award-winners *Southern Comfort* (2001, dir. Kate Davis) about a transgender cowboy living in the South, and *Blue Vinyl*, about the environmental dangers of vinyl (dirs. Judith Helfand and Daniel B. Gold).[46] But not all Docurama videos engaged in the discourse of sobriety. Like the variety of documentaries programmed by HBO, Docurama could appeal to more prurient interests, releasing some playful, sex-themed documentaries on home video. Its very first release, in 1999, was *Some Nudity Required*, about B-movies.[47] In 2003, Docurama released rated and unrated versions of *Porn Star: The Legend of Ron Jeremy*.[48]

Docurama executives understood the value of libraries: from the very beginning, the company released both new documentary films and older

---

[44] Seth Goldstein, "Indie Studios Take Different Path for Growth," *Billboard*, June 6, 1999, 101.
[45] Jill Kipnis, "Buyers Demand More Documentary DVDs," *Billboard*, February 21, 2004, 42.
[46] Jill Kipnis, "Picture This," *Billboard*, March 8, 2003, 52.
[47] Goldstein, "Indie Studios," 101, 104.
[48] Kipnis, "Picture This," 52.

documentary films. Marketing director Kim Hendrickson explained the logic of this strategy: "The premise is that documentaries are cool and that great ones are being made now, but they haven't been given the platform to strut their stuff. The only way to develop a label like this is to go backwards and forwards and find these great gems."[49] For example, in 2000, Docurama licensed three titles by D. A. Pennebaker. *Dont Look Back* was the first to be released, and Docurama packaged it with numerous extras, including a commentary track with Pennebaker and tour manager Bob Neuwirth, biographies of cast and crew, a Dylan discography, a Pennebaker filmography, and uncut versions of performances that are featured in part in the film.[50]

Docurama also partnered with television channels that have long shown documentaries—PBS and Sundance Channel—and an innovative "disrupter"—Netflix. Partnerships with PBS and the Sundance Channel date to the founding of the label, when Docurama released a five-tape set of PBS's miniseries *An American Love Story*, about a mixed-race couple, the week after the series aired on stations. Then, in 2005, Sundance Channel made a deal with Docurama to launch a branded label, the Sundance Channel Home Entertainment Documentary Collection. As reported in *Documentary* magazine, "Currently, the plan is to release six titles culled from both original productions and acquisitions which have already aired on the Sundance Channel."[51] This label's first release was the miniseries *The First Amendment Project*, which Sundance made with Court TV about the First Amendment. It included short documentaries from major directors including *Fox vs. Franken* (2004, dirs. Chris Hegedus and Nick Doob) and *Poetic License* (2004, dir. Mario Van Peebles). Docurama's success during this period speaks to the growth of both the DVD market in general and the maturity of the documentary film market.

While Docurama thrived, individual documentaries also sold well on DVD. One reason is that big companies were figuring out how and where to sell specialty DVDs. A film's festival screenings and awards gained cachet, and some home-video companies knew to exploit it. According to Sony's Lexine Wong, "Ten to 15 years ago, you kept festival awards stuff off the box cover, but now, if you say a film played at Sundance, it starts the

---

[49] Jim Bessman, "Famed Dylan Rockumentary Gets DVD Release on Docurama," *Billboard*, January 8, 2000, 83.
[50] The other two Pennebaker documentaries were *Moon over Broadway* and *Company*.
[51] "Short Takes," *Documentary*, May 2005, documentary.org/column/short-takes-may-2005.

buzz-making."[52] Tracey Garvin, another marketing expert at Sony, told *Variety* that the way to sell art-house films, including documentaries, on DVD is to reach consumers in high-brow locations. "You have to be much more targeted with these films," she says. "We like to go into bookstores where people might be hanging out for two hours.'"[53] Music documentaries were also sold at clothing and lifestyle retail outlets, not just at video stores. Paul DeGooyer, vice president of Warner Strategic Marketing Home Video, told *Billboard*, "We're seeing customers from Best Buy to Amazon to Hot Topic."[54] The strategy of promoting documentaries in myriad retail environments expanded significantly in the early 2000s.

The new arena of online shopping was also a boon for retailing documentary DVDs. Both *Bowling for Columbine* and *Winged Migration* were in the top fifty DVD sellers on Amazon in 2003. Though both films had performed well at the box office, neither reached the top fifty in theaters. DVD was different. One reason for this is the demographic of online shoppers: in 2003, Amazon had not yet achieved ubiquity. But the people who were likely to shop online in 2003 were also those who were interested in documentaries. "It was fairly unique to have two such strong documentaries," Amazon's DVD/video store group merchandising manager Stefan Pepe says. "Documentaries seem to be a great fit with our customers."[55] The success of Docurama, as well as the stunning performance of documentaries in theaters, inspired other companies to begin releasing more documentaries on DVD. Koch Lorber Films, a combination of Koch Entertainment Distribution and Lorber Media, was founded in 2003, with plans to distribute twenty to twenty-four titles on DVD per year, including world cinema and documentaries. In 2004, *Billboard* writer Jill Kipnis cautioned that other, larger home-video companies like HBO Video, Columbia TriStar Home Entertainment, and MGM Home Entertainment were entering the market that Docurama had dominated.

The growth in the DVD market for documentary films increased revenue opportunities for filmmakers. IFC Films purchased the theatrical rights to the documentary *Metallica: Some Kind of Monster* (dirs. Joe Berlinger and Bruce Sinofsky) and released it in theaters in July 2004. It earned $1.2 million

[52] Stuart Levine, "No Language Barrier: Subtitled Releases, Art Films Form Big Market Segment," *Variety*/ DVD Exclusive Bonus Feature, August 2005, 10.
[53] Levine, "No Language Barrier," 11.
[54] Jill Kipnis, "Music Documentary DVDs Reap Best of Both Worlds," *Billboard*, April 9, 2005, 40.
[55] Kipnis, "Buyers Demand More," 42.

at the box office. In a savvy move, the directors had sold the home-video rights separately, rather than bundling them with the theatrical rights. Berlinger told *Billboard*, "We have three studios offering us advances for the DVD rights. . . . The fact that we can get multimillion dollar offers for DVD changes the whole distribution landscape."[56] The filmmakers went with Paramount Home Entertainment and adopted a clever promotional gimmick described as follows: "For the Metallica project, Paramount is sponsoring a *Willy Wonka*-style giveaway: Through May 3, up to five winners who find special tickets in their copies of *Some Kind of Monster* will receive a trip to meet Metallica and see the studio where 'St. Anger' was recorded."[57]

Because of filmmakers' ability to split rights, theatrical distributors were sometimes deprived of the ancillary money, even after they invested significant sums in a theatrical release. As a result, successful indie theatrical distributors began to hold onto the home-video rights to some documentaries, rather than ceding the territory to other companies. Splitting the rights had surely wounded distributors of unexpected hits in the past. For example, Sony Pictures Classics released *Winged Migration* in theaters in 2004, to a total gross of $11.6 million in North America, while Columbia TriStar Home Entertainment reaped the rewards from the film's DVD release. By 2005, ThinkFilm president and CEO Jeff Sackman declared, "Going forward, you will see much more of the ThinkFilm home entertainment brand." Some of their initial releases on DVD were documentaries *Murderball* and *The Aristocrats*.[58] Other companies embraced the logic of the library, expecting that DVD sales would provide long-lasting residual revenue. Lexine Wong of Sony explained, "The expectations are lower on these smaller films, but it's important to have these kinds of filmmakers [Michael Moore, Errol Morris] in our library."[59]

While Docurama was mostly alone in releasing documentary films on DVD when it began in 1999, it was soon joined by distribution companies large and small. Though documentary films were being distributed in theaters in ever-greater numbers, the mostly limited release patterns of the films meant that audiences were not nearly exhausted by theatrical release. Because the marketing and publicity effort required to launch a theatrical

---

[56] Kipnis, "Buyers Demand More," 42.
[57] Kipnis, "Music Documentary DVDs," 40.
[58] Susanne Ault, "Indie Disc Jockeys," *Variety/DVD Exclusive*, June 2005, 10.
[59] Levine, "No Language Barrier," 11.

release is so large, there was much value left in the films for home-video audiences.

Netflix Delivers DVDs, Acts as Distributor, Breaks Windows

Netflix began as a DVD rental service. Using the affordances of internet connectivity, user data collection, and the US Postal Service, Netflix offered customers a home-video rental service with online ordering, customized recommendations, a wider selection of titles than most chain rental stores, and monthly subscription plans rather than individual title rentals and high late fees.[60] Netflix capitalized on the penetration of DVD players into American homes in the early 2000s, just as the documentary film market was buoyed by the growth of DVD retailing. In June 2003, rentals of DVDs exceeded the number of VHS rentals for the first time.[61] Netflix has grown into one of the most powerful and influential media companies since then. Though Netflix started small, Tim Havens points out that its brand strategy aimed for a general audience, unlike the increasing nichification of cable channels.[62]

According to Sudeep Sharma, Netflix "has made feature-length documentary a core pillar of its service, both as a way to highlight its connection to quality cinema and to distinguish its catalog from more mundane forms of television programming."[63] Considering the vast quantity of documentaries available to stream on Netflix in the early 2020s, this claim is uncontroversial. But Sharma addresses documentaries only within the context of streaming. In fact, Netflix's involvement in the documentary market began well before it launched its streaming service. When it was primarily a DVD subscription rental service, Netflix used documentary films in multiple ways to differentiate its service from traditional video rental stores and create

---

[60] When Netflix launched in April 1998, it used a single-rental plan, similar to brick-and-mortar video rental shops. In 1999, Netflix began offering subscription plans, and in 2000, it dropped the single-rental model altogether.
[61] Jill Kipnis, "DVD Video Net Rental Takes Off," *Billboard*, August 2, 2003, 1, 69.
[62] Timothy Havens, "Netflix: Streaming Channel Brands as Global Meaning Systems," in *From Networks to Netflix: A Guide to Changing Channels*, ed. Derek Johnson (New York: Routledge, 2018), 321–31.
[63] Sudeep Sharma, "Netflix and the Documentary Boom," in *The Netflix Effect: Technology and Entertainment in the 21st Century*, ed. Kevin McDonald and Daniel Smith-Rowsey (New York: Bloomsbury Academic, 2016), 143.

key partnerships with cable channels and independent distributors. Netflix pursued a strategy similar to HBO's. Like HBO, Netflix rose to prominence, and then dominance, as a subscription service.[64] Because Netflix does not sell its viewers to advertisers, its goal is to create the perception of value in the mind of the subscriber. From early on, Netflix mobilized documentary features as a unique part of its service, and as content with which it could experiment with release strategies.

Netflix First was one program that Netflix championed in order to create more value. With Netflix First, certain films would be available to rent exclusively from Netflix for a period of time. Netflix began this initiative in 2003, and its first partner was Docurama. Whether Docurama was the first partner because this was a low-risk way to introduce the service, or because Netflix executives were committed to promoting documentaries to its viewers, is less important than the fact that executives recognized they could use documentaries to offer a unique service to their subscribers. Later in 2003, Netflix First partnered with television companies that had long shown documentaries, PBS and Independent Film Channel. Through Netflix First, subscribers had an exclusive ninety-day rental windows for the documentaries *Daughter from Danang* and *Dinner for Five*, respectively.[65]

Netflix was invested in pushing specialty films to customers. As *Billboard* reported, "Through its recommendations feature, customers who have previously rented documentaries or other niche titles will be made aware of the exclusive [Netflix First] offer."[66] Familiarity has made Netflix's recommendations process seem obvious—of course Netflix functions as a "newsstand," pushing certain types of content to customers based on algorithms.[67] But this was a novel way of interacting with subscribers and publicizing films in an individual way in 2003. Even when the process was new, it was large scale: in 2003, Netflix was sending thirty million personal recommendations per day to its customers. This new way of publicizing home videos seemed to offer many benefits to distributors. Matt Lasorsa, senior VP of marketing for New Line Home Entertainment, praised the recommendation feature because it highlighted films other than the newest releases/tentpole films, saying, "These titles would get lost on a shelf in a

---

[64] Netflix surpassed HBO in number of subscribers in April 2013. "Netflix Subs Top HBO's," *Variety*, April 23, 2013, 11.
[65] Jill Kipnis, "Picture This," *Billboard*, November 29, 2003, 46.
[66] Kipnis, "Picture This," 46.
[67] "Newsstand" is different from "library"; see definitions in Timothy Havens and Amanda Lotz, *Understanding Media Industries* (New York: Oxford University Press, 2016).

brick-and-mortar store."[68] Speaking specifically of the partnership with Netflix First, which promised to push Docurama's videos even harder, Docurama president Steve Savage identified how the program could benefit both his company and Netflix. He told *Billboard*, "This is sort of the equivalent of opening a film in New York, Los Angeles and Chicago and getting the critics to create a buzz."[69] Savage framed Netflix First as a way to attract early attention to the video releases of specialty films.

But Netflix First was only one experiment that utilized documentaries. Netflix began to act as a producer and distributor of independent films. Like Docurama, Netflix executives saw the benefits of a library model, rather than one that emphasized new releases. As reported by *Variety* in 2006, "The company's rental ratio of library titles to new releases is thought to be an astonishing 70-30 (at most large rental outlets, new releases can easily account for 60%–70% of total rentals), as customers in search of brand-new titles are more likely to buy the DVD or rent locally."[70] To build its library, Netflix started acquiring indie films en masse. Netflix's film division company would eventually be called Red Envelope Films/Entertainment. Red Envelope lasted fewer than three years, but during that time, the company acquired 126 films.[71]

However, Red Envelope Films did not act like a typical theatrical distributor or home-video company. It acquired films principally to add to Netflix's library, and handed off the duties of a theatrical release to other companies. This is remarkably similar to the way cable channels produced and acquired documentaries during the same period. As *Variety* explained, "Each deal is structured differently, but in a typical case, Netflix will act as distributor of record for theatrical and homevid, paying a flat fee to a company like IFC to handle a limited theatrical release."[72] In this way, Netflix / Red Envelope used theatrical release as an explicit loss-leader for its main interest, the home-video market. The company worked with HBO on theatrical releases of documentaries *Born into Brothels* (2004, dirs. Zana Briski and Ross Kauffman) and *Balseros* (2002, dirs. Carles Bosch and Josep Maria Domènech), and with Magnolia Pictures on the release of *No End in Sight*

---

[68] Kipnis, "DVD Video Net Rental," 69.
[69] Kipnis, "DVD Video Net Rental," 69.
[70] Steven Zeitchik, "Netflix Adds Its Own Pix to Mix," *Variety*, February 27, 2006, 9.
[71] Anthony Kaufman, "Netflix Folds Red Envelope; Exits Theatrical Acquisition and Production Biz," *Indiewire*, July 23, 2008, indiewire.com/2008/07/netflix-folds-red-envelope-exits-theatrical-acquisition-and-production-biz-72010.
[72] Ian Mohr and Steven Zeitchik, "Little pix with lofty goals," *Variety*, June 19, 2006, 13.

(2007, dir. Charles Ferguson). Red Envelope also coproduced movies for IFC TV, including *The Film Is Not Yet Rated* (2006, dir. Kirby Dick).

In addition to working on its own films' theatrical releases, Red Envelope also used special-event screenings to drive DVD rentals of documentaries it did not own the rights to. In the case of *Super High Me* (2008, dir. Michael Blieden), a documentary on marijuana, Red Envelope held over one thousand private screenings to launch the DVD release. These screenings drove advanced buzz of the film in lieu of an official theatrical release. Netflix head Ted Sarandos boasted that Red Envelope's intervention made *Super High Me* popular among customers, saying, "It's done more business on Netflix than [Fox Searchlight's popular documentary] *Young@Heart*," which earned nearly $4 million at the box office.[73] Though there is no way to verify Sarandos's statement, it is clear that Red Envelope used the publicizing of even unaffiliated documentaries as a show of Netflix's power.

Just as filmmakers appreciated the documentary DVD market that Docurama helped grow, independent distributors realized that they stood to benefit significantly from the reach of Netflix and Red Envelope. According to a 2006 article, Netflix took credit for 70 percent of the DVD revenue for *Capturing the Friedmans*, a hit in theaters for distribution partners ThinkFilm and HBO.[74] ThinkFilm's Mark Urman confirms the importance of Netflix for his business: "Right now anything I can do to help Netflix do better means I'll do better."[75] Howard Cohen of Roadside Attractions, another distributor of documentaries, agreed. He said that Netflix is "the future.... They're the only major entity that really has a firsthand relationship with their consumers.... They have 4 million subscribers, with an interest in independent films, and they have their names and email addresses—and we don't and Hollywood doesn't."[76] This direct relationship with subscribers helped Netflix target film recommendations to specific subscribers, a very advanced form of niche marketing. It also helped Netflix benefit from the value of its increasingly deep library.

Documentary features are a fundamental part of Netflix's service and brand identity, and they have been since the company's early days. Netflix used documentary features to build its library, partner with other companies,

---

[73] Kaufman, "Netflix Folds Red Envelope."
[74] Steven Zeitchik, "Netflix adds its own pix to mix," *Variety*, February 27, 2006, 9.
[75] Steven Zeitchik, "Netflix adds its own pix to mix," *Variety*, February 27, 2006, 9.
[76] Anthony Kaufman, "Industry Beat: Netflix Becomes a Player in the Acquisitions Game," *Filmmaker*, Summer 2006, 26.

and experiment with release strategies. By elevating documentary features, Netflix created a perception of its subscription service as valuable to customers. Netflix's experimentation with documentaries also demonstrated to the film industry that it had the power to drive viewers to particular films. Netflix and Docurama confirmed the value of documentary on home video, thereby strengthening the market infrastructure for feature documentaries.

Self-Distribution and Direct Distribution in the Internet Age

During this period, theatrical distributors, film festivals, cable companies, and DVD purveyors were building a stable multilayered market for documentary features. This created a clear, regularized pipeline for documentary features to travel, and integrated documentary further into the mainstream film industry. But that does not mean that documentarians no longer engaged in individualized distribution and exhibition plans. The internet opened up many new possibilities for directly connecting with, and selling to, audiences.

As Howard Cohen suggested, one of Netflix's strengths was the direct relationship it had with its subscribers. But Netflix was not the only entity to use the affordances of internet connectivity and social media to build direct relationships with viewers. Individual filmmakers marketed their films online, and some even bypassed traditional distribution routes entirely by selling their films directly to consumers online. At the same time, Truly Indie, a distribution company, institutionalized the practice of self-distribution by offering distribution services to filmmakers for a price. Self-distribution, via four-walling individual theaters, was traditionally the way that independent documentarians could connect to viewers outside of the mainstream industry. But Truly Indie aimed to make the practice replicable as a business model in which filmmakers paid for their distribution and marketing services.

In the past, documentarians employed self-distribution tactics because established companies were not interested in distributing their work. From Leacock and Pennebaker forming their own distribution company to distribute *Dont Look Back*, to documentarians in the 1980s launching their films with the help of Film Forum before selling rights to distribution companies, self-distribution was a key part of documentary distribution for decades.

Some filmmakers continued to practice self-distribution in the 1990s, including Joe Berlinger and Bruce Sinofsky with *Brother's Keeper* and *Paradise Lost*, but with more and more distributors edging into the territory, it was no longer as necessary.

Success in self-distribution, more often than not, relied upon the film's subject matter being popular (Bob Dylan, William S. Burroughs) or appealing to an identifiable niche (gay and lesbian community for *Word Is Out*, veterans of antiwar movement for *The War at Home*). Such was the case with some of the most-discussed documentary films of the early 2000s: the films of Robert Greenwald, including *Uncovered: The Whole Truth about the Iraq War* (2003) and *Outfoxed: Rupert Murdoch's War on Journalism*. Appealing to politically engaged liberals, Greenwald and his associates went a step further than self-distribution—they employed direct distribution. They bypassed theatrical exhibition in favor of direct-to-video release. While direct-to-video is usually not accompanied by the kind of strong marketing scheme used for theatrical release, Greenwald mobilized progressive news websites and online political communities to publicize and sell DVDs of the film.

The direct distribution of *Uncovered: The Whole Truth about the Iraq War* reveals this method. Greenwald produced the film for $300,000, then organized house parties on MoveOn.org, meetUp.com, and other social networks to exhibit the film. Tryon describes this process: "Volunteers would offer to host screenings and would place messages on MeetUp.com in order to alert people in the community of a screening. Several days before the schedule premiere, the hosts received a DVD copy of the film, which they would play on the night of the premiere."[77] The film premiered at over twenty-six hundred private gatherings. On the same night, Greenwald hosted a teleconference that allowed people to discuss the film with him and ask questions. Documentarians had long seen the value of direct interaction with audiences—recall Julia Reichert's account of traveling around the country with a copy of *Growing Up Female*, in order to reach feminist viewers. However, the house party strategy allowed Greenwald to connect with viewers in twenty-six hundred places at once—an incredible feat of organizing. This strategy also drove sales of the DVD, which reached one hundred thousand copies, for a total of $1.5 million in sales. By combining traditional political organizing with networking via the internet, Greenwald was able to mobilize a large audience and circumvent theatrical exhibition.

---

[77] Tryon, *Reinventing Cinema*, 98.

There were other benefits to bypassing theatrical exhibition, like speed and urgency. As Tryon points out,

> Rather than releasing the film to art-house theaters, which requires that a filmmaker negotiate with national theater chains and distributors, the producers distributed the film through progressive news sources and web sites including *The Nation*, the Center for American Progress, Alternet.org, and MoveOn.org. As Greenwald himself comments, this distribution process allowed him to release the film much more quickly, which in turn permitted him to make a documentary film that could incorporate even the most recent events.[78]

The marketing of these documentaries often came in the guise of political organizing, with websites and blogs hailing audiences as activists. This was an effective way to sell DVDs, as well as to gather the contact information of supporters of future films. Though Greenwald's model was a significant phenomenon, the "house party" model should not be seen as the norm for documentaries in this time period. Rather, along with Netflix's experiments with distribution, Greenwald's strategies were precursors to the explosive growth of crowdfunding, grassroots marketing, and digital distribution via streaming video in the American documentary market.

Docbuster: Box Office Success and Beyond

When writing about the adoption of new media delivery technologies, optimistic journalists and critics tend to claim each change as a step toward more complete audience choice. This is doubly true for the concurrent diffusion of DVD technology and internet connectivity. DVD promised viewers higher-quality copies of films on home video, in addition to a host of supplemental material. Internet connectivity promised audiences a platform on which to share their opinions and tastes, and in doing so, make the media industry listen. With the promise of streaming video on the horizon, it seemed clear that the "celestial jukebox" was becoming a reality—with every film and television show available, finally there would be no gatekeepers to prevent

---

[78] Chuck Tryon, *Reinventing Cinema: Movies in the Age of Media Convergence* (Piscataway: Rutgers University, 2014), 100.

audiences choosing exactly what they wanted to view, when they wanted to view it. This is often the discourse used to describe the early 2000s, and it is easy to see how the popularity of documentary features during this time is wrapped in the same language.

Rather than technological change and audience taste driving the "docbuster" phenomenon, the industrial strategies deployed at every level of the feature documentary market drove documentaries to become valuable commodities. In the early 2000s, more organizations and companies recognized the benefits of investing in documentaries and joined the growing number of institutions that supported documentaries and their makers. Their investment in production and distribution created a strong infrastructure for documentary features. Gatekeepers like theatrical distributors, film festivals, and cable companies did not diminish in importance; rather, they purposefully partnered with new DVD companies to enhance the home-video market for their documentaries. This is a trend that has continued to the present day: while some documentarians continue to make and self-distribute their work, without aid or interference from a granting agency, cable company, or streaming service, for most filmmakers there is now an expectation of cooperation with powerful institutions. Tim Horsburgh, director of communications and distribution for Kartemquin Films, confirms that this is the case. In conversation in 2016, he noted that it was very rare for a documentary to succeed commercially if it has been rejected by major gatekeepers like the Sundance Institute, the MacArthur Foundation, CineReach, ITVS, and Film Society of Lincoln Center.[79]

The increased visibility and high box-office returns of feature documentaries during this era were not anomalous or sudden. They resulted from years-long initiatives undertaken by a constellation of organizations and companies. A larger number of theatrical distributors acquired and released documentaries than in previous decades, spurred by the lower cost of acquisition and strong box-office grosses of feature documentaries in the 1990s. Cable companies like HBO, Discovery, and A&E began to invest in documentaries earlier in their life cycle. Executives at cable companies said explicitly that these investments were meant to link their brand with a theatrically released film, adding a new twist to the tension between documentary film and television. The rapid diffusion of DVD technology

---

[79] Tim Horsburgh (Director of Communications and Distribution, Kartemquin Films) in conversation with the author, December 2016.

and simultaneous spread of internet connectivity allowed home-video companies like Docurama and Netflix to profit from the previously insignificant documentary genre, both newly released and library films. Netflix also began to act like one of the above cable companies by acquiring numerous independent films, including documentaries, and paying distributors to give them a run in theaters. Netflix was one of many companies, including Magnolia Films, that were using documentary films in a quest to disrupt traditional release windows. Because they were a relatively low-risk investment, compared to the average fiction film, documentaries were ripe fodder for distribution experimentation. At the same time as more institutions committed to documentaries, individual, activist filmmakers used the new affordances of DVD and internet connectivity to self-distribute their documentaries and target viewers in new, more direct ways.

6
Streaming Video Drives Documentary Production Trends and Private Investment (2008 to 2022)

In February 2020, *American Factory* won the Academy Award for Best Documentary Feature. Codirector Julia Reichert has made feminist and leftist documentaries since the 1970s—and *American Factory* is no exception in her filmography. But *American Factory* was financed and circulated in novel ways, as a result of the commercialization of documentary film. The film's Oscar win demonstrates the dual power of the two most significant new forces in documentary feature filmmaking in recent years: private financing and subscription video-on-demand services. Both forces, often operating in concert, have created a kind of fast track to visibility, awards, and profitability for the documentary films deemed commercially and culturally viable enough to merit the type of industry push given *American Factory*.

When Chinese glass manufacturer Fuyao took over a shuttered General Motors factory in Dayton, Ohio, the company asked Julia Reichert and Steven Bognar to capture the factory's reopening. The pair had documented the factory's closing in the award-winning short film *The Last Truck: Closing of a GM Plant* (2009), so it was a natural fit. Rather than accept the assignment, Reichert and Bognar proposed making a documentary over which they would have full editorial control. Fuyao agreed. Granted unlimited access to the plant, to workers both Ohioan and Chinese, to the company's Chinese executives, and to local government officials, the filmmakers created an observational documentary with a tapestry of characters navigating clashes in national culture and workplace culture. The story's ultimate conflict, and irony, is the Communist Chinese company's fight against the local workers' push to unionize.

When beginning the film, Reichert and Bognar were awarded production grants from Chicken & Egg Pictures Breakthrough Filmmaker Award and the Sundance Institute.[1] Grants continue to be an important source of financing for documentaries, even as the genre has become increasingly commercialized. The largest source of financing and support came from Participant Media, a private media company that produces and acquires socially conscious documentary and fiction films. Private investing in documentary films is a significant development in the documentary genre's march toward greater commercialization, proving a broad recognition that the financial benefit of investing in documentaries is more likely to outweigh the risk than in previous eras.

Following in the footsteps of many popular and award-winning documentaries, *American Factory* premiered in competition at the Sundance Film Festival in January 2019 and won the Directing Award for U.S. Documentary. Unlike documentaries even five years before, *American Factory* was not acquired by a theatrical distribution company, but by the subscription video-on-demand service Netflix. Netflix paid a little under $3 million for the documentary, a handsome sum to reward Participant Media's investment.[2] Former president Barack Obama and Michelle Obama added their imprimatur, as well, branding the documentary as the first project in their Higher Ground production company's partnership with Netflix.

Netflix released *American Factory* in a few theaters in August 2019 to qualify for film awards; then the documentary hit the streaming portal on August 21, 2019. This release circumvented theatrical distributors and exhibitors completely, demonstrating how subscription video on demand (SVOD) can reconfigure the traditional releasing pattern for a documentary. Over the autumn months of 2019, Participant Media funded a social-action campaign to accompany the film. This campaign was a blend of social advocacy and a publicity push for the documentary. Participant screened *American Factory* in six American cities plagued by postindustrial fallout,

---

[1] The Breakthrough Award is a $50,000 grant. The amount of the Sundance Institute Documentary Fund grant is undisclosed. "Chicken & Egg Pictures Announces Five Recipients of Inaugural Breakthrough Award," Chicken & Egg Pictures, January 19, 2016, https://chickeneggpics.org/chicken-egg-pictures-announces-five-recipients-of-inaugural-breakthrough-award/; "More Than $1.9 Million to Nonfiction Storytellers: Sundance Institute Announces Documentary Fund Grants Across Nonfiction Formats," September 26th, 2017, https://www.sundance.org/blogs/news/2017-documentary-fund-grantees-announced.

[2] Tatiana Siegel, "Sundance: Netflix Nabs 'American Factory' Doc for $3 Million," *Hollywood Reporter*, February 1, 2019, https://www.hollywoodreporter.com/news/netflix-nabs-american-factory-doc-3-million-1179673.

with postscreening discussions about the future of work.[3] Finally, in February 2020, the film won Academy Award for Best Documentary Feature. Financed with grants and private investment, circulated on a commercial streaming platform and through community groups, *American Factory* embodies the continued tension between public service and commodity in the documentary film market.

This example is significant because it demonstrates the power of private funding and streaming subscription services to push a documentary film to success, visibility, and prestige. While theatrical distribution is not "dead" and foundation grants are still important for documentary filmmakers, *American Factory*'s trajectory shows how the new, commercialized fast track circumvents traditional ways of bringing documentaries to market and audiences. The film did an end run around theatrical distributors, taking the $3 million deal with Netflix—a deal that required no risky rollout in theaters. Netflix became the film's distributor and promoter, along with production company Participant Media and the Obamas' brand. *American Factory*'s trajectory contrasts sharply with Julia Reichert's self-distribution practices early in her career, including her cofounding New Day Films. It also contrasts with the workings of the documentary film market just a decade prior.

In this chapter, I demonstrate how Netflix's acquisition of documentaries for its streaming service has driven production trends. Filmmakers and production companies have responded to Netflix by making documentaries to fit SVOD's preferred topics and formats. The promise of pickup by Netflix or another streaming service has also pushed private investors to finance documentary films, like Participant's investment in *American Factory*. Never before has the commercial market so directly shaped documentary filmmaking. Over the 2010s, as Netflix and other streaming video-on-demand services adjusted their strategies surrounding documentary film, the rest of the documentary ecosystem reeled. Small, independent distributors struggled to survive as streamers sidestepped theatrically released documentaries in favor of exclusive deals that made streamers the first exhibition window. Many filmmakers began making documentary series, rather than features, as streamers preferred the series format. And established documentarians founded their own production companies, eager to seize opportunities and benefit from economies of scale in this boom time. Finally, for the first time

---

[3] Talib Visram, "Exclusive: The Obamas' Netflix Doc 'American Factory' to Launch Nationwide Social-Impact Tour," *Fast Company*, August 29, 2019, https://www.fastcompany.com/90396477/exclusive-netflix-obamas-american-factory-launch-nationwide-social-impact-tour.

ever, private investors, like Participant Media and Impact Partners, financed the production of documentaries. This is a fundamental shift that reflects the strength of the market for documentary films as well as the maturity of the commercial infrastructure for documentaries.

Netflix

The Switch to Streaming and Original Content

Documentary features were a fundamental part of Netflix's service and brand identity since the company began delivering DVD rentals by mail. This continued with Netflix's distribution company, Red Envelope Entertainment. In operation from 2005 to 2008, Red Envelope acquired global rights to independent films, including documentaries. It acquired films principally to add to Netflix's library, and handed off the duties of a theatrical release to other companies, like mid-size distributors Magnolia Pictures and IFC. In addition to renting documentaries on DVD to customers, Netflix used documentary features as a way to partner with other companies and experiment with release strategies. In 2008, Netflix closed the three-year-old division. The company had acquired 126 films during its short life, but in spite of that volume, owning theatrical or all rights was only ever an experiment in the transition to internet-delivered video. As Netflix's chief content officer Ted Sarandos told *IndieWire* in 2008, "I often referred to our buying all rights to movies as a necessary evil, to get to the underlying rights we needed to innovate the release windows."[4] From then on, Netflix would acquire only streaming rights to films. This was part of its move to focus on streaming, and documentaries would continue to factor into the equation.

Netflix's Watch Instantly streaming service debuted in 2007, and by 2009 it was thriving. In July 2009, 31 percent of all Netflix subscribers streamed media; that percentage more than doubled, to 66 percent, by July 2010.[5] A Netflix subscription included both DVD rental by mail, from a huge catalog more comprehensive than any retailer with a physical rental storefront,

---

[4] Anthony Kaufman, "Netflix Folds Red Envelope; Exits Theatrical Acquisition and Production Biz," *IndieWire*, July 23, 2008, indiewire.com/2008/07/netflix-folds-red-envelope-exits-theatrical-acquisition-and-production-biz-72010.

[5] M. G. Siegler, "Netflix Now 15 Million Users Strong with over 60 Percent of Them Streaming Content," *TechCrunch*, July 21, 2010, https://social.techcrunch.com/2010/07/21/netflix-users/.

and video streaming, with a much smaller catalog of options. The service's addition to living-room devices like Roku, Blu-ray players, TiVo boxes, the Xbox, and the newest smart TVs, in 2008 and 2009, helped to drive this growth.

As Netflix's streaming video business grew, the company had to grapple with a change in how it acquired movies and TV shows. Rather than simply buying DVDs to rent to customers, like any video-rental business, Netflix had to license content for delivery by streaming. This necessitated a shift in Netflix's business model, becoming like a film distributor, exhibitor, and television channel. But rather than stay the course with Red Envelope Entertainment, acquiring all rights to a film in order to eventually place it on the streaming service, Netflix went a different route. The company licensed older films—"library titles"—for streaming. It also focused on licensing overlooked, undervalued films for streaming, since the traditional windowing process made most recent popular films unavailable for streaming licenses. Public relations framed this process of bargain hunting as a technological feat. Witness how Sarandos told *Wired* in 2009 that Netflix engineers mined data searching for film and television that could be acquired for a pittance. He said, "We have the rental history and the queue insight that enables us to go after things that other people may not be really even hunting."[6] The article cites Netflix's acquisition of a French film, *Tell No One* (2006, dir. Guillaume Canet) that had made only $6 million in American theaters, but which many subscribers had added to their DVD queue. The discrepancy between theatrical gross and subscriber interest led Netflix to license the film for streaming, and it immediately became the fourth-most-watched piece of content on the service, according to the company.

Netflix's interest in content overlooked and undervalued by the mainstream industry led to the company licensing documentary films for streaming. It fit with the company's "conglomerated niche" strategy, in which the company "develops offerings with distinct segments of subscribers in mind" rather than trying to reach the broadest possible audience.[7] Netflix had proof, from years of DVD rentals, customers' queues and ratings, and releases from its own Red Envelope Entertainment, that its subscribers had an unfulfilled demand for documentaries. Conveniently, documentaries

---

[6] Daniel Roth, "Netflix Everywhere: Sorry Cable, You're History," *Wired*, September 21, 2009, https://www.wired.com/2009/09/ff-netflix/.

[7] Amanda Lotz, *Portals: A Treatise on Internet-Distributed Television* (Ann Arbor: Michigan Publishing, University of Michigan Library, 2017), http://dx.doi.org/10.3998/mpub.9699689.

were little valued by the mainstream industry in the late 2000s and early 2010s, so they were an obvious choice for Netflix to license for streaming. In spite of the "docbuster" boom, documentary films were relatively inexpensive to license and unlikely to be subject to the strict windowing of studio fiction films. Netflix's strategy of pushing documentary DVD rentals continued on its streaming service, when the company padded its streaming catalog with inexpensive documentaries.

Interestingly, Netflix continued to acquire documentaries as it moved decisively into television series development and production. As Netflix's streaming service thrived, it started to develop "Originals"—television shows and films that would be exclusive to the service. The first series, *Lilyhammer*, a Norwegian coproduction, premiered in February 2012, and *House of Cards* was the first major Netflix Originals hit, premiering in 2013. While Netflix was releasing numerous television series, the company also began to acquire documentaries to be branded as Originals. This strategy maintained Netflix's branding as a home for documentaries and specialty films, remaining essential to that audience niche, while the company simultaneously built a huge library of original television series.

This strategy immediately paid dividends to Netflix in terms of prestige. The first high-profile documentary film "Original" was *The Square* (2013, dir. Jehane Noujaim).[8] An on-the-ground account of how Egypt was rocked by the Arab Spring uprising in Tahrir Square, *The Square* was nominated for an Academy Award for Best Documentary Feature. This was the first Oscar nomination for Netflix. Netflix's first win came from a Best Documentary Short Subject, *The White Helmets* (dir. Orlando von Einsiedel) in 2017. Its second win was the Best Documentary Feature for *Icarus* (dir. Bryan Fogel) in 2018. And in 2020 *American Factory* took home the prize. These prestigious awards cemented Netflix's status as a haven for documentary film, earning the company praise and publicity. They also confirmed that Netflix's investment in documentary film Originals had worked.

During the first half of the 2010s, Netflix dealt with documentary films in two ways. First of all, the company licensed streaming rights to documentary films, many through output deals with distribution companies. In an output deal, also known as a pay-one deal, an SVOD service pays to license the films

---

[8] Sarah Salovaara, "Netflix Originals 'Exclusively' Acquires *The Square*," *Filmmaker Magazine*, November 4, 2013, https://filmmakermagazine.com/77115-netflix-originals-exclusively-acquires-the-square/.

that a distribution company has released in theaters. Netflix had output deals with numerous distribution companies in the early to mid-2010s, including those, like Kino Lorber, Cinema Guild, and Zeitgeist Films, that released a high volume of documentary films. It worked with aggregators like New Video and Cinedigm, which had partnered with Sundance Artist Services, so films on the festival circuit could find a way to this major platform even if they did not have a theatrical distributor. Netflix also acquired streaming licenses for individual documentaries, opening a new ancillary window for documentary films. The availability of documentaries on Netflix is reflected in the number of them added to the streaming service each year. In 2014, Netflix added 49 licensed documentaries to the service.[9] That steadily increased to 72 in 2015 and 119 in 2016.

The second way Netflix handled documentaries in the early 2010s is by acquiring completed documentary films as Originals. These documentaries are exclusive to Netflix subscribers. So even though Netflix did not originate and produce these projects, they are called Originals. This is an intentionally ambiguous distinction that has allowed Netflix to take credit for successful, award-winning documentary films, without taking on the great risk of producing them. Originals generally do not go through the theatrical releasing process. Netflix began acquiring documentaries as Originals in 2012, and began releasing them in 2013. Netflix released seven documentary Originals annually in 2014 and 2015, then ten in 2016. Since then, Netflix has exclusively acquired a growing number of documentary films to be Netflix Originals.

Licensing streaming rights and doing negative pickup deals are the main ways Netflix puts feature documentaries on its service. In addition to these tactics, which grew Netflix's catalog and delivered a ballooning number of documentaries into subscribers' homes, Netflix also defined itself, to the public and to the entertainment industry, as a leader in documentary film exhibition. In 2006, the company had touted its power to get people watching documentaries, taking credit for 70 percent of DVD revenue on *Capturing the Friedmans*.[10] Even though, as shown in last chapter's account, *Capturing the Friedmans* was a hit in theaters and garnered an enormous amount of press, Netflix claimed responsibility for the film's home-video success. In

---

[9] Numbers calculated from *Vulture*'s monthly "New on Netflix" column (https://www.vulture.com/news/new-on-netflix/) and *What's on Netflix*'s "What's New on Netflix" column (https://www.whats-on-netflix.com/whats-new/).
[10] Steven Zeitchik, "Netflix Adds Its Own Pix to Mix," *Variety*, February 27, 2006, 9.

2008, Sarandos claimed that "Netflix routinely provides some 75 percent of DVD and electronic revenue for specialty films, 'and for foreign and documentary, even more than that.'"[11] This is how Netflix defined itself to the public—as a distinctive service that offers variety, partly by stocking documentary film DVDs—and to the entertainment industry—as having the ability to funnel customers toward specialty films.

This self-definition persisted as Netflix transformed its business into a streaming subscription service. Netflix had helped pioneer an audience for documentaries with its DVD service, and the company continued to build on this by licensing documentaries for its streaming service.

Documentary filmmakers were generally amenable to working with Netflix. They saw monetary and accessibility benefits to selling their work on Netflix, rather than pursuing a traditional release strategy that began in theaters and moved through windows. First of all, in financial terms, selling to Netflix is attractive. Documentary films generally have much lower production budgets than fiction features, even independent ones, so an acquisition fee from Netflix might be enough to cover production costs. And since theatrical release of documentaries is quite risky, getting an upfront payout from Netflix is a very appealing prospect.

Second of all, for many documentarians, a documentary film is both a commodity and a public service. Exposure and accessibility for their films is as important as the financial reward of a potential box-office bonanza (and profits from later windows). By the late 2010s, filmmakers themselves were repeating Netflix's public relations points. As director Ava DuVernay pointed out, "I'm told by the system that [theatrical release] is what matters, but then people aren't seeing your movies. Take the number of people who saw *Selma*, a Christmas release with an Oscar campaign about Dr. Martin Luther King. Well, more than a quadruple amount of people saw [my Netflix documentary] *13th*, about the prison-industrial complex. If I'm telling these stories to reach a mass audience, then really, nothing else matters."[12] This was once how documentarians discussed their desire to play on PBS—a free channel broadcast over the air to any American with a television. Now the conventional wisdom is that Netflix is the great democratizer, bringing niche films to people who do not or cannot see movies in theaters.

---

[11] Kaufman, "Netflix Folds Red Envelope."
[12] Kyle Buchanan, "How Will Movies Survive the Next 10 Years?," *New York Times*, June 20, 2019, sec. Movies, https://www.nytimes.com/interactive/2019/06/20/movies/movie-industry-future.html.

On the surface, this makes sense—if you are a socially conscious documentarian, take your wares to where the people are. Let them watch it in the place they expect it to be, bundled in with the subscription that also delivers access to favorite old sitcoms and the animated movies their kids watch over and over. In this way, Netflix's strategy dovetails with documentarians' public service aims, theoretically helping them reach wider audiences. The problem arises when Netflix's licensing fee does not replace revenue lost from releasing a documentary in other channels. Yet the appeal of being on a platform with so many subscribers can outweigh concerns over a fair price, lost revenue from video-on-demand and educational sales, all of which suffer when a film is available on Netflix streaming.

The Netflix Documentary

Executives' stated goal for Netflix is to be anything to anyone, by building a vast library of streaming content and using data to customize the content presented to each subscriber. As Sarandos is often quoted as saying, "Our brand is personalization." Catherine Johnson has pointed out how this is branding on the basis of service, rather than programming.[13] Amanda Lotz refines this idea, showing how the service branding translated to Netflix's programming strategies. She calls it a "conglomerated niche strategy," made possible by the lack of a broadcast schedule and the addition of precise data mining. Lotz writes, "Importantly, it is the attributes of nonlinearity that enable Netflix and others using a conglomerated niche strategy to be different things to different people—without anyone really noticing—and make this strategy effective. Netflix's curation strategy is guided by mass customization and its ability to market and recommend to subscribers is highly individualized."[14] Mass customization means that Netflix can license and acquire programming, including documentary films, for a variety of niche audiences. It also means that the service highlights award-winning political documentaries for some subscribers, while spotlighting celebrity profiles documentaries for others.

To understand this programming strategy, consider the common types of documentary films Netflix adds to its streaming service. Netflix acquires

---

[13] Catherine Johnson, *Branding Television* (New York: Routledge, 2012).
[14] Lotz, *Portals*.

four main types of documentaries for streaming: political documentaries, character documentaries, celebrity profiles (specifically popular music related), and soft documentaries (films on light topics that do not engage in a discourse of sobriety). This carries over to both the licensed documentaries and the Originals. Rather than genres, these categories offer a large-scale impression of the documentaries Netflix added to it streaming service.

For those subscribers interested in documentary films about political movements, underexplored moments in history, and interesting people, Netflix acquires documentary features that fulfill a public service mandate—political and character documentaries. Political documentaries are those concerned with an issue, an investigation, or a potent piece of history. Examples include *Mission Blue* (2014, dirs. Robert Nixon, Fisher Stevens), *(T)ERROR* (2015, dirs. Lyric R. Cabral, David Felix Sutcliffe), *Let the Fire Burn* (2013, dir. Jason Osder), *Icarus, Edge of Democracy* (2019, dir. Petra Costa), *Crip Camp* (2020, dirs. James Lebrecht, Nicole Newnham), and *Whose Streets?* (2017, dirs. Sabaah Folayan, Damon Davis). Character documentaries are those that introduce a noncelebrity character, such as *Finding Vivian Maier* (2013, dirs. John Maloof, Charlie Siskel), *Shirkers* (2018, dir. Sandi Tan), *Dick Johnson Is Dead* (2020, dir. Kirsten Johnson), or *Father Solder Son* (2020, dirs. Leslye Davis, Catrin Einhorn). Netflix particularly acquires political and character documentaries dealing with identity—racial, gender, and sexual orientation—like *One of Us* (2017, dirs. Heidi Ewing, Rachel Grady), *I Am Not Your Negro* (2016, dir. Raoul Peck), *Disclosure* (2020, dir. Sam Feder), *Mercury 13* (2018, dirs. David Sington, Heather Walsh), and *Feminists: What Were They Thinking?* (2018, dir. Johanna Demetrakas).

Theatrical release has long been a risky undertaking for political and character documentaries, with very few earning large box-office grosses or playing in many theaters. In the past, PBS series *P.O.V.* and *Independent Lens* were the only reliable ancillary outlets for these documentaries. Netflix changed this, allowing many political and character documentaries to attract a wider audience when they earn notice from critics or are nominated for major awards. As HBO has long done, Netflix uses the buzz and awards generated by documentaries to make its subscription service seem essential to subscribers, even if those subscribers do not watch the documentaries.

For those subscribers who are more interested in a peek behind the curtain at stars, athletes, or subcultures, Netflix acquires celebrity profile documentaries and soft documentaries. By interspersing a wide variety of documentary film, Netflix transfers the sheen of prestige from serious, political documentaries to lighter documentaries. In turn, the entertainment value of celebrity profiles and soft documentaries permeates the cultural currency of the documentary genre. This intermingling is a key part of Netflix's effect on documentary film.

Licensing or acquiring celebrity profile documentaries is one tactic Netflix used to fill its streaming library inexpensively. Celebrity profile documentaries boast an obvious star, but they are cheaper to acquire than a fiction film with a major actor. They are also much easier to market than documentaries structured around a political issue or a nonfamous character because stars have built-in fans and name recognition. These stars could be actual, current superstars, like Taylor Swift in *Miss Americana* (2020, dir. Lana Wilson), or pop culture legends, like George Takei in *To Be Takei* (2014, dir. Jennifer M. Kroot) or Nina Simone in *What Happened Miss Simone?* (2015, dir. Liz Garbus). Though they might not count as movie stars in Hollywood, Donald Rumsfeld, in *The Unknown Known* (2013, dir. Errol Morris), Malala Yousafzai, in *He Named Me Malala* (2015, dir. Davis Guggenheim), Conor McGregor in *Conor McGregor: Notorious* (2017, dir. Gavin Fitzgerald), and Steve Jobs in *Steve Jobs: The Man in the Machine* (2015, dir. Alex Gibney), are stars in documentary terms because of their name recognition and notoriety. Celebrities have fans, who are likely to watch, as are subscribers curious to know more about a notorious cultural figure.

Netflix acquires many music-related celebrity documentaries, which have the added benefit of containing musical performances. It also licenses celebrity documentaries about sports, including those in ESPN's *30 for 30* series. Celebrity profile documentaries are a key plank of HBO's documentary programming, and they have other outlets as well, in theaters and on PBS's long-running series *American Masters*. Netflix acquiring celebrity profile documentaries expands the number of outlets that documentarians can sell them to, another place for them to end up after, or instead of, theatrical release.

In addition to celebrity profile documentaries, the service also acquires many soft documentary films. Soft documentaries explore topics like sports, leisure, and scandal with a light tone. Soft documentaries promise easy viewing; they occupy the opposite end of the scale from "hard" documentaries that investigate acute issues like climate change or detail a celebrity's heart-wrenching struggle with addiction. Examples of soft documentaries on Netflix include *The Battered Bastards of Baseball* (2014, dirs. Chapman Way, Maclain Way), *CounterPunch* (2017, dir. Jay Bulger), *Fyre: The Greatest Party That Never Happened* (2018, dir. Chris Smith), *The Legend of Cocaine Island* (2018, dir. Theo Love), *Have a Good Trip: Adventures in Psychedelics* (2018, dir. Donick Cary), *Burlesque: Heart of the Glitter Tribe* (2018, dir. Jon Manning), and *The American Meme* (2018, dir. Bert Marcus). By acquiring soft documentaries, Netflix embraces the documentary as fun and easy to watch, beyond the discourse of sobriety that permeates political documentaries, character documentaries, and even many celebrity profiles.

The large quantity and wide variety of documentaries, along with its own branding as a home for documentaries, further shifted the discourse around documentary film in the 2010s. Netflix accomplished, on a much broader scale, what HBO did with its mix of the serious and salacious on *America Undercover*: "incorporate popular pleasure into a discourse of quality," as Susan Murray puts it.[15] Soft documentaries about memes and exotic dancing bump up next to more sober documentary features about migrants crossing the Mediterranean Sea and protests for racial justice in Ferguson, Missouri. While some claim that Netflix has neutered the radical potential of documentary film by making the genre more commercial, the truth is murkier. Netflix has made many types of documentary films more widely accessible than before, and the service's simultaneous promotion of the serious and frivolous has imbued the genre with higher entertainment value.[16] This is a continuation/intensification of a process begun even before Netflix existed, and certainly before the company founded its streaming service.

[15] Susan Murray, "'I Think We Need a New Name For It': The Meeting of Documentary and Reality TV," in *Reality TV: Remaking Television Culture*, ed. Susan Murray and Laurie Ouellette (New York: New York University Press, 2004), 53.
[16] Netflix also acquires classic documentaries for streaming. This boosts its credibility as a library for documentaries, a "home" for them. At various times, cinéma vérité opuses *Paris Is Burning* and *Hoop Dreams* and essay film *Los Angeles Plays Itself* were available for streaming on Netflix. More recent popular documentaries also became available on the streaming service some years after their release: *Bowling for Columbine*, *An Inconvenient Truth*, *Exit through the Gift Shop*, *Enron: The Smartest Guys in the Room*, *20 Feet from Stardom*, *Dogtown and Z-Boys*, *Grizzly Man*. Some older documentaries Netflix licensed to accompany its newer originals. For example, around the time Netflix released original documentary limited series *Five Came Back*, it licensed World War II–era documentaries *Why We Fight*, *Battle of San Pietro*, and *Memphis Belle*, all made by the subjects of *Five Came Back*.

The Expansion of Original Content and Exclusivity

Netflix's acquisition of documentary Originals was part of its streaming strategy, building up the streaming catalog inexpensively and providing differentiation from TV shows. But there was a decisive shift in the mid-2010s.

Exclusivity became an increasingly important programming strategy for Netflix over the second half of the 2010s. Netflix had a legacy as a video-rental service, from its DVD delivery days, and it enjoyed years of dominance in the streaming space. But in the mid-2010s, Netflix faced the threat of studios and broadcasters creating their own streaming services that could siphon away subscribers and content. Having the exclusive rights to films and series was one strategy Netflix used to thwart other contenders in the streaming wars.

This growing focus on exclusivity affected Netflix's documentary film strategy in two main ways. First, the balance between Netflix Original documentaries and licensed documentaries changed. In 2017, the ratio between Original documentaries added to the service and documentaries licensed for streaming was one to six. Netflix released twenty Original documentaries and added 128 nonexclusive documentaries to the service in 2017. By 2019, this ratio changed drastically to one to two. That year, Netflix released twenty-one Original documentaries and added fifty-one nonexclusive documentaries. Netflix maintained the same level of Original documentary features, stamped with its brand and bringing awards to its name. And the service drastically reduced the number of documentary features it acquired from theatrical distributors.

For documentarians and theatrical distributors, this change meant less likelihood of Netflix licensing their films. Only by submitting to exclusive deals with Netflix could filmmakers access Netflix subscribers, and these deals remained limited to a very small number each year. The result was many fewer independently produced documentary films on Netflix, reducing the number of outlets likely to deliver these films to a wide audience. For subscribers, this strategic shift meant that Netflix-branded documentaries became more prominent on the service.

The second result of this growing focus on exclusivity was the increased importance of documentary series at the end of the 2010s. There were few documentary series released on Netflix during much of the 2010s. Netflix released a single documentary series in 2015, *Making a Murderer* (dirs. Moira Demos, Laura Ricciardi), which became a cultural sensation.[17] The

---

[17] Viewership was estimated at 19.3 million viewers in the first thirty-five days the series was available, though Netflix will not confirm the numbers. Jethro Nededog, "Here's How Popular Netflix's

Table 6.1 Documentaries added to Netflix streaming

Year	Licensed	"Originals"	Series
2014	49	7	
2015	72	7	1
2016	119	10	1
2017	128	20	4
2018	64	15	2
2019	51	21	11
2020	81	23	17

popularity of the series enhanced the appeal of documentary series and true-crime genre of documentary. Netflix moved to acquire many more series, most of them in the true-crime genre, all of them exclusive to the service. There were four series released in 2017, two in 2018, and then a huge jump. In 2019, Netflix released at least eleven series, and in 2020, it released at least seventeen series (Table 6.1).

But the popularity of a single series is not the only reason Netflix pivoted its documentary strategy toward series. Documentaries are ideal for being made into series. Documentaries are fungible—it is much easier to take a feature documentary and spin it into a series than to do the same with a narrative feature film. Documentarians shoot a large amount of footage, generally resulting in a high ratio between footage shot and film length. The long shooting period and the challenge of editing so much footage are usually a detriment for the regularity and efficiency of documentary production, but they can be an advantage: a planned feature can be retrofitted to a series, with more episodes. Documentaries are ideally suited for expansive serialization.

In addition, Netflix is ideally suited to hosting limited documentary series. Netflix programming is not beholden to a broadcast schedule, so series length can vary without disrupting linear programming. Documentary series complement Netflix's television series, rather than replacing them on a broadcast schedule. Another benefit of Netflix's nonlinear delivery is that the service can release all series episodes at once. If the documentary series is a hit, this strategy enables binge-watching and organic engagement.

'Making a Murderer' Really Was according to a Research Company," *Business Insider*, February 12, 2016, https://www.businessinsider.com/netflix-making-a-murderer-ratings-2016-2.

Finally, premiering and heavily marketing documentary series on its platform allows Netflix to reify its status as a primary exhibition window. Programming and developing series is another way for Netflix to exclude theatrical distributors, retaining exclusivity and strengthening its brand. Indeed, it is one way Netflix drains audiences, buzz, and power from theaters and the traditional theatrical windowing system in general. Documentary series are developed in-house or with close supervision by Netflix, similar to the way HBO produced the series *America Undercover*. They can also be picked up upon completion, though Netflix need not compete with theatrical distributors for these Originals—the format of a limited series largely precludes theatrical release. Instead, Netflix competes only with the few other outlets that pick up limited documentary series, namely HBO, ESPN, Hulu, and other streaming services and cable channels.

Documentary series about characters, sports, celebrities, and even political issues replace some of the documentary features Netflix would have licensed. For example, the series *Last Chance U* (2016–20), *Basketball or Nothing* (2019), and *Maradona in Mexico* (2019, dir. Angus MacQueen) are sports documentaries exclusive to Netflix, so the company need not license the latest *30 for 30* documentary films from ESPN.[18] The series *Living Undocumented* (2019, dirs. Anna Chai, Aaron Saidman) and *Immigration Nation* (2020, dirs. Christina Clusiau, Shaul Schwarz) can theoretically replace political documentaries about the United States' immigration crisis that Netflix would license or acquire. *Tiger King* (2020, dirs. Rebecca Chaiklin, Eric Goode) and *Cheer* (2020–22) do the same for character documentaries. *Inside Bill's Brain* (2019, dir. Davis Guggenheim) and *Pretend It's a City* (2021, dir. Martin Scorsese) do the same for celebrity profile documentary films.

But true-crime documentaries outpace the above categories, by far, and they represent Netflix's embrace of a different strain of documentary. Prior to the series era, Netflix did not license or acquire as Originals many true-crime documentary *features*. The most high-profile true-crime features were *Strong Island* (2017, dir. Yance Ford) and *Amanda Knox* (2016, dirs. Rod Blackhurst, Brian McGinn), both Originals exclusive to the service. A big shift took place late in the decade, simultaneous with Netflix's emphasis on exclusive content. From 2017 to 2021, Netflix released at least twenty-five true-crime documentary series, including *Wormwood*, the second season of *Making a*

---

[18] Netflix partnered with ESPN on *The Last Dance* (dir. Jason Hehir, 2020). The series premiered weekly on ESPN, then was available on Netflix soon after.

Murderer, *Wild Wild Country* (2018, dirs. Chapman Way, Maclain Way), *Evil Genius: The True Story of America's Most Diabolical Bank Heist* (2018, dirs. Trey Borzillieri, Barbara Schroeder), *The Devil Next Door* (2019, dirs. Yossi Bloch, Daniel Sivan), *Don't F**k with Cats: Hunting an Internet Killer* (dir. Mark Lewis), and *Carmel: Who Killed Maria Marta?* (2020, dir. Alejandro Hartmann). As Tanya Horeck argues, "The long-form true crime serial is one of the genres that Netflix has mined and developed in order to construct and promote the notion—central to its business model—of audience participation through 'binge-watching.'"[19] Generating a communal feeling through orchestrated outrage and participation is remarkably similar to the way that activists use explicitly social-issue documentaries. But in this case, Netflix's goal is to drive business. The buzz created through binging true-crime series and building outrage gives the sense that the streaming service is indispensable and worth the subscription price. Activating publics is an essential element of publicity for documentaries, especially true-crime and political documentaries.

The ballooning number of true-crime documentary series represents Netflix's delicate balance between prestige and popularity. This is both Netflix embracing a type of documentary storytelling long associated with television (*Unsolved Mysteries*, *Forensic Files*, other lowbrow episodic investigative shows), and adjusting the terms of engagement with the genre. True-crime documentaries lie at the nexus of public service documentaries and popular soft documentaries. The subgenre of true-crime documentary had few but significant prestige films—*The Thin Blue Line*—and these influence the way that Netflix positions its series. Horeck points out, "The *Paradise Lost* films, along with *The Thin Blue Line*, provide extraordinarily powerful examples, then, of the kind of change that documentaries can affect in righting egregious social wrongs. While not all crime documentaries result in such dramatic action occurring, I would suggest that these historical examples help to fuel a fantasy of the cultural purchase of the documentary form, which is also further energized by the rise of participatory media culture."[20] This fantasy provides the legitimate cover needed for Netflix to invest heavily in true-crime documentary series, while remaining a venue for serious, less-lurid documentary features.

---

[19] Tanya Horeck, *Justice on Demand: True Crime in the Digital Streaming Era* (Detroit: Wayne State University Press, 2019), 24.
[20] Horeck, *Justice on Demand*, 21.

Exclusivity as a programming strategy resulted in a sharp drop in the number of documentary films Netflix licenses and an increase in the number of documentary series Netflix acquires. The number of Netflix Originals documentaries has plateaued, around twenty annually, and they are heavily marketed, along with Netflix documentary series, particularly true-crime series. This has allowed Netflix to consolidate its documentary strategy around content exclusive to its service, both prestige—political docs—and popular—bingeable true-crime series.

Consequences for Streaming Services, Filmmakers, and Distributors

Streaming Services
In the 2010s, cable channels and television networks alike moved to distribute their content nonlinearly, over the internet. They also turned toward subscription models to replace the advertising revenue lost with fewer linear television viewers. Amanda Lotz argues,

> Dominant funding practices of advertiser and public service funding do persist, but subscriber funding . . . has become far more prevalent in the post-network competitive field. The increased reliance on subscriber payment substantially adjusts the goals and practices of television services utilizing this funding model, especially in the cases of services relying only on subscriber fees.[21]

One way television services adjusted their goals and practices is by imitating strategies used by Netflix and HBO. They have invested in documentary as a less expensive and reliable form of programming, which can generate subscriber value through binge-built buzz and the prestige of awards. ESPN was on the bleeding edge of this trend, developing the acclaimed documentary film series, *30 for 30*, years before ESPN had a streaming platform.[22] In 2018, ESPN Films vice president and executive producer Libby Geist confirmed

---

[21] Amanda D. Lotz, "Teasing Apart Television Industry Disruption: Consequences of Meso-Level Financing Practices before and after the US Multiplatform Era," *Media, Culture & Society* 41, no. 7 (October 2019), 925, https://doi.org/10.1177/0163443719863354.
[22] Travis Vogan, "ESPN Films and the Construction of Prestige in Contemporary Sports Television," *International Journal of Sport Communication* 5, no. 2 (June 2012), 137–52, https://doi.org/10.1123/ijsc.5.2.137.

the value of this investment for the streaming age, saying, "I can tell you that we know for a fact that *30 for 30* is one of the strongest brands at ESPN.... We are the #1 reason people are subscribing to [SVOD service ESPN] Plus and coming back to it."[23]

Like television services' investment in documentary, most general audience streaming services have documentary programming. And in the latter half of the 2010s, they started consolidating their content to focus on exclusivity, like Netflix. These efforts entangled the public service element of documentary ever more tightly with the commercial element, both in the documentaries' production origin and in subject. The streamers acquired a mix of documentaries, including soft documentaries, celebrity profiles, and political and character documentaries. For example, in 2016 Hulu announced an initiative to have its own branded documentary films.[24] Its most high-profile documentary acquisition was *Minding the Gap* (dir. Bing Liu, 2018), which led Hulu to partner with Kartemquin Films, the non-profit documentary production house that incubated *Minding the Gap*.[25] Hulu pledged funds to accelerate documentary projects by people of color, through Kartemquin's already-existing Diverse Voices in Docs, KTQ Labs, and KTQ Internship programs.[26] Amazon also stepped into the fray, acquiring Sundance Grand Jury Prize winner *One Child Nation* (dir. Nanfu Wang) in 2019 for a deal in the high six figures.[27] The documentary captures the long-term effects of China's policy that forcefully limited maternity to one child per family. Amazon got headlines for this deal, and an Academy Award nomination for Best Documentary Feature, but little mentioned was the fact that the Independent Television Service coproduced the film.[28] Apart from acquiring PBS-affiliated films, Amazon played into the public service element

---

[23] Ben Koo, "AA Q&A: ESPN's Libby Geist Outlines the Future of *30 for 30*," *Awful Announcing* (blog), August 14, 2018, https://awfulannouncing.com/espn/aa-qa-espns-libby-geist-outlines-the-future-of-30-for-30.html.

[24] Jacob Kastrenakes, "Hulu Is Getting into Documentaries, Starting with Ron Howard's Beatles Film," *The Verge*, May 4, 2016, https://www.theverge.com/2016/5/4/11589950/hulu-documentaries-ron-howard-the-beatles-eight-days-a-week; Kelly Anderson, "Hulu Takes Streaming Rights to 'Minding the Gap,'" *RealScreen* (blog), June 6, 2018, https://realscreen.com/2018/06/06/hulu-takes-streaming-rights-to-minding-the-gap/.

[25] Anderson, "Hulu Takes Streaming Rights."

[26] Daniele Alcinii, "Kartemquin Films, Hulu Launch Accelerator Program for Filmmakers of Color," *RealScreen* (blog), January 27, 2020, https://realscreen.com/2020/01/27/kartemquin-films-hulu-launch-accelerator-program-for-filmmakers-of-color/.

[27] Brent Lang, "Sundance: Amazon Buys Grand Jury Prize Winner 'One Child Nation' (EXCLUSIVE)," *Variety* (blog), February 3, 2019, https://variety.com/2019/film/markets-festivals/sundance-amazon-china-one-child-nation-1203126866/.

[28] ITVS, "*One Child Nation*," http://www.itvs.org/films/one-child-nation, accessed May 29, 2021.

with political investigation docs: Amazon Studios also financed *Citizen K*, a documentary by Alex Gibney about a Russian oligarch-turned-dissident who accused Putin's government of corruption. The film played festivals in 2019 and was released theatrically by Greenwich Entertainment, ending up on Amazon Prime in 2020.[29] Apple TV made clear its intentions to do documentaries when it hired Molly Thompson away from A&E IndieFilms, which she founded in 2005 and where she has developed numerous documentary films.[30] The simultaneous growth in subscriber funding and internet distribution accelerated the adoption of Netflix's and HBO's strategies around documentary film in the multiplatform era.

Filmmakers and Producers
Netflix's focus on Originals, as opposed to licensed films, and growing investment in documentary series has significantly influenced how documentarians navigate the film industry. Streamers' demand for series has driven many established documentarians to pivot to making series. This is a market-driven production trend, which is highly unusual and a new development in the documentary industry. The increased perceived demand for documentary films and series has also resulted in documentary production on a studio scale, another new development in the industry.

Because streamers and cable channels started spending heavily on documentary series, numerous well-established documentarians have begun making documentary limited series in the second half of the 2010s. These are filmmakers who, traditionally, have made documentary features that premiere at film festivals, play in theaters, and then are broadcast on HBO or one of PBS's strands. Now, in addition to making documentary features, they seized the opportunity to produce series exclusive to the streamer or cable channel. Errol Morris, director of the highly influential true-crime documentary *The Thin Blue Line*, made the series *Wormwood* for Netflix (2017). Joe Berlinger, codirector of the *Paradise Lost* trilogy, has also turned to series. He made the series *Conversations with a Killer: The Ted Bundy Tapes* (2019) and *Crime Scene: The Vanishing at the Cecil Hotel* (2021) for Netflix.[31] Jehane

---

[29] Scott Feinberg, "Alex Gibney Doc 'Citizen K' Sells to Greenwich Entertainment, Will Get Oscar Push," *Hollywood Reporter*, September 30, 2019, https://www.hollywoodreporter.com/race/alex-gibney-doc-citizen-k-sells-greenwich-films-will-get-oscar-push-1244381.

[30] Anne Thompson, "Apple Poaches A&E Veteran Molly Thompson in Pursuit of Documentary Dominance," *IndieWire*, April 15, 2019.

[31] Berlinger also made a Netflix Original fictionalized film about Ted Bundy, *Extremely Wicked, Shockingly Evil and Vile* (2019).

Noujaim's documentary feature *The Square* was an early Netflix Original documentary, earning Netflix its first Oscar nomination ever. In 2020, Noujaim made the series *The Vow* (2020), about the NXIVM cult, for HBO. Kirby Dick, director, and Amy Ziering, producer, have made documentary films like *The Invisible War* (2012) and *The Hunting Ground* (2015). Recently the two codirected the documentary series *Allen vs. Farrow* (2021) for HBO. Liz Garbus, director of documentary features like *The Farm: Angola USA* (1998), *Girlhood* (2003), and *What Happened, Miss Simone?* (2015) has also been making series recently. *The Fourth Estate* (2018), about how the *New York Times* covered the first year of the Trump presidency, played on Showtime. *I'll Be Gone in the Dark* (2020), based on the best-selling book by Michelle McNamara, about the hunt for the Golden State Killer, played on HBO.

In conjunction with the market-driven production trend of series, the documentary industry has grown in response to an increase in perceived demand. This resulted in documentary production on a studio scale, for the first time ever. In the past, a very select few documentarians benefited from steady production funds, primarily from PBS. This is how Frederick Wiseman has maintained a high output of documentaries, making forty-five independent documentaries since 1967. Similarly, Ken Burns relied on continuous funding from PBS and corporate sponsors to maintain a stable of employees, with multiple teams working on various projects at once. The new studio scale of documentary productions was funded by commercial media, not by public television funds or governmental grants. Documentary production companies began to make a large volume of films and series, as in the case of Alex Gibney's Jigsaw Productions, and the entrance of Hollywood production companies into the arena, in the case of Imagine Entertainment.

Alex Gibney's career arc illustrates the vast changes the documentary film industry has undergone in the twenty-first century. With injections of private investment in documentary and a growing number of outlets acquiring documentary films and series, Gibney has become a prolific director and producer, with dozens of credits to his name. Gibney began making films before the "docbuster" era, when a theatrical release and play on PBS or HBO was the best possible outcome for a documentary film. He first gained notice for *The Trials of Henry Kissinger*, made with Eugene Jarecki and released theatrically in 2002. He then won the Academy Award for Best Documentary Feature for *Taxi to the Dark Side* (2007). This honor turned sour, however, when Gibney took the film's distribution company to arbitration. As he told press at the time, "I'm upset because the whole commercial strategy of the film was predicated on the idea of winning awards. . . . The fact that they were fiscally unable to capitalize on the Oscar infuriated me."[32] This episode showed that Gibney had industry savvy and the ability to focus on financial returns, even when promoting a film about the United States' torture and interrogation practices in the war on terror.

Despite this frustration, Gibney continued making documentary films. The stability of nonfiction television beckoned, but the highly standardized nature of cable series did not appeal. As he told a reporter in 2008, "If you flick through Discovery or the History Channel or A&E . . . they all have a brand, and they make the programs they do conform to that brand. There's not much choice for the filmmaker—you're another link in the sausage chain."[33] Rather than moving into the homogenized, narrowly branded basic cable nonfiction series, Gibney and his Jigsaw Productions continued to focus on documentary features. He succeeded by focusing on exactly the types of documentary films most favored by Netflix, HBO, and other outlets: celebrity profiles and political documentaries. Gibney has directed several celebrity profile documentaries, including *Sinatra: All or Nothing* (2015), *Mr. Dynamite: The Rise of James Brown* (2014), and *Robin Williams: Come Inside My Mind* (2018), all for HBO, and *The Armstrong Lie* (2013) and *Steve Jobs: The Man in the Machine* (for CNN Films). Gibney also makes films that combine the investigative structure of true crime with the scope of political documentaries, like *Enron: The Smartest Guys in the Room* (2005), *We Steal Secrets: The Story of Wikileaks* (2013), *Zero Days* (2016), *Casino Jack and the United States of Money* (2010), *Going Clear: Scientology and the Prison of Belief* (2015), *Citizen K* (2019), and *Totally Under Control* (2020). Many of them are funded by cable film units like CNN Films and A&E IndieFilms or private investors like Impact Partners. If distributed theatrically, most are distributed by Magnolia Pictures. Recently Gibney has produced limited series and television series for outlets like Netflix, HBO, National Geographic, and AMC, reflecting the surge in demand for documentary series.

Setting aside Jigsaw Productions series, Gibney has directed more than fifteen documentaries since 2006. This number seems nearly impossible, but this high volume is a direct result of the explosion of interest in documentary films by streaming video services and cable channels in the 2010s. It has

---

[32] ThinkFilm ended operation in 2008. Charles Lyons, "Filmmaker Says Distributor Failed Him," *New York Times*, June 26, 2008, sec. Movies, https://www.nytimes.com/2008/06/26/movies/26thin.html.

[33] Daniel Frankel, "'Taxi' Driver Steers Wider Course for Documakers," *Variety*, April 7, 2008.

removed the risk of producing documentaries because there is guaranteed funding and guaranteed outlet, either in theaters, on premium cable, or on an SVOD. To make this many films, Gibney works collaboratively. He runs multiple teams, each of which works on a single project, and shuttles between them. Some have questioned whether Gibney is an active creator on all these projects, or a mere figurehead for Jigsaw. He admits that his working method is different from almost all documentarians', but says, "On the films that I direct, I'm there, I'm asking the questions, I'm going out and doing the research. I surround myself with a team that only does one thing."[34] This mode of production is highly unusual for documentary film. Instead, it echoes the classical Hollywood producer-unit system, wherein a studio's producers each managed their own film projects simultaneously, under the control of an executive.

Gibney's success and working method has attracted Hollywood, including production companies primarily concerned with big-budget, star-driven fiction features. Headed by Ron Howard and Brian Grazer, Imagine Entertainment is a major Hollywood production company in business since 1985.[35] Its recent feature films include *Solo: A Star Wars Story* (2018, dir. Ron Howard) and *Hillbilly Elegy* (2020, dir. Ron Howard). Imagine made its first foray into documentary in 2016 with *The Beatles: Eight Days a Week*, a Howard-directed film about the band's early days. Released in theaters by Abramorama Films, it earned $2.9 million domestically. Shortly after, it premiered on Hulu as a Hulu Documentary Film.[36] Since then, Imagine has produced seven documentary features and a handful of documentary series. Following the most popular documentary genres, Imagine has produced mainly celebrity profile documentaries—*Pavarotti* (2019, dir. Ron Howard), *D. Wade: Life Unexpected* (2020, dir. Bob Metelus)—along with some true-crime documentary series—*Crime Scene: The Vanishing at the Cecil Hotel* (2021, dir. Joe Berlinger).[37] The company also hired Sara Bernstein,

---

[34] Scott Feinberg, "Alex Gibney on 'Fever of Rage' That Motivated the COVID-19 Doc 'Totally under Control,'" *Hollywood Reporter's Awards Chatter*, November 10, 2020, https://www.hollywoodreporter.com/news/alex-gibney-on-fever-of-rage-that-motivated-the-covid-19-doc-totally-under-control.

[35] Imagine Entertainment has produced such fiction films as *Solo*, *The Da Vinci Code*, *Cinderella Man*, *Liar Liar*, *The Nutty Professor*, and *Apollo 13*.

[36] While Hulu Documentary Films are meant to be exclusive to the service, Hulu acquired only the digital rights to *The Beatles: Eight Days a Week*, so it played in theaters first. Kastrenakes, "Hulu Getting into Documentaries."

[37] Imagine, "Documentaries," https://imagine-entertainment.com/documentary/, accessed May 29, 2021.

a veteran of HBO Documentary, as an executive vice president of Imagine Documentaries and signed a first-look deal with Apple, creating a direct pipeline to streaming for its films and series.[38]

Then, in 2020, Imagine Entertainment invested in Jigsaw Productions. Upon announcing Imagine's investment, Grazer declared, "It's our goal and intention to be the premiere documentary film company in the world. . . . To be able to get Alex Gibney just fortifies that creative ambition."[39] Grazer's bold announcement indicates the company's commitment to producing documentaries on a studio scale. It also tacitly acknowledges Gibney's expertise in producing a high volume of documentaries and series, while maintaining a high journalistic standard and winning awards. Imagine Entertainment's move into documentary filmmaking is a major signal that Hollywood production companies understand the commercial potential of documentary film.

Distribution Companies

Netflix's licensing and acquisition of documentary films and series has driven studio-scale working methods and Hollywood production companies to enter the documentary realm. At the same time, Netflix and other streaming services have savaged the existing documentary ecosystem. The small distribution companies that brought the most documentary films to theaters (and home video) experienced major pressure in Netflix's recent focus on exclusive content. Owning exclusive content is key to Netflix's dominance, as legacy companies with massive libraries of content open their own streaming portals. But it has also meant that Netflix competes for films with film distributors. In addition, Netflix and others sign output deals with mid-level distribution companies, while pulling back on one-off licenses for individual films. The promise of playing on Netflix is a powerful incentive for filmmakers and their sales agents to sign with these distribution companies. With this structure, the final streaming home can determine which distributor releases the film in theaters. This collusion often means cutting out small distributors who used to benefit from Netflix licensing.

---

[38] Cynthia Littleton, "Imagine's Documentary Arm Sets First-Look Pact with Apple (EXCLUSIVE)," *Variety* (blog), January 18, 2019, https://variety.com/2019/tv/news/imagine-apple-documentary-first-look-pact-1203112356/.

[39] Mike Fleming Jr, "Imagine Entertainment Makes 'Substantial Investment' in Jigsaw Productions as Alex Gibney Becomes Cornerstone Filmmaker in Documentary Growth Plans," *Deadline*, June 16, 2020, https://deadline.com/2020/06/alex-gibney-imagine-entertainment-substantial-investment-jigsaw-productions-documentary-expansion-plans-1202960576/.

Netflix and other streamers compete with distribution companies for documentary films. For example, in 2019, Netflix paid $10 million for exclusive rights to the documentary *Knock Down the House* (dir. Rachel Lears). This was the highest price ever paid for a documentary at the Sundance Film Festival.[40] But making the film a Netflix Original meant it would not play in theaters. Netflix, Hulu, Amazon, and HBO regularly make splashy deals for potentially popular documentaries. By releasing them exclusively on their portals, they excise the traditional theatrical windowing process—and remove distribution companies' potential profits.

Mid-level distribution companies like NEON, IFC Films, and Magnolia continue to acquire and release documentary films in theaters. Because they have output deals (also known as pay-one deals) with streamers, their films are guaranteed a place on the dominant streaming libraries.[41] These deals give the distributors an advantage in acquisition because placement on Netflix or Hulu is prized by filmmakers. Sales agents acknowledge that output deals play a big role in selling the rights to a film, even very early in the process. Kevin Iwashina, senior associate at Endeavor Content, explains,

> When we are selling a film to a theatrical distributor . . . we will simultaneously approach their "pay one" partner to gauge their interest as well. The pay cable or SVOD output partner may end up driving an acquisition if they like a particular film, and they will have a preference as to which of their theatrical distribution partners will release the title.[42]

According to this account, even when a film does not go directly to Netflix or another streamer to be branded as an "Original," the streamer can determine whether and which theatrical distributor acquires the film. This practice is certainly not limited to documentary films, but its impact on the documentary film market and ecosystem is significant.

---

[40] Mike Fleming, Jr, "Sundance Festival Favorite 'Knock Down the House' Sold for Record $10 Million; Why This Golden Age for Docus?," *Deadline*, February 6, 2019.

[41] Premium cable channels like HBO and Showtime were long the default pay-one window. Now streaming portals are the main pay-one window. Cynthia Littleton, "Hulu Nabs 'Weiner,' 'King Georges' in Broad Documentary Output Deal with IFC Films," *Variety*, January 27, 2016, https://variety.com/2016/digital/news/hulu-ifc-films-weiner-documentary-output-deal-1201690195/; Selina Chignall, "Hulu and Distributor Neon Ink Licensing Deal," *RealScreen*, April 21, 2017, https://realscreen.com/2017/04/21/hulu-and-distributor-neon-ink-licensing-deal/.

[42] Anthony Kaufman, "Digital Haves and Have-Nots: Disappearing SVOD Deals and Independent Film," *Filmmaker Magazine*, March 14, 2019, https://filmmakermagazine.com/107124-digital-haves-and-have-nots-disappearing-svod-deals-and-independent-film/.

For a time, small, independent distributors like Zeitgeist Films, Cinema Guild, and Icarus Films had output deals with Netflix, so their films would eventually end up on the platform. But these deals expired as streamers concentrated instead on building up proprietary content. Ryan Krivoshey confirms this, saying that Cinema Guild's output deal with Netflix ended in the mid-2010s, which "coincided with a major shift internally at Netflix where they decided that they didn't need every film on the planet, they just needed films that they could recommend to people. They started buying a lot less from us and others like us."[43] The streaming services' focus on exclusivity, rather than scope, has caused the chasm between the big distributors and small ones to grow.

In the latter half of the 2010s, these streaming behemoths ended their output deals with independent distributors. This practice gives the small distribution companies a competitive disadvantage in acquiring films, since they have no guaranteed streaming platform. As Emily Russo, copresident of Zeitgeist Films, acknowledged,

> It's definitely given a lot of people pause . . . and [made them consider] what it takes to acquire a film without that output deal. Sometimes you can gauge interest from an SVOD company on a one-off basis, but if you don't have that, you have to navigate the deal more cautiously with your potential downside.[44]

If a small distributor acquires a documentary and releases it in theater, the distributor may end up not being able to sell the film to any streaming service. Despite this major downside, theatrical release remains important for legitimizing and raising awareness of a documentary film. It is a necessary step to increase the documentary's value as it moves into other windows. As Marcus Hu of Strand Releasing declared in 2016, "I'm very much a believer in still trying to get [specialty films] to go theatrical. . . . It's still the best way to generate publicity and press for the films."[45] The need to generate publicity and awareness for documentaries remains, since they rarely have large advertising budgets. Yet the profit center for documentaries is not in

---

[43] Author's interview with Ryan Krivoshey, February 15, 2021.
[44] Kaufman, "Digital Haves and Have-Nots."
[45] Graham Winfrey, "Harvey Weinstein Isn't Alone: Why Independent Film Distributors Are Taking a Beating," *IndieWire*, September 7, 2016.

theatrical release; the largest revenue source is in the eventual licensing to a streaming service.

So theatrical releasing is a nearly untenable risk for small, independent distribution companies, which means that they will not be able to acquire as many documentary films. Collusion between streaming services and mid-level distribution companies means the bigger documentary films will dominate screens, box office, and conversation. There is a fast track, which involves going straight to a streamer or having theatrical release with a streaming home locked in. And there is a slow track, with high risk at every step as small distributors and documentarians fight for attention and deals. This is strikingly analogous to the classical studio system's vertical integration practices. Like the streaming services, which claim an enormous number of subscribers and "eyeballs," the studios' own theaters were the most profitable theaters in the best locations. They offered preferential booking to the studios' own films and largely excluded classical-era independent producers and distributors from booking their films in these theaters. Boxed out of the largest revenue source, small distributors face a similar situation. In 2019, Jonathan Miller, president of Icarus, stated, "If you talk to any of the smaller distributors, they're fucked because they can't sell films for any money to anybody."[46] While viewers have long expected to find documentary films on Netflix, and now on other streamers, the documentaries they find there are now mostly work made *for* Netflix. This ghettoizes the more unusual, experimental, radical documentaries, and those made by new filmmakers, from the streamers' newsstand.

To survive in this environment, smaller distributors have turned back to the nontheatrical and educational market to release bold, experimental documentaries. Krivoshey elucidates the benefits of doing so: "What helps with Cinema Guild and Grasshopper is that we had this educational division, so we could acquire slightly more adventurous work, so we could cover some of the basic costs, to soften the blow a little bit if it didn't work in theaters."[47] When founding Grasshopper Films, Krivoshey established a nontheatrical division immediately. For an example of how this kind of alternative acquisition works, take the case of *A Prison in Twelve Landscapes* (2016, dir. Brett Story). Winner of Best Canadian Features prizes at Hot Docs and DOXA Documentary Film Festival, Grasshopper first acquired only educational

---

[46] Kaufman, "Digital Haves and Have-Nots."
[47] Author's interview with Ryan Krivoshey, February 15, 2021.

rights to the film. Grasshopper propelled it to be a top seller on the educational market. Satisfied with the results, the company then acquired all digital rights to the film, and subsequently placed it on transactional video-on-demand sites like iTunes, Amazon, Mubi, as well as smaller/niche subscription services like the Criterion Channel. While large distributors place a low value on the educational market, often selling the educational rights to an aggregator, taking an active role in the educational market can be a hedge against the riskier theatrical market and the now-closed streaming platforms.

Private Investment in Documentary

If Netflix changed the marketplace, giving documentaries a more central seat at the table and fortifying a popular audience for those films, the consequences of that commercialization process might be more revolutionary. By making the market visible, Netflix drastically mitigated the risk factor of investing in documentaries because producers know they can sell documentaries to streamers and television portals. Distribution is now so profitable that the money comes up front. For the first time ever, private investors are financing the production of documentaries. This is a fundamental shift that reflects the strength of the market for documentary films as well as the maturity of the commercial infrastructure for documentaries. It is the most significant innovation in how documentaries are produced in the last thirty years.

Over the past fifteen years, many of the most popular and award-winning documentaries have been funded by two companies, Participant Media and Impact Partners. These include Academy Award winners *An Inconvenient Truth*, *The Cove* (2009, dir. Louie Psihoyos), *Citizenfour* (2014, dir. Laura Poitras), *Icarus*, and *American Factory*. They have also financed numerous documentaries that earned more than $1 million in theatrical release, including *Food, Inc.* (2008, dir. Robert Kenner), *Waiting for Superman* (2010, dir. Davis Guggenheim), *Queen of Versailles* (2012, dir. Lauren Greenfield), *Citizenfour*, *The Eagle Huntress* (2016, dir. Otto Bell), *The Biggest Little Farm* (2018, dir. John Chester), *Won't You Be My Neighbor* (2018, dir. Morgan Neville), and *RBG* (2018, dirs. Julie Cohen, Betsy West).

This is a significant change from the way documentaries were produced for much of their history. Documentarians have long cobbled together production funds with grants from public broadcasting, foundations, state and federal governments, and other organizations with a mission-based stake in the making of documentaries. These grants came from organizations that saw supporting documentary films as a method of enhancing the public good, creating public history, and drawing attention to important social issues and marginalized voices.

The other way documentary filmmakers financed their work is through commissions or direct financing from broadcasters. This way, documentarians gained financing as well as a guaranteed distribution and exhibition platform for their work. This closed system meant that broadcasters lowered the risk of funding documentaries.

Neither grants or broadcast licenses are investments meant to turn a profit, through sale to a theatrical distributor or streaming service. Grantees do not reimburse the foundations or organizations that supply them. Broadcasters get broadcast rights in exchange for their financing. In contrast, private investment in documentary is a gamble based on the likelihood of selling the resulting film to theatrical distributors, broadcasters, or streaming services.

The market for documentary films has become sturdy enough for private investors to take this high-risk gamble on nonfiction films. The odds have become more favorable. One reason for this is that income streams for documentaries became more varied—DVDs became a reliable revenue stream, a way to reach people that did not require competing in theatrical space with narrative films. An explosion of film festivals helped create a stronger infrastructure for documentaries, as well as creating an audience attuned to documentary films. The introduction of streaming services was a massive accelerant. Streaming services were hungry for content, and audiences responded positively to documentary features. All these factors helped entrench the documentary market. The question about documentary films used to be, "Who wants to go see that?" Now the answer is obvious: documentary film fans.

Commercially oriented companies are now induced to invest in documentary films. But it is significant that those companies that did invest in documentaries during the 2000s follow the traditions of the field: they are committed to social projects that they extend through their financing of films. This philanthropic approach is known as "filmanthropy." To understand how documentary features are produced, marketed, and distributed, it is necessary not to see them as analogous to independent fiction features or as overlapping with reality TV or nonfiction series. There is a distinctive mode of production and motive for production that extends far back in documentary film history and continues to the streaming era.

There are very legitimate critiques to be made of filmanthropy. Sherri Ortner has called out Participant Media for producing films that suggest superficial, technocratic solutions to social problems and for designing pointedly apolitical impact campaigns. Angela Aguayo treats the entire notion of "impact" with suspicion, and rightly so. As she puts it, "In the new century, emerging documentaries received industry funding based on measurable impact, regardless of whether the actions served the injustices on the screen."[48] The use of short-term, usually uncritical metrics to judge which films deserve funding and which films "succeeded" is inadequate to the complex matrix of art, craft, and social change in the real world. Though she critiques Participant Media's films for being apolitical, Ortner acknowledges that "some more 'political' films do get through the company's antipolitics filters, despite being quite 'controversial.'"[49] She can offer no clear explanation for Participant's investment in *Citizenfour* and other hard-hitting, politically engaged films. In addition, Ortner admits that the impact of specific films is very unpredictable as well.

> For example, it seems clear that a highly political and controversial film like Michael Moore's (2002) *Bowling for Columbine* (not produced by Participant), and a film stripped of politics like *An Inconvenient* Truth can both have a lot of impact, not only in the sense of box office success and winning awards (both films won Oscars) but also in the larger sense of provoking discussion and maybe even action.[50]

Aguayo agrees, stating, "The connection between story, action, and material forces is still obscure."[51] Neither an explicit political message nor a well-funded social impact campaign is a foolproof way of judging a documentary's worth.

While the task of judging the legitimacy of Participant and Impact is beyond this book's scope, the companies' effect on the commercialization of documentary film is not. Participant Media and Impact Partners injected

---

[48] Angela Aguayo, *Documentary Resistance: Social Change and Participatory Media* (New York: Oxford University Press, 2019), 8.
[49] Sherry Ortner, "Social Impact without Social Justice: Film and Politics in the Neoliberal Landscape," *American Ethnologist* 44, no. 3 (2017), 528–39, https://doi.org/10.1111/amet.12527.
[50] Ortner, "Social Impact," 537.
[51] Aguayo, *Documentary Resistance*, 8.

financial liquidity into documentary filmmaking while maintaining a connection to traditional social-issue documentary motives. A wider range of funding sources means that more projects are made, and those projects have greater flexibility as they enter the marketplace. While non-repayable grants from nonprofits and government have been important to the production of documentary films, the nature of grants and nonprofit modus operandi clashes with the increasingly commercialized nature of the documentary film industry. Participant and Impact's investment in documentary films is a necessary counterweight to the outsized power wielded by streaming service behemoths. It also increases the sustainability of documentary filmmaking as a career.

Formed around the same time with similar goals, Participant and Impact Partners invest in documentaries in different ways. Impact Partners does not develop and produce documentary films. Instead, the fund supports films being developed independently and films that are in postproduction. Impact acts as a broker for documentary films looking for financing. Documentarians apply for financing—approximately seven hundred film projects are submitted per year—and Impact chooses about twelve to support annually. This support comes in the form of investment, rather than grants. Abbie Morfoot explains in *Variety*, "If a project uses Impact's money and recovers that money, investors get paid back. If a doc does not recoup Impact funds, filmmakers don't owe anything."[52]

Impact helps documentarians design and implement plans to maximize a film's social and cultural influence. They want a film's impact to ripple out beyond the people who view the film. They want the film to be a tool in larger campaigns to change the world. This is part marketing, part community outreach. For example, Impact worked to get the military chain of command to watch *The Invisible War*, about sexual assault in the armed forces. Impact also campaigned to get colleges to show college freshmen *The Hunting Ground*, about campus rape and sexual assault. For films about trafficked children, *The Day My God Died* (2003, dir. Andrew Levine) and *Born into Brothels* (2004, dir. Zana Briski, Ross Kauffman), Impact sold photographs made by the subjects and used the proceeds to send all the children to college.[53] These campaigns reveal how Impact focuses on getting documentaries seen

---

[52] Addie Morfoot, "Documentary Patrons Impact Partners Make Splashes at Sundance," *Variety*, January 17, 2018.
[53] "Private Investment in Documentary: How and Why?," TIFF Doc Conference, 2017, https://www.youtube.com/watch?v=-PZbnZ8OgoM.

by audiences who could take action, and on delivering aid directly to film subjects.

There are benefits to both filmmakers and investors in Impact's structure. First of all, it allows documentarians to maintain editorial independence. Filmmakers are not beholden to the whims of an investor. By aggregating investors, Impact takes the challenge of managing relationships with investors off filmmakers' shoulders. Morgan Neville, director of *Won't You Be My Neighbor?*, says,

> There are a lot of documentaries that get funded by a rich person who has an issue that they care a lot about.... So they fund a film and are breathing down the neck of the film director. What is so great about Impact is you pitch your film exactly like you want and if they say, "We like it and we will fund it," there is no interference. They have zero agenda other than we believe in your agenda.[54]

Investors benefit because they can trust Impact to administer the investment professionally and translate the film world to them and vice versa. Impact's investment in documentaries at a later stage in production is one example of this: investing in films at that point means that the film's story and budget are less likely to shift than if one invested early in the process. Thus, the risk is reduced. Impact's strong track record itself reduces the risk of investing in film. As Geralyn Dreyfous pointed out, investors

> can create the same back office in their foundations to search for suitable films, staffing this for around $300,000 a year, or they can pay us $35,000 a year to cover our overhead. That way, they draw upon our expertise and avoid reinventing the wheel. They can test the waters and make sure any mistakes they make are not million-dollar mistakes but, say, $25,000 mistakes.[55]

And it is an appealing model. According to Cogan, in 2015 there was a waitlist of a dozen people who wanted to join Impact.[56]

---

[54] Morfoot, "Documentary Patrons."
[55] Geralyn Dreyfous, "Pivotal Funding," *The State of SIE* (blog), February 14, 2019, https://thestateofsie.com/impact-partners-geralyn-dreyfous-funding-models-equity-investing-social-impact-films/.
[56] Anthony Kaufman, "Reality Checks: How Rich People Are Influencing the Documentary World," *IndieWire*, January 8, 2015, 6.

Participant is a more traditional media company, founded by Jeff Skoll, employee 1 at eBay and tech billionaire.[57] Participant produces and acquires documentaries connected to social and environmental causes. It takes on films at various stages, some in the development stage, some after the film is finished and being shopped around. It developed *An Inconvenient Truth* and *The World according to Sesame Street* (2006, dirs. Linda Goldstein Knowlton, Linda Hawkins) in-house, while Participant joined with Magnolia Films to pick up the more recent *RBG* once it was completed. Then Participant guides these films through the marketplace, hooking them up with theatrical distributors and streaming services. It designs philanthropic and political campaigns connected to each film. Participant takes a heavier hand with the documentary films it finances.

As a major philanthropist, Skoll endowed the Skoll Foundation and the UCLA Center for Social Impact Entertainment, and he could have easily made grants to documentary films through those mechanisms. But instead, Skoll and Participant executives see that the market for documentary films is robust enough to support the enterprise.

Participant invests in documentary films with less risk than Impact. One way the company lowers its risk is by financing documentaries by proven, award-winning documentarians Errol Morris (*The Unknown Known*, *Standard Operating Procedure*), by Alex Gibney (*Zero Days*, *Citizen Jack*, *Totally Under Control*). Another way is by producing portraits of beloved public figures: *He Named Me Malala*, *RBG*, and *John Lewis: Good Trouble* (2020, dir. Dawn Porter). Participant occasionally produces and acquires more daring documentaries like *The Look of Silence* (2014, dir. Joshua Oppenheimer) and *Citizenfour*.

The introduction of private investment brought more stability and routinization to the world of documentary film. The very public success of many of these documentaries encouraged filmmakers to follow certain paths that are paved and easy to travel along. It encouraged the expansion of the documentary ecosystem, with many new production companies formed and more streamers and cable channels forming documentary film units. As much as private investment and commercialization tend toward centralization,

---

[57] In addition to documentaries, Participant produces fiction films like *Spotlight, No, Lincoln*, and *Green Book*. The company has also invested in other media companies like Summit Entertainment and DreamWorks and was a founding partner in Amblin Partners. For a time, Participant expanded into web publishing and social media with TakePart, a news website for those interested in social change, and a television network, Pivot.

corporatization, and banality, those on the lower rungs in the documentary world also benefit.

These companies have been so successful that they have spawned other organizations that invest in documentary film. Founded in 2014, CMP I/I (Community, Media, Philanthropy; formerly the Chicago Media Project) is an equity investing fund for "commercially viable documentaries."[58] This is the same model that Impact Partners uses, and cofounder Steve Cohen acknowledges their example, declaring, "I like to say that [Impact Partners cofounder] Dan Cogan changed my life."[59] Then there is Concordia Studio, which is patterned after Participant Media and is run by former Participant Media personnel. In 2020, Davis Guggenheim, director of *An Inconvenient Truth*, and Jonathan King, former head of production at Participant, announced the formation of Concordia Studio, which will produce both documentary and fiction content.[60] Like Participant, Concordia was founded by a tech billionaire, Laurene Powell Jobs, widow of Steve Jobs. Also, like Participant, Concordia's initial investment in documentary films led to a meteoric rise: at the 2020 Sundance Film Festival, one-quarter of the documentary films in competition were produced by Concordia Studios.[61]

Being vetted and chosen by Impact Partners and Participant gives documentaries a leg up earlier in their journey than ever before. It also gives documentary filmmakers more powerful backing, so they are not limping to the finish line. The private investment companies connect the filmmakers to theatrical distributors and cable channels, and these distributors come calling way before the films play at festivals. The festival premiere and run become a publicity ramp up to theatrical distribution or drop on streaming and cable. Private investment companies grab some of the power away from festival programmer kingmakers and film critics; these companies become the earliest gatekeepers, and ones that continue to be committed to the film as it moves through the marketplace.

But there is still variation in what happens to the documentaries financed by Impact and Participant. And they continue to interact with all the nodes

---

[58] CMP I/I, "Our Mission," https://cmpii.com/#our-mission-section, accessed May 28, 2021. CMP I/I is part of a larger organization called CMP. CMP supports documentary films through community philanthropy and events like the Great Chicago Pitch and Doc10 and Doc5 Film Festivals. CMP, "Hi, We're CMP," https://wearecmp.org/, accessed May 28, 2021.

[59] Kaufman, "Reality Checks."

[60] Dino-Ray Ramos, "Davis Guggenheim and Jonathan King Launch Concordia Studio with Laurene Powell Jobs," *Deadline*, January 20, 2020.

[61] Nicole Sperling, "A New Player at Sundance, Backed by Laurene Powell Jobs," *New York Times*, January 20, 2020, 4.

in the network, to make contact with all the pieces of infrastructure that have been built up before. Many documentaries, like *American Factory*, begin production with foundation grants, before Impact or Participant sign on. The films may premiere at film festivals in hopes of earning glowing reviews and attracting the attention of theatrical distributors, cable channels, streaming services, and public television. For an example of this, we can turn to the film *Bisbee '17* (2018, dir. Robert Greene). The formally daring film tells the history of a 1917 labor dispute known as the Bisbee Deportation, in the New Mexico town of Bisbee. Bisbee residents discuss how the Bisbee Deportation echoes in their town to the present day. The documentary builds to the event's centennial anniversary when the current Bisbee residents reenact the 1917 events.

Greene was not new to making documentaries—*Bisbee '17* was his fifth feature-length documentary film—but making documentaries was not a source of income. Many documentarians are on the margins of the entertainment industry, working more regularly as photojournalists, anthropologists, film editors, or professors. Thus, the financing by Impact Partners or Participant helps them enter and sustain their livelihoods in the resource-intensive world of film. Such was the case with Greene. Impact financed *Bisbee '17* on a tight deadline, and allowed the director to earn income from making the film. Greene says, "[My producing partners and I] were finally, like, okay, we all need to get paid to do this work because we'd been doing feature documentaries as side work in a way. So we pitched it to Impact Partners at Sundance 2017, just six months before we shot most of the film. . . . They came on board pretty quickly and then off to the races."[62] CMP also supported the film's production, and Concordia Studios came on as producers once *Bisbee '17* had been accepted in to the 2018 Sundance Film Festival. These investments stabilized the production and allowed the filmmakers to finish the film in a timely manner, by paying them to make it.

Despite these investments from Impact, CMP, and Concordia, *Bisbee '17* was still subject to the tumultuous distribution landscape of the late 2010s. No theatrical distributor acquired *Bisbee '17* out of the Sundance Film Festival. As a result, the filmmaker had to put together a distribution plan. "We basically piecemealed the rights out in various ways," says Greene.[63]

---

[62] Author's interview with Robert Greene, December 2, 2020.
[63] Author's interview with Robert Greene, December 2, 2020.

The film was released in theaters with the help of distribution consultant Michael Tuckman. Broadcast rights sold to *P.O.V.* and Grasshopper Films took the home-video rights. The largest payout came from Amazon: the company paid $250,000 for the streaming rights to *Bisbee '17*, as part of Amazon Video Direct Festival Stars. This now-defunct program offered an upfront bonus to Sundance filmmakers for placing their films on Amazon's self-publishing platform, Amazon Video Direct.[64] As Greene says, "We took that deal so we got Amazon built in from the top. . . . They were really flexible because, frankly, they didn't care, but they didn't promote the film at all."[65] While visibility on Amazon's video platform is significant, *Bisbee '17* did not benefit from the publicity push that a Netflix Original would have received.

This example shows both the promise and the limits of private investment in documentary. Private investment can power documentarians to create radical and boundary-pushing work on politically sensitive subjects. Private investment also moves faster than a grant application process, so it can support work in a tighter time frame. It can stabilize documentary filmmakers and help them have a sustainable career as they continue to make independent work. However, private investment does not guarantee a documentary's commercial success or political impact. Some films produced by Impact and Participant have entered the fast track—gaining a major distribution deal with a theatrical distributor or streaming service. Recent examples include *Won't You Be My Neighbor?* (Impact), which Focus Features acquired and released in theaters, earning nearly $23 million at the box office, and *American Factory* (Participant), which Netflix acquired as an Original. But most documentaries still contend with distribution and exhibition headwinds.

---

[64] Amazon Video Direct Festival Stars ran in 2017 and 2018. In 2021, Amazon removed all documentary films from the Amazon Video Direct platform. Jane Schoenbrun, "Sundance: Exploring the Implications of Amazon's New Distribution Play," *Filmmaker Magazine*, January 20, 2017, https://filmmakermagazine.com/101359-sundance-exploring-the-implications-of-amazons-new-distribution-play/; Chris O'Falt, "Sundance Market Maybe Hurt by Amazon Film Festival Stars Absence," *IndieWire*, January 4, 2019, https://www.indiewire.com/2019/01/sundance-2019-market-amazon-video-direct-festival-stars-likely-pulled-1202032051/; Chris Lindahl and Dana Harris-Bridson, "Amazon Prime Video Direct and the Dystopian Decision to Stop Accepting Documentaries," *IndieWire* (blog), February 24, 2021, https://www.indiewire.com/2021/02/amazon-prime-video-direct-stop-accepting-documentaries-1234617608/.

[65] Author's interview with Robert Greene, December 2, 2020.

Conclusion

The advent and evolution of Netflix's streaming video service has had an enormous impact on the documentary film market and the cultural currency of documentary film. As the company went from being a subscription video-rental company, with a catalog more comprehensive than any physical rental shop, to a subscription video-on-demand service, Netflix continued to act as an important ancillary market for documentary films. Netflix licensed documentaries for streaming because it was a relatively low-cost way to stock its new streaming library. The main types of documentaries Netflix licensed were celebrity profiles, political documentaries, character documentaries, and soft documentaries. This wide variety played into Netflix's mass customization strategy—the service's use of algorithmic personalization to cater to numerous niche audiences.

Then, in the mid-2010s, Netflix shifted its strategy to emphasize exclusive content, including documentary. Rather than acting as ancillary market, the company increased its acquisition of all rights to documentary films, branding them "Originals" and being the films' primary and only window. By 2019, about one-third of the documentaries being added to Netflix were Originals. In addition, the company invested heavily in documentary series, which are also exclusive to Netflix.

These changes have reconfigured the way many documentarians and film distributors work. In response to Netflix's interest in series, documentarians who have long made feature films have pivoted to making series. Some have also pursued working methods more consistent with studio fiction filmmaking than the documentary field. Netflix competes with theatrical distributors for documentary films. The company also has output deals with a select few distributors, which has allowed Netflix to determine which films theatrical distributors pick up.

Making Netflix the primary release window means there is no chance for filmmakers to recoup budget from a traditional succession of windows—theatrical, VOD and premium cable, home-video release and SVOD, and television broadcast. Once a film is on an SVOD like Netflix, other revenue streams dry up. This has concentrated even more power in Netflix's hands.

At the same time, private investment companies have begun investing in documentary films. This investment helps bring documentaries to the market more quickly and gives a measure of sustainability to documentarians' precarious careers. Private investment in documentary also provides a balance to the power wielded by streaming behemoths. Because Impact Partners and Participant Media invest in documentaries for public service aims, at least nominally, they send support to films that might not be commissioned or acquired by a commodity-focused streaming platform.

The increasing commercialization of documentary film in the twenty-first century has modified audience expectations for the genre and increased the volume of documentaries being made. Professionals in the documentary field confirm this growth, with a majority reporting in 2018 that there are more opportunities than there were even two years prior.[66]

However, average documentarians are not substantially better off than they were in the 1960s and 1970s. Many documentarians remain solely committed to public service, and they circulate their work through educational and nontheatrical markets, as documentarians did when the campus market first blossomed. The difference is that now filmmakers license streaming rights to platforms available to students or library card-holders, like Kanopy. They have more options for obtaining funding and more ways to experiment with distribution, but the mode of production for documentary film remains closer to independent film than mainstream commercial movies. And the more personal or political the documentary is, the more the filmmaker must rely on grassroots funding and circulation. The 2018 *Study of Documentary Professionals* by the Center for Media and Social Impact testified, "About 4 in 10 documentary filmmakers (42 percent) reported that their most recent film did not generate any revenue. Less than a quarter of documentary filmmakers (22 percent) reported that their most recent documentary film made enough revenue to cover unpaid production costs and make a profit."[67] With less than a quarter of documentary filmmakers able to cover production costs and turn a profit, it must be acknowledged that the commercial and critical success of *American Factory* or *RBG* is anomalous and does not represent the vast majority of those making documentaries.

---

[66] Caty Borum Chattoo and William Harder, "The State of the Documentary Field: 2018 Study of Documentary Professionals" (Washington, DC: Center for Media and Social Impact, American University School of Communication, 2018), 9.

[67] Chattoo and Harder, "State of the Documentary Field," 12.

Conclusion

Documentary Film Inches Closer to the Center, but Core Tensions Remain

The commercial value and cultural significance of documentary films have grown prodigiously over the past sixty years. In the 1960s, documentary films were rarely released in theaters, and most documentaries made independently were not welcome on network television. Now documentaries are regularly released in theaters alongside fiction films and on streaming video platforms intermingled more conventionally "entertaining" content. While independent filmmakers fought for support from public television in the 1980s, private investors and commercial production companies now eagerly finance documentary films and limited series. In addition to theatrical distributors and broad-audience streaming services, a diverse set of outlets have made documentary films a fundamental part of their content libraries, ranging from basic cable channels like FX to premiere journalism institution like the *New York Times* to worldwide free video-sharing sites like YouTube.[1]

More seismic changes in documentary film distribution are still to come. At the time of this writing, the world has been rocked and reordered by the coronavirus pandemic. Those in the documentary film field responded by accelerating existing trends. Major documentarians, including Liz Garbus, David France, and Matthew Heinemann, stampeded to create films about the pandemic. In April 2020, *Vulture* tallied twenty coronavirus-related documentaries in production.[2] The number of projects speaks to both the nimbleness of documentary filmmakers to act in a crisis and the perceived

---

[1] "FX and Hulu Launch 10-Episode Documentary Series 'The New York Times Presents,'" The New York Times Company, July 7, 2020, https://www.nytco.com/press/fx-and-hulu-launch-10-epis ode-documentary-series-the-new-york-times-presents/; Janet W. Lee, "'Demi Lovato: Dancing with the Devil' Docuseries to Debut on YouTube in March," *Variety*, January 13, 2021, https://variety.com/2021/tv/news/demi-lovato-documentary-youtube-1234884762/.

[2] Chris Lee, "The Race to Make the First Coronavirus Documentary Has Begun," *Vulture*, April 30, 2020, https://www.vulture.com/2020/04/the-race-to-make-the-first-coronavirus-documentary-has-begun.html.

strength of the market to absorb so many documentary films. In response to the shuttering of schools, Netflix made ten documentary features, series, and short films free to stream on YouTube, including *13th*, *Knock Down the House*, and *Chasing Coral*.[3] The press release pointed to educational resources for each title, and read, "We hope this will, in a small way, help teachers around the world."[4] This was a surprising nod to the educational use of documentary film, a discursive position usually ignored by entertainment companies. It was also a gesture toward the public service value of documentary. At the same time, Netflix benefited from buzz surrounding its documentary miniseries *Tiger King: Murder, Mayhem and Madness*. The salacious story was decidedly more entertaining than educational, and its rise to number one most-watched content on Netflix was fueled by audience engagement on social media in the early days of the pandemic.[5] *Tiger King*'s popularity was clear evidence of the commodity value of documentary to Netflix. The documentary market continued to hold public service and commodity value in high tension.

The pandemic also kickstarted the creation of a novel network of alternative video-on-demand services. With movie theaters closed and in-person events banned, distributors and film festivals pivoted to virtual screenings at a startling rate. Distributors like Magnolia Pictures, NEON, Bleecker Street, and Greenwich Entertainment partnered with theaters, including Arclight Cinemas, Laemmle Theaters, and Facets, to run virtual cinemas.[6] Virtual-cinema-goers could purchase a ticket to stream a new-release film at home, the ticket revenue shared between distributor and theater. This was a remarkably transparent move to help art-house and independent movie theaters stay in business while closed indefinitely. It was a public acknowledgment that film distributors and cinemas depend on one another. This cooperative response to crisis contrasted strongly with the way the behemoth streaming

---

[3] Todd Spangler, "Netflix Releases 10 Documentary Films and Series for Free on YouTube," *Variety*, April 17, 2020, https://variety.com/2020/digital/news/netflix-free-streaming-10-documentary-films-and-series-youtube-1234583317/.

[4] Spangler, "Netflix Releases 10."

[5] According to Nielsen, thirty-four million viewers streamed the series in its first ten days on Netflix. Todd Spangler, "'Tiger King' Ranks as TV's Most Popular Show Right Now, according to Rotten Tomatoes," *Variety*, March 29, 2020, https://variety.com/2020/digital/news/tiger-king-most-popular-tv-show-netflix-1203548202/; Todd Spangler, "'Tiger King' Nabbed over 34 Million U.S. Viewers in First 10 Days, Nielsen Says," *Variety*, April 8, 2020, https://variety.com/2020/digital/news/tiger-king-nielsen-viewership-data-stranger-things-1234573602/.

[6] Kate Erbland, "Streaming Wars: Virtual Cinemas Offer Haven for Cinephiles and Struggling Theaters Alike," *IndieWire*, April 24, 2020, https://www.indiewire.com/2020/04/virtual-cinema-guide-1202226844/.

services steamroll the documentary ecosystem to break windows and become the original exhibition site for documentary films and series. Whether virtual cinemas will continue to be significant alternatives to in-person theatrical releasing remains to be seen.

Other current events have also prompted responses from the documentary field. In the wake of the murder of George Floyd and the international Black Lives Matter movement, multiple stakeholders worked together to make three documentaries about black thinkers and civil rights protests widely available at no cost. The John S. and James L. Knight Foundation paid rental fees to Magnolia Pictures for people around the country to watch *I Am Not Your Negro*, *Toni Morrison: The Pieces I Am* (2019, dir. Timothy Greenfield-Sanders), and *Whose Streets?* online, for free. The art house O Cinema helped coordinate community-led virtual discussions in eight cities.[7] This partnership between those in the nonprofit world and the commercial world affirmed the public service value of documentary film.

The dual aspects of the documentary film market—commodity exchange and public service—have become more tightly intertwined because of commercialization. As documentary film's commercial viability has grown, so has the number of filmmakers aiming to enfold their public service goals within commercial structures of production, distribution, and exhibition. But commercialization has not fundamentally shifted the documentarian's motive for production. As Caty Borum Chattoo and William Harder reported in the 2018 *Study of Documentary Professionals*, 58 percent of documentary directors and producers describe themselves as social issue advocate filmmakers. And 38 percent of documentary professionals list "positive impact on social issues" as the most meaningful aspect of their work.[8]

The tension between television and cinema has continued. In 2017, one year after the eight-hour documentary from ESPN Films *O.J.: Made in America* won the Oscar for Best Documentary Feature, the Academy barred multipart documentaries from competing for the film awards.[9] This quick action showed the industry's eagerness to police the boundaries of film and

---

[7] Brent Lang, "'I Am Not Your Negro,' Toni Morrison, Ferguson Uprising Docs Made Available for Free," *Variety*, June 4, 2020, https://variety.com/2020/film/news/i-am-not-your-negro-whose-streets-toni-morrison-the-pieces-i-am-available-free-james-baldwin-1234625617/.

[8] Caty Borum Chattoo and William Harder, "The State of the Documentary Field: 2018 Study of Documentary Professionals," Center for Media and Social Impact, American University School of Communication, 2018, 9–10.

[9] Dave McNary, "Oscars: New Rules Bar Multi-part Documentaries Like 'O.J.: Made in America,'" *Variety*, April 7, 2017, https://variety.com/2017/film/news/oscars-new-rules-documentary-oj-made-in-america-barred-1202026406/.

television, especially now that documentaries are more integral to the commercial industry. Even PBS's investigative journalism series *Frontline* has pushed into theaters, eager for the buzz and awards possibilities built by theatrical release. In 2019, *Frontline* executive producer Raney Aronson-Rath noted, "This era has been called the golden age of documentaries, and I increasingly felt that at the right time and with the right film, it made sense for us to be in this space.... Seeing a documentary on a big screen is a different experience, and there are documentaries that *Frontline* supports that should be seen in the theater and festival environment."[10] Aronson-Rath recognizes that the theater experience and film festival circuit can confer an affective power and cultural cachet to documentaries.

But the tension between film and television is a different tension now that internet distribution has transformed television in fundamental ways. Portals, including Netflix, HBO Max, and Peacock are generally subscriber funded, rather than advertiser funded, and they offer subscribers libraries of content, not scheduled delivery of that content. As portals produce both features and series, and viewers access feature films, limited series, and television series from the same home-viewing platforms, it is likely that audiences will distinguish less and less between documentary film and television. Instead, this differentiation will be meaningful only to industry insiders.

The downsides of commercialization are real and severe. Huge, global technology companies Netflix and Amazon tightly control access to their streaming services. After licensing large quantities of documentaries to fill their libraries and becoming the de facto place to watch documentaries, they shifted focus to exclusivity and specific genres. This has driven production trends and siloed unwelcome types of documentaries to smaller, less visible platforms. One example of this is Amazon tightening control over Amazon Prime Video Direct. Prime Video Direct is a self-distribution platform, to which anyone can upload content available to Prime subscribers or for rental or purchase. In February 2021, Amazon stopped accepting, and began purging, documentary films from Amazon Prime Video Direct.[11] No longer could filmmakers or specialty distributors like Kino Lorber upload documentary films to Prime Video Direct. Done without warning, or even

---

[10] Jill Goldsmith, "With More Docs in Theaters, 'Frontline' Makes Play for New Audiences," *Current*, August 22, 2019.
[11] Chris Lindahl and Dana Harris-Bridson, "Amazon Prime Video Direct and the Dystopian Decision to Stop Accepting Documentaries," *IndieWire*, February 24, 2021, https://www.indiewire.com/2021/02/amazon-prime-video-direct-stop-accepting-documentaries-1234617608/.

notifying filmmakers and distributors, this move was a chilling reminder that independent filmmakers are at the mercy of powerful platforms.

Boxed out by streaming behemoths Netflix, Hulu, and Amazon Prime, core distributors of documentaries are left without a public streaming platform for many of their films. In response, small independent distributors like Zeitgeist Films, Grasshopper Films, and Oscilloscope Laboratories have launched their own streaming platforms. These platforms, such as OVID.tv and Projectr.tv, keep the distribution infrastructure intact rather than capitulating to streaming behemoths overthrowing theatrical releasing and traditional distributors. OVID and Projectr create continuity and visibility for the filmmakers they work with. And they help filmmakers reach their public service goals, by hosting their documentaries on a publicly available platform. These sites are home to both robust catalogs of documentaries and the virtual cinemas that highlight new documentary films and art-house films. They play to the educational market by providing access to a wide range of documentaries, and to the cinephile audience, by offering rare finds and quality curation. This new constellation of distribution strategies could be an area of transformation in a landscape dominated by global conglomerate streamers.

In another frightening turn in the commercialization of documentary, filmmakers publicly claimed that their work was rejected by major platforms for political reasons. The most chilling of these is the story of *The Dissident*, a documentary on the murder of Jamal Khashoggi, allegedly ordered by Saudi crown prince Mohammed bin Salman. Bryan Fogel's follow-up to the Academy Award–winning *Icarus*, it premiered at the Sundance Film Festival and earned rave reviews. But no major distributors or streaming services acquired *The Dissident*, not even Netflix, which had paid $5 million for *Icarus*. Fogel savvily analyzed the reason Netflix pounced on *Icarus*, which explores state-sponsored sports doping in Russia. Fogel noted,

> When *Icarus* came out, they had 100 million subscribers. . . . And they were in the hunt to get David Fincher to do movies with them, to get Martin Scorsese to do movies with them, to get Alfonso Cuarón to do movies with them. That's why it was so important that they had a film they could win an award with.[12]

---

[12] Nicole Sperling, "An Oscar Winner Made a Khashoggi Documentary. Streaming Services Didn't Want It," *New York Times*, December 24, 2020, sec. Business, https://www.nytimes.com/2020/12/24/business/media/dissident-jamal-khashoggi-netflix-amazon.html.

CONCLUSION 193

Having achieved those goals and earned the brand prestige, and anxious to remain on good terms with foreign governments, Netflix was less inclined toward risky, controversial acquisitions. Fogel declared, "Sadly, they are not the same company as a few years ago when they passionately stood up to Russia and Putin [by acquiring *Icarus*]."[13] Indeed, as streamers' businesses evolve, so too do their strategies around documentary films. Where once a portal's strategies performed a public service, a pivot might lead the company toward embracing documentary as commodity alone.

Nevertheless, there are undeniable upsides to the commercialization of documentary film. More documentaries are being made. There is more funding available and more avenues of distribution to earn returns. The growth of funding means documentarians can finish projects faster. One newer institution, Field of Vision, made it a mandate to speed the production of investigative documentary work, to bring it to viewers more quickly.[14] This initiative combines the best aspect of commercialization—potentially more sustainable careers, wider audiences—with the public service motive that drives so many documentarians. Documentary filmmaking remains a precarious career, but commercialization has undoubtedly stabilized it for some.

With so many documentary films being produced, scholars face a significant challenge in attending to them. The work of describing and analyzing documentaries made at different production levels and for different motives has only just begun. Chris Cagle's festival documentary project is one promising avenue for this task, as is the collection *Reclaiming Popular Documentary*.[15] *Documentary's Expanded Fields: New Media and the Twenty-First-Century Documentary*, Jihoon Kim's study of documentary media in new spaces, like galleries and online, and the use of new tools, like virtual reality environments and drone cameras, is also a step in the right direction.[16]

As documentary film has moved closer to the commercial media industry, there has been increased attention to labor conditions. Those working

---

[13] Sperling, "Oscar Winner."

[14] Chris O'Fait, "How Field of Vision's Quick Production Turnaround Is Changing the Way Documentaries Are Made and Seen," *IndieWire*, May 26, 2016, https://www.indiewire.com/2016/05/how-field-of-visions-quick-production-turnaround-is-changing-the-way-documentaries-are-made-and-seen-288739/.

[15] Chris Cagle, "Film Festival Documentary," https://festivaldocumentary.com/. Chris Cagle, "Color Correction and the Film Festival Documentary," *Velvet Light Trap* 88 (Fall 2021), 38–48; Christie Milliken and Steve F. Anderson, *Reclaiming Popular Documentary* (Bloomington: Indiana University Press, 2021).

[16] Jihoon Kim, *Documentary's Expanded Fields: New Media and the Twenty-First-Century Documentary* (New York: Oxford University Press, 2022).

on documentaries that premiere in theaters and are hosted on the largest platforms demand better compensation and working conditions. Labor organizing is a new frontier in documentary filmmaking, and it is likely to expand in the coming years. The Writers' Guild of America–East is making concerted push to organize those who work in documentary film and nonfiction media. Jigsaw Productions, Alex Gibney's production company, joined the WGAE in 2021.[17] A new organization called the Documentary Producers Alliance is also working on issues of labor and crediting in the documentary world, to standardize the titles assigned to those who guide films through production and those who merely provide financing.[18]

Holistic examinations of the careers of documentarians would also help. The overlap between the documentary film world and the worlds of fine art and advertising is large. Film and media scholars are apt to focus on a filmmaker's documentaries, naturally, but ad work and industrial filmmaking can be significant elements of a career. They can also influence filmmaking decisions. Similarly, the art world has taken a great interest in documentary film over the past two decades. However, the relations between documentary and contemporary art are obscure. Tracing the movement between these nodes would help illuminate the recent history of documentary film.

And despite the drastically changed media landscape, full of "disrupters," certain mission-oriented institutions continue to support documentary film, like PBS's *P.O.V., Independent Lens*, and Independent Television Service. Indeed, documentary filmmakers acknowledged the importance of PBS's place in the ecosystem when they advocated against changes to the national broadcast schedule in 2011 and late 2014 and 2015. Documentary filmmakers banded together as Indie Caucus / PBS Needs Indies to keep independently made nonfiction films on an important PBS station's prime-time schedule. This advocacy paid off—Indie Caucus's demands were met. It also resulted in a reciprocal relationship with the network: the group has written to Congress advocating for continued funding of PBS.

The continued support from granting foundations and legacy organizations is significant when looking toward the future of documentary. PBS and

---

[17] Kate Kilkenny, "Alex Gibney's Jigsaw Productions Recognizes Writers Guild East Union," *Hollywood Reporter*, October 27, 2021, https://www.hollywoodreporter.com/business/business-news/jigsaw-productions-union-wga-east-1235037891/.

[18] Documentary Producer's Alliance, "A Guide to Best Practices in Documentary Crediting," January 2019, https://www.documentaryproducersalliance.org/_files/ugd/446e61_8f6a014f26084f4ab3efbdd5880cda92.pdf.

other nonprofits stopped supporting independent fiction film once indie cinema was bankable and embraced by Hollywood. Knowing that trajectory, it is possible that the entrance of private investment and studio-style production into documentary will end grants and other nonprofit support. However, this is unlikely to happen. For one, PBS's brand identity is inextricably linked to documentary film. For another, the mission-driven nature of much documentary filmmaking matches the mission-driven organizations that offer grants. This convergence of goals makes the nonprofit support of documentary filmmaking self-reinforcing and likely to continue.

That said, the history of twenty-first-century documentary would benefit from sustained attention to funding models, including crowdfunding. Many documentary films have benefited from crowdfunding campaigns on platforms like Kickstarter, Indiegogo, and Seed&Spark, yet there are few scholarly accounts of this financing strategy.

In an unexpected turn, the higher visibility of documentary films has made them valuable in a new way: as intellectual property. Over the past ten years, film producers and others in the media industry have been acquiring the rights to adapt documentary films into scripted films. While it was still in theaters in 2018, producers announced that they were adapting the hit documentary *Three Identical Strangers* into a fiction film.[19] Major fiction directors have also been attached to these projects: in 2020 alone, press releases touted that Barry Jenkins would adapt *Virunga* (2014, dir. Orlando von Einsiedel) and Justin Lin would adapt *Abacus: Small Enough to Jail* (2017, dir. Steve James).[20] This trend has created new value for older documentaries as well. For example, the documentary *The Eyes of Tammy Faye* was released in 2000. The fictionalized version was released in 2021, and it won Jessica Chastain the Academy Award for Best Actress for the title role. The use of documentary films as the basis for derivative works is unlikely to abate. Instead, the potential intellectual property value is probably already steering which documentary films are financed and made.

---

[19] Henry Chu, "Hit Documentary 'Three Identical Strangers' to Be Adapted into Feature Film," *Variety*, July 19, 2018, https://variety.com/2018/film/news/three-identical-strangers-docuemtnary-adapted-feature-film-1202878246/.

[20] Brian Welk, "Barry Jenkins to Write Adaptation of 'Virunga' Doc Produced by Leonardo DiCaprio," *TheWrap*, June 23, 2020, 2.

Mike Fleming Jr, "Participant Boards 'Abacus,' Justin Lin-Directed Adaptation of 2016 Toronto Docu on Sung Family: Chinatown Bankers Were Only Ones Charged Criminally after 2008 Financial Collapse," *Deadline*, August 11, 2020, https://deadline.com/2020/08/justin-lin-abacus-participant-2016-documentary-sung-family-chinatown-bank-only-bank-criminal-charges-2008-financial-collapse-1203010104/.

Thus, commercialization has caused a ballooning at one end. The grassroots documentarians remain on the other end, and they are likely helped by greater interest in documentary film. Yet the road is hard and revenue for documentarians is "low—and inconsistent," as Borum Chattoo and Harder report in *The State of the Documentary Field: 2018 Study of Documentary Professionals*. Making a documentary is a highly risky undertaking, unless the filmmaker works with a well-established production company or gets a large amount of private financing. But the model of the independent documentary filmmaker remains attractive. As Robert Greene notes, "My model was always Wiseman. He's never gonna make a lot of money, but he's always gonna get to do what he wants to do."[21] The sustainability, productivity, and editorial control of Wiseman's career are incredibly rare, but many still strive for this combination, using all the tools of the commercialized documentary landscape to achieve it.

[21] Author's interview with Robert Greene, December 2, 2020.

Bibliography

Aguayo, Angela. *Documentary Resistance: Social Change and Participatory Media.* New York: Oxford University Press, 2019.

Anderson, Carolyn. "Theatricals." In *The Essential HBO Reader*, edited by Gary R. Edgerton and Jeffrey P Jones. Lexington: University Press of Kentucky, 2008.

Aufderheide, Patricia. "Documentary Filmmaking and US Public TV's Independent Television Service, 1989–2017." *Journal of Film and Video* 71, no. 4 (2021), 3–14.

Baker, Michael Brendan. "Rockumentary: Style, Performance, and Sound in a Documentary Genre." PhD diss., McGill University, 2011.

Balio, Tino. *The Foreign Film Renaissance on American Screens, 1946–1973.* Madison: University of Wisconsin Press, 2010.

Balio, Tino, ed. *Hollywood in the Age of Television.* Boston: Unwin Hyman, 1990.

Barsam, Richard. *Nonfiction Film: A Critical History, Revised and Expanded.* Bloomington: Indiana University Press, 1992.

Baughman, James Lewis. "ABC and the Destruction of American Television, 1953–1961." *Business and Economic History* 12 (1983), 56–73.

Bennett, James, Paul Kerr, and Niki Strange. "Cowboys or Indies? 30 Years of the Television and Digital Independent Public Service Production Sector." *Critical Studies in Television* 8, no. 1 (March 2013), 108–30. https://doi.org/10.7227/CST.8.1.9.

Borum Chattoo, Caty. *Story Movements: How Documentaries Empower People and Inspire Social Change.* New York: Oxford University Press, 2020.

Borum Chattoo, Caty, and William Harder. "The State of the Documentary Field: 2018 Study of Documentary Professionals." Center for Media and Social Impact, American University School of Communication, 2018.

Boyle, Raymond. "The Television Industry in the Multiplatform Environment." *Media, Culture & Society* 41, no. 7 (October 2019), 919–22. https://doi.org/10.1177/0163443719868389.

Brooks, Carolyn N. "Documentary Programming and the Emergence of the National Educational Television Center as a Network, 1958–1972." PhD diss., University of Wisconsin–Madison, 1994.

Buehler, Branden. "The Documentary as 'Quality' Sports Television." In *Sporting Realities: Critical Readings of the Sports Documentary*, edited by Samantha Sheppard and Travis Vogan, 11–34. Lincoln: University of Nebraska Press, 2020.

Bullert, B. J. *Public Television: Politics and the Battle over Documentary Film.* New Brunswick, NJ: Rutgers University Press, 1997.

Chris, Cynthia. "All Documentary, All the Time? Discovery Communications Inc. and Trends in Cable Television." *Television and New Media* 3, no. 1 (February 2002), 7–28.

Comiskey, Andrea. "The Campus Cinematheque: Film Culture at U.S. Universities, 1960–1975." *Post Script—Essays in Film and the Humanities* 30, no. 2 (Winter–Spring 2011), 36–52.

Couret, Nilo. "Under Fyre: Debt Culture in the Streaming Era." *Film Quarterly* 74, no. 1 (September 1, 2020), 57–63. https://doi.org/10.1525/fq.2020.74.1.57.
Curtin, Michael. *Redeeming the Wasteland: Television Documentary and Cold War Politics.* New Brunswick, NJ: Rutgers University Press, 1995.
Curtin, Michael, and Kevin Sanson, eds. *Voices of Labor: Creativity, Craft, and Conflict in Global Hollywood.* Oakland: University of California Press, 2017.
Day, James. *The Vanishing Vision: The Inside Story of Public Broadcasting.* Berkeley: University of California Press, 1995.
Edgerton, Gary R. "Charles E. Sellier, Jr. and Sunn Classic Pictures: Success as a Commercial Independent in the 1970s." *Journal of Popular Film and Television* 10, no. 3 (Fall 1982), 106–18.
Edgerton, Gary R. *Ken Burns' America.* New York: Palgrave, 2001.
Edgerton, Gary R., and Jeffrey P Jones, eds. *The Essential HBO Reader.* Lexington: University Press of Kentucky, 2008.
Fenwick, James. "Urban Regeneration and Stakeholder Dynamics in the Formation, Growth and Maintenance of the Sheffield International Documentary Festival in the 1990s." *Historical Journal of Film, Radio and Television* 41, no. 4 (May 10, 2021), 1–39. https://doi.org/10.1080/01439685.2021.1922035.
Fuhs, Kristen. "The Legal Trial and/in Documentary Film." *Cultural Studies* 28, nos. 5–6 (September 3, 2014), 781–808. https://doi.org/10.1080/09502386.2014.886484.
Glick, Joshua. *Los Angeles Documentary and the Production of Public History, 1958–1977.* Berkeley: University of California Press, 2018.
Hadida, Allègre L., Joseph Lampel, W. David Walls, and Amit Joshi. "Hollywood Studio Filmmaking in the Age of Netflix: A Tale of Two Institutional Logics." *Journal of Cultural Economics* 45 (2021), 213–28. https://doi.org/10.1007/s10824-020-09379-z.
Havens, Timothy. "Netflix: Streaming Channel Brands as Global Meaning Systems." In *From Networks to Netflix: A Guide to Changing Channels*, edited by Derek Johnson, 321–31. New York: Routledge, 2018.
Hessler, Jennifer. "Quality You Can't Touch: Mubi Social, Platform Politics, and the Online Distribution of Art Cinema." *Velvet Light Trap* 82 (Fall 2018), 3–17. https://doi.org/10.7560/VLT8202.
Hilderbrand, Lucas. *Paris Is Burning.* Vancouver: Arsenal Pulp Press, 2013.
Horeck, Tanya. *Justice on Demand: True Crime in the Digital Streaming Era.* Detroit: Wayne State University Press, 2019.
Iordanova, Dina. "The Film Festival as an Industry Node." *Media Industries Journal* 1, no. 3 (January 1, 2015). https://doi.org/10.3998/mij.15031809.0001.302.
Jaeckle, Jeff, and Susan Ryan, eds. *ReFocus: The Films of Barbara Kopple.* Edinburgh: Edinburgh University Press, 2019.
Johnson, Catherine. "The Appisation of Television: TV Apps, Discoverability and the Software, Device and Platform Ecologies of the Internet Era." *Critical Studies in Television* 15, no. 2 (June 2020), 165–82. https://doi.org/10.1177/1749602020911823.
Johnson, Catherine. *Branding Television.* New York: Routledge, 2012.
Johnson, Derek, ed. *From Networks to Netflix: A Guide to Changing Channels.* London: Routledge, 2018.
Juhasz, Alexandra, ed. "Interview with Julia Reichert." In *Women of Vision: Histories in Feminist Film and Video*, 121–35. Minneapolis: University of Minnesota Press, 1997.
Kamir, Orit. "Why 'Law-and-Film' and What Does It Actually Mean? A Perspective." *Continuum* 19, no. 2 (June 2005), 255–78. https://doi.org/10.1080/10304310500084558.

Kepley, Vance, Jr. "The Origins of NBC's Project XX in Compilation Documentaries." *Journalism Quarterly* 61, no. 1 (1984), 20–26.

King, Geoff. *American Independent Cinema*. London: I.B. Tauris, 2005.

Knight, Julia, and Peter Thomas. *Reaching Audiences: Distribution and Promotion of Alternative Moving Image*. Bristol: Intellect, 2011.

Kreul, James. "New York, New Cinema: The Independent Film Community and the Underground Crossover, 1950–1970." PhD diss., University of Wisconsin-Madison, 2004.

Labuza, Peter. "Under the Electric Cloud: Cinema at Paramount 's Twilight." *Framework: The Journal of Cinema and Media* 62, no. 2 (Fall 2021), 242–60.

Lang, Brent. "How WarnerMedia Siblings HBO Max and CNN Films Formed Their Documentary Production Partnership." *Variety*, August 19, 2020. https://variety.com/2020/streaming/features/hbo-max-cnn-films-1234739080/.

Leverette, Marc, Brian L. Ott, and Cara Louise Buckley, eds. *It's Not TV: Watching HBO in the Post-television Era*. New York: Routledge, 2008.

Levy, Emanuel. *Cinema of Outsiders: The Rise of American Independent Cinema*. New York: New York University Press, 1999.

Lotz, Amanda. *Portals: A Treatise on Internet-Distributed Television*. Ann Arbor: Michigan Publishing, University of Michigan Library, 2017. http://dx.doi.org/10.3998/mpub.9699689.

Lotz, Amanda. "Teasing Apart Television Industry Disruption: Consequences of Meso-Level Financing Practices before and after the US Multiplatform Era." *Media, Culture & Society* 41, no. 7 (October 2019), 923–38. https://doi.org/10.1177/0163443719863354.

Lotz, Amanda. *We Now Disrupt This Broadcast: How Cable Transformed Television and the Internet Revolutionized It All*. Cambridge, MA: MIT Press, 2018.

Lotz, Amanda, and Timothy Havens. *Understanding Media Industries*. New York: Oxford University Press, 2016.

Mamber, Stephen. *Cinema Verite in America: Studies in Uncontrolled Documentary*. Cambridge, MA: MIT Press, 1974.

McCracken, Chelsea. "Rethinking Television Indies: The Impact of American Playhouse." *Screen* 57, no. 2 (June 2016), 218–34. https://doi.org/10.1093/screen/hjw018.

McDonald, Paul, and Janet Wasko, eds. *The Contemporary Hollywood Film Industry*. Hoboken, NJ: Wiley-Blackwell, 2008.

McLane, Betsy. *A New History of Documentary Film*. 2nd ed. London: Continuum, 2012.

Miller, Elizabeth. "Building Participation in the Outreach for the Documentary *The Water Front*." *Journal of Canadian Studies* 43, no. 1 (Winter 2009), 59–86.

Murray, Susan. "'I Think We Need a New Name for It': The Meeting of Documentary and Reality TV." In *Reality TV: Remaking Television Culture*, edited by Susan Murray and Laurie Ouellette, 65–81. New York: New York University Press, 2004.

Musser, Charles. "Film Truth in the Age of George W. Bush." *Framework: The Journal of Cinema and Media* 48, no. 2 (2007), 9–35. https://doi.org/10.1353/frm.2007.0015.

Newman, Michael Z. *Indie: An American Film Culture*. New York: Columbia University Press, 2011.

Nichols, Bill. *Newsreel: Documentary Filmmaking on the American Left*. New York: Arno Press, 1980.

Nichols, Bill. "Newsreel: Film and Revolution." Master's thesis, University of California, Los Angeles, 1972.

Ortner, Sherry. "Social Impact without Social Justice: Film and Politics in the Neoliberal Landscape." *American Ethnologist* 44, no. 3 (2017), 528–39. https://doi.org/DOI: 10.1111/amet.12527.

Owczarski, Kimberly. "Becoming Legendary: Slate Financing and Hollywood Studio Partnership in Contemporary Filmmaking." *Spectator*, Fall 2012, 50–59.

Peranson, Mark. "First You Get the Power, Then You Get the Money: Two Models of Film Festivals." *Cineaste*, Summer 2008, 8.

Perren, Alisa. *Indie, Inc.: Miramax and the Transformation of Hollywood in the 1990s.* Austin: University of Texas Press, 2012.

Perren, Alisa. "Rethinking Distribution for the Future of Media Industry Studies." *Cinema Journal* 52, no. 3 (2013), 165–71. https://doi.org/10.1353/cj.2013.0017.

Ramírez, Gracia. "The March of Time in Britain and the International History of Documentary Film." *Film History* 32, no. 2 (2020), 1. https://doi.org/10.2979/filmhistory.32.2.01.

Resha, David. *The Cinema of Errol Morris*. Middletown, CT: Wesleyan University Press, 2015.

Rizzo, Sergio. "The Left's Biggest Star: Michael Moore as Commercial Auteur." In *Michael Moore: Filmmaker, Newsmaker, Cultural Icon*, edited by Matthew Bernstein, 27–50. Ann Arbor: University of Michigan Press, 2010.

Sharma, Sudeep. "Netflix and the Documentary Boom." In *The Netflix Effect: Technology and Entertainment in the 21st Century*, edited by Kevin McDonald and Daniel Smith-Rowsey, 143–54. New York: Bloomsbury Academic, 2016.

Sheppard, Samantha, and Travis Vogan. "Introduction." In *Sporting Realities: Critical Readings of the Sports Documentary*. Lincoln: University of Nebraska Press, 2020.

Smits, Roderik, and E. W. Nikdel. "Beyond Netflix and Amazon: MUBI and the Curation of On-Demand Film." *Studies in European Cinema* 16, no. 1 (January 2, 2019), 22–37. https://doi.org/10.1080/17411548.2018.1554775.

Stover, John Abraham. "The Intersections of Social Activism, Collective Identity, and Artistic Expression in Documentary Filmmaking." PhD diss., Loyola University Chicago, 2012.

Strain, Ellen. *Public Places, Private Journeys: Ethnography, Entertainment, and the Tourist Gaze*. Piscataway, NJ: Rutgers University Press, 2003.

Tryon, Chuck. *Reinventing Cinema: Movies in the Age of Media Convergence*. Piscataway, NJ: Rutgers University Press, 2009.

Tzioumakis, Yannis. *American Independent Cinema*. 2nd ed. Edinburgh: Edinburgh University Press, 2017.

Tzioumakis, Yannis. *Hollywood's Indies: Classics Divisions, Specialty Labels, and American Independent Cinema*. Edinburgh: Edinburgh University Press, 2012.

Valck, Marijke de. "Sites of Initiation: Film Training Programs at Film Festivals." In *The Education of the Filmmaker in Europe, Australia, and Asia*, edited by Mette Hjort, 127–45. New York: Palgrave Macmillan US, 2013. https://doi.org/10.1057/9781137070388_7.

Vogan, Travis. "ESPN Films and the Construction of Prestige in Contemporary Sports Television." *International Journal of Sport Communication* 5, no. 2 (June 2012), 137–52. https://doi.org/10.1123/ijsc.5.2.137.

Vogan, Travis. "HBO Sports: Docu-Branding Boxing's Past and Present." In *Sporting Realities: Critical Readings of the Sports Documentary*, edited by Samantha Sheppard and Travis Vogan, 193–215. Lincoln: University of Nebraska Press, 2020.

Warren, Shilyh. *Subject to Reality: Women and Documentary Film*. Champaign: University of Illinois Press, 2019.

Wasko, Janet, and Eileen R. Meehan. "Critical Crossroads or Parallel Routes? Political Economy and New Approaches to Studying Media Industries and Cultural Products." *Cinema Journal* 52, no. 3 (2013), 150–57. https://doi.org/10.1353/cj.2013.0028.

Whedbee, Karen. "Reverend Billy Goes to Main Street: Free Speech, Trespassing, and Activist Documentary Film." *Journal of Film and Video* 71, no. 2 (2019), 30. https://doi.org/10.5406/jfilmvideo.71.2.0030.

Wilinsky, Barbara. *Sure Seaters: The Emergence of Art House Cinema*. Minneapolis: University of Minnesota Press, 2000.

Winston, Bryan. "'A Riddle Wrapped in a Mystery inside an Enigma': Wiseman and Public Television." *Studies in Documentary Film* 3, no. 2 (2009), 95–111.

Winton, Ezra. "Good for the Heart and Soul, Good for Business: The Cultural Politics of Documentary at the Hot Docs Film Festival." PhD diss., Carleton University, 2014. https://doi.org/10.22215/etd/2014-10051.

Wyatt, Justin. "From Roadshowing to Saturation Release: Majors, Independents, and Marketing/Distribution Innovations." In *The New American Cinema*, edited by Jon Lewis, 64–86. Durham, DC: Duke University Press, 1998.

Index

For the benefit of digital users, indexed terms that span two pages (e.g., 52–53) may, on occasion, appear on only one of those pages.
Tables are indicated by *t* following the page number

Abacus: Small Enough to Jail, 195
ABC, 13–14, 27
ABC News, 106
Abortion: Desperate Choices, 107–8
Abramorama Films, 172–73
Academy Awards, 90–91, 93–94, 128
  American Factory, 151, 152–53, 156, 177
  Bowling for Columbine, 116
  Buena Vista Social Club (nominated), 100–1
  Children Underground (nominated), 138
  Citizenfour, 177
  Common Threads: Stories from the Quilt, 109
  The Cove, 177
  Crack USA: County under Siege (nominated), 108
  Death on the Job (nominated), 108
  Doing Time: Life inside the Big House (nominated), 108
  Down and Out in America, 102, 108
  The Eyes of Tammy Faye, 195
  Genocide, 57
  I Am a Promise: The Children of Stanton Elementary School, 108
  Icarus, 156, 177
  An Inconvenient Truth, 177
  Jesus Camp (nominated), 135
  LaLee's Kin: The Legacy of Cotton (nominated), 107–8
  Let's Get Lost (nominated), 95–96
  March of the Penguins, 123
  Mondo Cane (nominated), 21
  Murder on a Sunday Morning, 138
  O.J.: Made in America, 190–91
  One Child Nation (nominated), 168–69
  rule change for nomination qualification, 8, 91, 91n.6, 92, 102, 108–9, 111, 112–13
  The Sky above, the Mud Below, 21n.24
  Soldier in Hiding (nominated), 108
  The Square (nominated), 156, 169–70
  Taxi to the Dark Side, 170–71
  The Times of Harvey Milk, 58–59
  When We Were Kings, 98
  The White Helmets, 156
  Who Killed Vincent Chin?, 69
Achbar, Mark, 96–97
Adair, Peter, 19–20n.19, 39–40, 48, 50, 78–79
adult content in films, 10, 20–22, 31–32, 138
advertising. *See also* marketing
  of independent films, 45, 46
  prohibited on public television, 71
  television, 47–48, 56–57
advocacy, 52–53
A&E, 118, 132, 135–36, 149–50
A&E IndieFilms, 135–36, 168–69, 171
AFI Docs, 129
Agee, 55t
Agenda (*Independents* segment), 81
Aguayo, Angela, 179
AIDS epidemic, 110–11
Air Power, 11–12
AIVF. *See* Association for Independent Video and Filmmakers
Ali, Muhammed, 98
Alive Enterprises, 59
Allen vs. Farrow, 169–70
Alliance Française, 62

All My Babies, 14–15
Alpert, Jon, 104–5, 107–8
Altamont Raceway, 26–27
Altman, Robert, 57, 58
Alvarez Roman, Santiago, 19–20n.19
Amanda Knox, 165–66
Amazon, 168–69, 174, 176–77, 184–85, 191–92
Amazon Prime, 168–69, 192
Amazon Studios, 168–69
Amazon Video Direct, 184–85, 191–92
Amazon Video Direct Festival Stars, 184–85
AMC, 171
America Is Hard to See, 61n.43, 66t
American Documentary, Inc., 83–84
American Documentary, The (original title of *P.O.V.*), 84
American Experience, 103–4
American Factory, 151–54, 183–84, 185, 187
   Academy Award win, 151, 152–53, 156, 177
   financing of, 151–52
American Family, An, 104–5
American Film, 43–44, 79
American Film Institute's Exhibition Services, 50–51
American Independent Cinema (King), 42
American Love Story, An, 139
American Masters, 70–71, 103–4, 161
American Meme, The, 161–62
American Movie, 100
American National Enterprises, 47–48
American Playhouse, 82–83, 85–86
American Splendor, 134
America Today series, 33–34
America Undercover, 102, 103–7, 108, 109, 162, 165
   narrative strategies in, 106–7
   structure and content of, 103
Andersen, Fay, 66t
Andersen, Thom, 66t
Anderson, Carolyn, 109
Anderson, Chris, 117
Anderson, Laurie, 58
Angela: A Portrait of a Revolutionary, 61, 66t

Angelika Film Center, 125
Anthem, 96–97
anthology series, 75, 76, 77–79
Antiques Roadshow, 70–71
Anything You Want to Be, 36–37
Apocalypse Now, 46, 48, 63
Apollo 13, 172n.35
Appalshop, 50–51
Apple TV, 168–69, 172–73
Apted, Michael, 55t, 90, 99, 134–35
Arclight Cinemas, 189–90
Aristocrats, The, 141
Armstrong Lie, The, 171
Army-McCarthy hearings, 17–18
Aronofsky, Darren, 100–1
Aronson-Rath, Raney, 190–91
art houses, 7, 10, 15–16, 20–21
Artisan Entertainment, 99, 100–1
Arts & Entertainment Network, 101–2. See also A&E
Asher, Japhet, 108
Association for Independent Video and Filmmakers (AIVF), 41–42, 50, 53, 72–74, 76, 77, 83, 84, 85–86
   Frontline criticized by, 80–81
   PBS vs., 71, 72, 82
Association of Public Broadcasting Stations of New York, 74
Atlanta DocuFest, 129
Atomic Cafe, The, 7–8, 51–52, 62–63, 66t, 78–79
At the Max, 90
Attica, 34n.62
audiences. See core audience; general audiences; niche audiences
Audio Brandon, 30
Aufderheide, Patricia, 85

Baez, Joan, 24, 27n.42
Bahr, Fax, 66t
Bailey, Fenton, 99n.21
Baillie, Bruce, 33–34
Balio, Tino, 23
Ballot Number 9, 96–97
Balseros, 144–45
Barbato, Randy, 99n.21
Bar-Lev, Amir, 136
Barron, Art, 29

Baseball, 87
Basic Training, 75
Basketball or Nothing, 165
Battered Bastards of Baseball, The, 161–62
Battle of Midway, The, 11n.3
Battle of San Pietro, 162n.16
BBC, 71, 90–91
Beatles, 25–26
Beatles, The: Eight Days a Week, 172–73
Beaver, Christopher, 68–69
Before Stonewall, 55t
Before the Nickelodeon: The Cinema of Edwin S. Porter, 55t
Beineix, Jean-Jacques, 57
"Being Homosexual" (*America Undercover* episode), 103, 106–7
Bell, Otto . 177
Belzberg, Edet, 138
Bennett, William J., 77–78, 80–81
Bergman, Ingmar, 15–16
Berkeley, Busby, 18n.16
Berlin Film Festival, 9–10, 100
Berlinger, Joe, 109–10, 140–41, 146–47, 169–70, 172–73
Berman, Shari Springer, 134
Bernstein, Sara, 172–73
Best Boy, 43–44, 43t
Best Canadian Features prizes, 176–77
Bethune, Lee, 19–20n.19
Beyond the Mat, 99n.21
Biggest Little Farm, The, 3, 177
Big Sky Documentary Film Festival, 129
Billboard, 26, 139–41, 143–44
Bill Cunningham New York, 95, 96–97
Billy Jack, 47–48
binge-watching, 164, 165–66
bin Salman, Mohammed, 192
Biography, 12n.6, 135–36
Bird, Lance, 51–52
Bird, Stewart, 43t, 45, 53, 55t
Birth Film, 66t
Birth without Violence, 66t
Bisbee '17, 183–85
Blackhurst, Rod, 165–66
Black Lives Matter movement, 190
Black Natchez, 19–20n.19, 20
Blackwell, Chris, 59
Blair Witch Project, The, 100–1

Blasetti, Alessandro, 20–21
Blaustein, Barry W., 99n.21
Bleecker Street Cinema, 16, 189–90
Blieden, Michael, 145
Blitz, Jeffrey, 121
Bloch, Yossi, 165–66
Blue Planet, 90
Blue Vinyl, 138
Bognar, Steve, 151–52
Born into Brothels, 116, 144–45, 180–81
Borum Chattoo, Caty, 190, 196
Borzillieri, Trey, 165–66
Bosch, Carles, 144–45
Bowles, Eamonn, 125–26
Bowling for Columbine, 119, 126, 132, 140, 162n.16
  Academy Award win, 116
  impact of, 179
Boxoffice, 25, 28, 53–54, 59–60
Boys Don't Cry, 112
Brakhage, Stan, 18n.16
Brandon, Liane, 36–37
Brandon Teena Story, The, 96–97
Breakthrough Filmmaker Award, 151–52, 152n.1
Brief History of Time, A, 63–64, 90, 99–100
Briski, Zana, 144–45, 180–81
Broadcasting, 80
Broadcasting & Cable, 109
Broderick, Peter, 92–93
Brokaw, Cary, 59
Brookner, Howard, 58
Brooks, Carolyn, 73–74
Broomfield, Nick, 55t
Brother's Keeper, 109–10, 146–47
Brown, Barry Alexander, 43t, 46, 48–49, 54
Brown, Bruce, 24
Brown, James, 98
Brown, Jim, 57
Brown v. Board of Education, 134–35
Bruce, Donald C., 19–20n.19
Buena Vista Social Club, 88–89, 100–1
Bulger, Jay, 161–62
Bullert, B. J., 68–69
Bullfight at Malaga, 13
Burlesque: Heart of the Glitter Tribe, 161–62
Burnett, Carol, 14

Burns, Ken, 86–87, 90, 170
Burstein, Nanette, 134–35
Burroughs, 58
Burroughs, William S., 58, 147
Burstyn Releasing, 20–21
Bush, George W., 126–27
Bus 174, 133–34
Bute, Mary Ellen, 31

cable television, 1–2, 5, 7, 8, 81–82, 90–91, 118
   documentaries used to enter theatrical market, 133–36
   popularity of nonfiction programming on, 86, 101–2
Cabral, Lyric R., 160
Cagle, Chris, 193
Cain, Julian, 76–77
Camden International Film Festival, 129
CameraPlanet, 134–35
campus market, 30–32, 38
Canada, 129
Canadian Broadcasting Corporation, 19
Canal Zone, 75n.11
Canby, Vincent, 19
Canet, Guillaume, 155
Cannes Film Festival, 126–27, 132
Capra, Frank, 11, 11n.3
Capturing the Friedmans, 8, 124–26, 133–34, 145, 157–58
   audience for, 121
   commercial success of, 116
   controversy surrounding, 120–21, 124–25
Cardoso, Patricia, 134
Carmel: Who Killed Maria Marta?, 165–66
Carpenter, John, 43–44
Carrigan, Ana, 77–78
Cary, Donick, 161–62
Casino Jack and the United States of Money, 171
Cassavetes, John, 46
Cavalcanti, Alberto, 14–15
Cavara, Paolo, 20–21
CBS, 13–14, 104–5
CBS News, 1–2, 13
celebrity profile documentaries, 159–62, 165, 168–69, 171, 172–73, 186

Celluloid Closet, The, 66t, 100, 109
censorship, 22, 126–27
Center for Media and Social Impact, 187
Chai, Anna, 165
Chaiklin, Rebecca, 165
Chair, The, 17–18
Changing World, 73–74
character documentaries, 159–60, 165, 168–69, 186
Chariots of the Gods, 47–48
Charlie Rose, 125–26
Chase, Barry, 79
Chasing Coral, 188–89
Chastain, Jessica, 195
Chavez, Cesar, 9–10
Cheer, 165
Chelsea Girls, The, 33
Chester, John, 177
Chicago Media Project, 183
Chicken & Egg Pictures, 151–52
Chicken Ranch, 55t
Children Underground, 138
Chomsky, Noam, 96–97
Chopra, Joyce, 14
Choy, Christine, 69, 104–5
Chris Marker, 61–62
Christian audiences, 124
Churchill, Winston, 23
Cinda Firestone, 34n.62
Cinderella Man, 172n.35
Cinderella Season, A: The Lady Vols Fight Back, 107–8
cine-clubs, 16
Cinecom, 56–57, 58–59
Cinedigm, 156–57
Cinema du Reel, 129
Cinema V, 24, 26–27, 53–54, 56, 60
Cinema Guild, 156–57, 175, 176–77
Cinema of Errol Morris, The (Resha), 4–5
Cinema of Outsiders (Levy), 42
Cinema 16, 14–16, 31
cinema-television tension, 2, 8, 37–38, 88–89, 101–2, 190–91
cinéma vérité, 129–30
Cinemax, 133
CineReach, 149
Cinetrees, 34
Citizenfour, 177, 179, 182

Citizen Jack, 182
Citizen K, 168–69, 171
Civil War, The, 86–87
Clark, Malcolm, 106–7
Clarke, Shirley, 16, 32, 33–34, 66t
classics divisions. *See* studio classics divisions
Clinton, Bill, 99–100
clip shows, 11–14
Close Up!, 13–14
Clusiau, Christina, 165
CMP. *See* Community, Media, Philanthropy
CNN Films, 171
Coffin, Andrew, 124
Cogan, Dan, 181, 183
Cohen, Howard, 145, 146
Cohen, Julie, 177
Cohen, Maxi, 43–44, 43t, 53
Cohen, Steve, 183
collectives, 10–11, 34–37, 38, 45–46, 75–76
Collins, Judy, 27n.42
Columbia, 23, 41–42, 94–95
Columbia Records, 26, 59–60
Columbia TriStar Home Entertainment, 140, 141
Come Back to the Five and Dime, Jimmy Dean, Jimmy Dean, 58
Coming Home, 48
Coming Out under Fire, 96–97
Comiskey, Andrea, 30
commercialization, 2, 3, 151–52, 187, 190, 196
  downsides of, 191–93
  explaining, 4–8
  private investment and, 179–80
  upsides of, 193
Common Threads: Stories from the Quilt, 109
Community, Media, Philanthropy (CMP), 183, 184–85
Concordia Studio, 183, 184–85
conglomerated niche strategy, 155–56, 159
Conor McGregor: Notorious, 161
conservative Christian audiences, 124
Conte, Felice, 107–8
Continental, 15–16

controversy
  in docbuster era, 120–21, 124–25, 126–27
  fear of, 70, 73–74, 77
  freedom from, 80–81
Conversations with a Killer: The Ted Bundy Tapes, 169–70
Cooper, Kevin, 51–52
Coppola, Eleanor, 63, 66t
Coppola, Francis Ford, 63
core audience, 92–94, 95, 96, 98
core tensions, 2–3
coronavirus pandemic, 188–90
Corporation, The, 95, 96–97, 116
Corporation for Public Broadcasting (CPB), 75, 77–78, 80, 85
Costa, Petra, 160
CounterPunch, 161–62
Cove, The, 177
CPB. *See* Corporation for Public Broadcasting
CPH: Dox, 129
Crack USA: County under Siege, 108
Crime Scene: The Vanishing at the Cecil Hotel, 169–70, 172–73
Crip Camp, 160
Crisis: Behind a Presidential Commitment, 17–18
Crisis to Crisis, 77–78, 80, 83
Criterion Channel, 176–77
Cronenberg, David, 43–44
crowdfunding, 195
Crowther, Bosley, 22
Crumb, 62–63, 66t, 88–89, 100
Crumb, Robert, 63
Cuarón, Alfonso, 192
Cuba: Battle of the Ten Million, 66t
customization, mass. *See* mass customization

D. Wade: Life Unexpected, 172–73
Dark Circle, 68–69
Dark Glow of the Mountains, 61, 66t
DAS, 98
Daughter from Danang, 143
David, 18
David Holtzman's Diary, 18, 66t
Da Vinci Code, The, 172n.35
Davis, Bruce, 90

Davis, Damon, 160
Davis, David, 83
Davis, Kate, 138
Davis, Leslye, 160
Day, James, 80–81
Day My God Died, The, 180–81
Dead of Night, 14–15
de Antonio, Emile, 16, 17–18, 34, 61n.43, 66t
Death on the Job, 108
Deer Hunter, The, 46
DeGooyer, Paul, 139–40
DeLeo, Maryann, 104–5, 107–8
de Lestrade, Jean-Xavier, 138
Demetrakas, Johanna, 160
Demme, Jonathan, 58
Demos, Moira, 163–64
Denmark, 129
Department of Justice, 14–15
de Rochemont, Louis, 14–15
de Valck, Marijke, 128, 130
Devil Next Door, The, 165–66
DiBitetto, Robert, 135–36
Dick, Kirby, 144–45, 169–70
Dick Johnson Is Dead, 160
Dickson, Deborah, 107–8
Dinner for Five, 143
Direct Cinema, 7, 9–38, 78–79
　feature documentaries and film culture, 14–20
　film industry reactions and predictions, 28–29
　fragmentary market for films, 10–14
　growing appreciation for, 16–18
　nontheatrical market for, 30–37, 38
　on television, 11–14, 18
　in theaters, 20–29
direct distribution, 147–48
Directing Award for U.S. Documentary, 152
Disclosure, 160
Discovery Channel, 65, 86, 101–2, 111–12, 118, 132, 134–35, 136, 149–50
Discovery Communications, 101–2
Discovery Docs, 134–35, 136
Disney, 94–95
Disney Decade, 94–95
Disney/Miramax, 126

Dis/Patches (*Independents* segment), 81
Dissident, The, 192–93
distribution. *See also* collectives; self-distribution
　direct, 147–48
　experiments in, 32–37
　in the internet age, 146–48
　Netflix's role, 142–46
distribution companies. *See also individual companies*
　in docbuster era, 120
　independent films and, 40–41, 52–60
　streaming video and, 173–77
Diva, 57
Diverse Voices in Docs, 168–69
docbuster era, 8, 116–50
　box office success and beyond, 148–50
　cable television in, 118, 133–36
　DVDs in, 118, 136–42, 148–49
　film festivals in, 117–18, 128–32
　theatrical release in, 118–27
Doclisboa, 129
Doc Shop, 131
Documentary (magazine), 139
Documentary Film Program, 130
Documentary Now!, 9–10
Documentary Producers Alliance, 193–94
Documentary's Expanded Fields: New Media and the Twenty-First-Century Documentary (Kim), 193
Docurama, 137–38, 139, 140, 141–42, 143–44, 145–46, 149–50
Doerfer, John, 11–12
Doerfer Plan, 11–12
Dogtown and Z-Boys, 162n.16
Doing Time: Life inside the Big House, 108
Domènech, Josep Maria, 144–45
Dong, Arthur, 96–97
Donovan, 24
Don't F**k with Cats: Hunting an Internet Killer, 165–66
Dont Look Back, 7, 10–11, 24, 25–26, 27, 28–29, 59–60, 138–39, 146–47
Doob, Nick, 139
Dope Sick Love, 107–8
Dore, Kathleen, 112–13
Down and Out in America, 102, 108

DOXA Documentary Film Festival, 129, 176–77
Drew, Robert, 7, 10, 13–14, 16–17, 18, 71, 78–79, 92
Drew Associates, 12–14, 17–18, 80, 103–4
Dreyfous, Geralyn, 181
DuLuart, Yolande, 66t
DuVernay, Ava, 158
DVDs, 8, 96–97, 148–49, 178
  house party model and, 147
  Netflix delivery of, 142–46, 154–56, 157–58
  as new ancillary market, 136–42
  prominance in documentary market, 118
Dylan, Bob, 24, 25–26, 27n.42, 138–39, 147
DysFunkTional Family, 116

Eadweard Muybridge, Zoopraxographer, 61, 66t
Eagle Huntress, The., 177
Ed Sullivan Show, 13
Einhorn, Catrin, 160
Eisenstein, Sergei, 14–15
Elephant, 134
El Norte, 58
Embassy Pictures, 15–16, 20–21
Emmy Awards, 110
Empire of the Air, 87, 90
Endeavor Content, 174
Endless Summer, The, 7, 24, 25
Energy and How to Get It, 78–79
Enron: The Smartest Guys in the Room, 162n.16, 171
Epstein, Jean, 18n.16
Epstein, Robert, 58–59, 66t, 91, 100, 104–5, 109
ESPN, 161, 165, 167–68
ESPN Films, 167–68, 190–91
Essene, 75n.11
Être et avoir (To Be and To Have), 116
European Nights, 20–21
Evergreen, 31
Every Seventh Child, 19–20n.19
Evil Genius: The True Story of America's Most Diabolical Bank Heist, 165–66
Ewing, Heidi, 160

Exit through the Gift Shop, 162n.16
exploitation films, 47–48, 55–56
Eyes of Tammy Faye, The, 99n.21, 195

Faces of November, 18
FACETS, 61–62, 189–90
Fahrenheit 9/11, 8, 99n.21, 119, 121, 126–27, 132
  commercial success of, 116
  controversy surrounding, 120–21, 124–25
  subject of, 126
family films, 47–48
family sector, 120
Fanning, David, 80, 83
Far from Vietnam, 66t
Farm, The: Angola USA, 169–70
Fassbinder, Rainer Werner, 57, 60
Fast, Cheap, and out of Control, 63–64, 100
Father Soldier Son, 160
feature documentaries, 131–32
  Direct Cinema and, 14–20
  increase in, 113–14
Feder, Sam, 160
Federal Communications Commission, 11–12
Fellowship Adventure Group, 126
feminist documentaries, 36–37
Feminists: What Were They Thinking?, 160
Ferguson, Charles, 144–45
Festival, 26–27
Field, Connie, 55t
Field of Vision, 193
"Film and Reality," 14–15
filmanthropy, 178–79
film culture, 14–20
Film Culture, 16, 17
film festivals, 7, 8, 117–18, 178. *See also individual festivals*
  Direct Cinema and, 16–18
  number of worldwide, 128–29
  as quasi-industrial players, 128–32
Film Forum, 40–41, 51–52, 88–90, 110, 121, 127, 146–47
Film Is Not Yet Rated, The, 144–45
Filmmaker Magazine, 118–19, 125–26
filmmakers, streaming video and, 169–73
Film-Makers' Cinematheque, 33–34

Film-Makers' Cooperative, 16–17, 32–33
Filmmakers' Distribution Center, 32–34, 54
Film News Now Foundation, 69
Film Society of Lincoln Center, 149
Films of the World, 15–16
Fincher, David, 192
Finding Vivian Maier, 160
Fine Line Features, 36–37, 56–57, 94–95, 99
Finest Hours, The, 23
Finnegan's Wake, 31
Fiore, Robert, 33–34
First Amendment Project, The, 139
First Run Features, 40–41, 53–56, 95–96
First Statement of the New American Cinema, 16–17
Fisher, Morgan, 66t
Fitzgerald, Gavin, 161
Five Came Back, 162n.16
Flaherty, Robert, 13, 14–15
Florentine Films / American Documentaries, 87
Floyd, George, 190
Focus Features, 94–95, 185
Fogel, Bryan, 156, 192–93
Fog of War, The, 116
Folayan, Sabaah, 160
Follows, Stephen, 128–29
Food, Inc., 177
Ford, John, 11, 11n.3
Ford, Yance, 165–66
Ford Foundation, 75, 78, 83
foreign films, 20–22, 23, 58
  adult content in, 20–22
  campus market for, 30, 31
  increased market for, 14, 15–16
  scarcity of, 20–21, 22
Foreman, George, 98
Forensic Files, 166
Forum, 21
Four Days in November, 23
4 Little Girls, 110
four-quadrant films, 123–24, 123n.13
Fourth Estate, The, 169–70
four-walling, 24, 39–40, 47–48, 146
Fox, 41–42
Fox, Beryl, 19–20n.19

Fox Searchlight, 93–95
Fox vs. Franken, 139
France, 129
France, David, 188–89
Frank, Robert, 78–79
Freed, Arthur, 18n.16
Freedman, Lewis, 77–78
Freedom to Love, 31–32
Freeman, Morgan, 122
Free Solo, 1–2
Friedman, Jeffrey, 66t, 109
Friedman, Peter, 96–97
Froemke, Susan, 107–8
From Mao to Mozart: Isaac Stern in China, 57
From Networks to Netflix: A Guide to Changing Channels (Johnson), 6
Frontier, 76, 81
Frontline, 80–81, 103–4, 190–91
Fruchter, Norman, 33–34
Fugees, 98
Full Frame Documentary Film Festival, 129
Fuyao, 151
FX, 188
Fyre: The Greatest Party That Never Happened, 161–62

Gabel, Shainee, 96–97
Gaisseau, Pierre-Dominique, 20–21
Gallery of Modern Art, 18
Game, The, 31
Garbus, Liz, 161, 169–70, 188–89
Garvin, Tracey, 139–40
Gast, Leon, 88–89
gatekeeping, 117–18, 148–49
Gates of Heaven, 63–64, 66t
Gaumont, 41–42
Geist, Libby, 167–68
general audiences, 92–94, 95, 98, 100, 118–19, 121, 123
General Motors, 40, 151
"genius" grant (MacArthur Foundation), 75
Genocide, 57
Georg, 18
Gerstman, Nancy, 95–97
Gessner, Peter, 33–34

Get Rollin, 43t
"Getting Even: When Victims Fight Back" (*America Undercover* episode), 103
Gibney, Alex, 161, 168–69, 170–73, 182, 193–94
Gide, Andre, 14–15
Gilbert, Peter, 134–35
Gimme Shelter, 26–27, 60n.42
Girlfight, 112
Girlhood, 169–70
Glass, Philip, 59–60
Gleaners and I, The, 95, 96–97
Glucksman, Mary, 118–19
Godard, Jean-Luc, 57
Going Clear: Scientology and the Prison of Belief, 171
Gold, Daniel B., 138
Gold, Joel, 43–44, 43t
golden age of documentary, 1–2
Goode, Eric, 165
Gordon, Shep, 59
Grady, Rachel, 160
Gramercy, 94–95, 98, 99
Grand Jury Prize (Sundance), 68–69, 89, 168–69
Grant, Lee, 102, 108
grants, 153, 177–78. *See also* rich uncle / grant pictures
Grasshopper Films, 176–77, 184–85, 192
Gray, Spaulding, 58, 112
Gray's Anatomy, 112
Grazer, Brian, 172–73
great-man history, 23–24, 38
Greeley, Bill, 29
Green Book, 182n.57
Greene, Robert, 183–85
Greenfield, Lauren, 177
Greenfield-Sanders, Timothy, 190
Greenwald, Robert, 147–48
Greenwich Entertainment, 168–69, 189–90
Grey Gardens, 46
Grierson, John, 14–15
Grizzly Man, 99n.21, 134–35, 162n.16
Grove Press, 31–32, 33–34, 49, 75
Growing Up Female, 36, 147
Guggenheim, Davis, 161, 165, 177, 183
Guns of August, The, 23

Guttentag, Bill, 108

Hahn, Kristin, 96–97
Halleck, Dee Dee, 76
Handcarved, 50–51
Hanson, John, 43–44, 43t, 53
Happy Mother's Day, 14, 18
Happy Valley, 136
Hard Day's Night, A, 25–26
Harder, William, 190, 196
Harlan County USA, 60n.42
Harron, Mary, 134
Hartmann, Alejandro, 165–66
Hart-Williams, Nick, 83
Have a Good Trip: Adventures in Psychedelics, 161–62
Havens, Tim, 142
Hawking, Stephen, 64, 99–100
Hawkins, Linda, 182
Haynes, Todd, 95–96
HBO, 8, 88, 90–91, 112–13, 114–15, 137, 145, 149–50
  in docbuster era, 118, 119, 121, 125, 127, 136
  Netflix compared with, 142–43, 162, 165
  Netflix partnership with, 144–45
  partnerships with theatrical distributors, 133–34
  streaming video and, 160, 161, 167–70, 174
HBO Documentary, 1–2, 101–12, 172–73
  characteristics of documentaries on, 105–7
  documentaries as original programming on, 102–5
  producing for, 107–8
  shift in emphasis from television to film, 108–11
HBO Films, 134
HBO Max, 191
HBO Theatrical Films Releasing, 109
HBO Video, 140
HDNet, 132
Healthy Baby Girl, A, 85
Hearts of Darkness: A Filmmaker's Apocalypse, 62–63, 66t, 90, 99
Hegedus, Chris, 100–1, 134–35, 139

Heinemann, Matthew, 188–89
Helfand, Judith, 138
He Named Me Malala, 161, 182
Hendrickson, Kim, 138–39
Herzog, Werner, 66t, 99n.21, 112, 134–35
Hester Street, 46
HGTV, 111–12
Hickenlooper, George, 66t
High Ground, 152
High on Crack Street: Lives Lost in Lowell, 107–8
High School, 75
Hill, Gary Leon, 78–79
Hillbilly Elegy, 172–73
Hollywood: The Fabulous Era, 12n.6
Hollywood: The Golden Years, 12n.6
Hollywood: The Great Stars, 12n.6
Holy Ghost People, The, 19–20n.19
Home for Life, 19–20n.19
Home of the Brave, 58
home video, 5, 7. *See also* DVDs; streaming video
　independent films and, 41–42
　as new ancillary market, 136–42
Hoop Dreams, 36–37, 88–89, 99, 162n.16
Hooper, Tobe, 43–44
Horeck, Tanya, 165–66
Horsburgh, Tim, 149
Horvath, Imre, 104–5
Hospital, 75
Hot Docs Film Festival, 129, 131, 176–77
Hot Docs Forum, 131
Hot Springs Documentary Festival, 129
House of Cards, 156
house party model, 147–48
House Subcommittee on Telecommunications and Finance, 82
Howard, Ron, 172–73
Hu, Marcus, 175–76
Hulu, 165, 172–73, 174, 192
Hulu Documentary Films, 172–73
Humphrey, Hubert, 13
Hunting Ground, The, 169–70, 180–81
Hurricane Katrina, 110

I Am a Promise: The Children of Stanton Elementary School, 99n.20, 108
I Am Curious (Yellow), 31–32
I Am Not Your Negro, 160, 190
I Am What My Films Are: A Portrait of Werner Herzog, 61, 66t
Icarus, 156, 177, 192
Icarus, Edge of Democracy, 160
Icarus Films, 175, 176
IDFA (International Documentary Filmfestival Amsterdam), 129
IFC. *See* Independent Film Channel
IFC Films, 111–12, 119, 140–41, 174
IFC Productions, 111–12, 114–15
If God Is Willing and da Creek Don't Rise, 110
IFP. *See* Independent Feature Project
I'll Be Gone in the Dark, 169–70
Image Union, 76
Imagine Entertainment, 170, 172–73
Immigration Nation, 165
Impact Films, 34
Impact Partners, 153–54, 171, 177, 179–81, 182, 183–85, 186–87
Inconvenient Truth, An, 119, 162n.16, 177, 179, 182, 183
Independent, The, 50, 51–52, 57–58, 71, 72, 74, 76–78
Independent Documentary Fund (of TV Lab), 77, 78, 83
Independent Feature Project (IFP), 50–51, 53
Independent Film Channel (IFC), 111–13, 114–15, 126–27, 143, 144–45, 154
Independent Filmmaker Project, 41–42
independent films, 39–67
　convincing exhibitors to play documentaries, 44–47
　explosion of and documentary success, 65–67
　growth of movement, 16–17
　increased competition in, 92
　indie TV, 111–13
　marketing documentaries, 47–50
　Netflix and, 144
　new institutions supporting documentaries, 50–53
　public television and, 68–87 (*see also* public television)
　specialty labels and (*see* specialty labels)
　underexplored documentaries, 41–44

Independent Lens, 85–86, 160, 194
Independents, The, 81–82, 83–84
Independent Television Service (ITVS), 7–8, 75, 149, 168–69, 194
  importance to airing of independent films, 70
  path to, 85
Indie Caucus / PBS Needs Indies, 194
"Indie Filmmakers Go Commercial" (Klain), 42–43, 43t
indie films, 7–8
Indiegogo, 195
indie TV, 111–13
Indie Wire, 154
indiewood, 94–95
Insdorf, Annette, 43–44
In Search of Noah's Ark, 47n.16
Inside Bill's Brain, 165
intellectual property, 195
International Documentary Filmfestival Amsterdam (IDFA), 129
internet, distribution and, 146–48
In the Year of the Pig, 34, 61n.43, 66t
Into Great Silence, 95
investigative journalism, 11–14
Invisible War, The, 169–70, 180–81
Irving, Judy, 68–69
Island/Alive, 56, 59–60
Island Alive Releasing, 62–63
Island Pictures, 59
Island Records, 59–60
It Happens to Us, 36–37
iTunes, 176–77
ITVS. *See* Independent Television Service
Ivory, James, 58
Iwashina, Kevin, 174

Jacopetti, Gualtiero, 20–21
Jacquet, Luc, 122
Jaeckle, Jeff, 4–5
James, Steve, 36–37, 88–89, 195
Japan Society, 62
Jarecki, Eugene, 125–26, 170–71
Jarmusch, Jim, 99
Jaws, 47–48
Jazz on a Summer's Day, 61n.43, 66t
Jefferson Airplane, 27
Jenkins, Barry, 195

Jesus Camp, 135
Jigsaw Productions, 170, 171–72, 173, 193–94
Jim Brown: All American, 110
Jimi Hendrix Experience, 27
Jobs, Laurene Powell, 183
Jobs, Steve, 161, 183
Joe and Maxi, 43–44, 43t, 53
"John Birch Society" (*Regional Report* episode), 73–74
John D. and Catherine T. MacArthur Foundation. *See* MacArthur Foundation
John Lewis: Good Trouble, 182
John S. and James L. Knight Foundation, 190
Johnson, Catherine, 159
Johnson, Derek, 6
Johnson, Kirsten, 160
Johnson, Tom, 51–52
journalism
  expectations of, 77–79, 85–86
  investigative, 11–14
  move away from, 84
Juvenile Court, 75n.11

Kanopy, 187
Kartemquin Films, 36–37, 77, 149, 168–69
Kauffman, Ross, 144–45, 180–81
Kaye, Stanley, 18
Kennedy, John F., 13, 18, 23
Kenner, Robert . 177
Kepley, Vance, 11–12
Kernochang, Sarah, 60n.42
Keshishian, Alek, 88
Keusch, Erwin, 66t
Key Picture, 13
Khashoggi, Jamal, 192
Kickstarter, 195
Kim, Jihoon, 193
King, Allan, 19–20n.19, 28–29
King, B. B., 98
King, Diana, 98
King, Geoff, 42
King, Jonathan, 183
King, Martin Luther, 158
Kipnis, Jill, 140
Kips Bay Theater, 24, 27

Kirby, William, 83–84
Kirchheimer, Manfred, 55t
Kirsanoff, Dimitri, 18n.16
Klain, Stephen, 42–43, 43t
Kleckner, Susan, 66t
Klein, Jim, 36–37
Knight, Julia, 6
Knight Foundation, 190
Knock Down the House, 1–2, 174, 188–89
Knowlton, Linda Goldstein, 182
Koch Entertainment Distribution, 140
Koch Lorber Films, 140
Koko: A Talking Gorilla, 61, 66t
Kopple, Barbara, 60n.42, 134–35
Koyaanisqatsi, 59, 62–63, 66t, 78–79
KQED, 68–69
Kreul, James, 16, 32–33
Krivoshey, Ryan, 175, 176–77
Kroot, Jennifer M., 161
KTCA, 81–82
KTQ Internship, 168–69
KTQ Labs, 168–69
Kusama, Karyn, 112
Kwit, Nathaniel, 56–57

labor conditions, 193–94
Laemmle, Greg, 123–24
Laemmle Theaters, 123–24, 189–90
LaLee's Kin: The Legacy of Cotton, 107–8
Landy, Ruth, 68–69
Lanzmann, Claude, 66t
Lasorsa, Matt, 143–44
Last Chance U, 165
Last Metro, The, 57
Last Truck, The: Closing of a GM Plant, 151
Latin Kings: A Street Gang Story, 107–8
Laughlin, Tom, 47–48
Law and Order, 75
Lay My Burden Down, 19–20n.19
Leacock, Richard, 13, 14, 17, 18, 25, 92, 146–47
Leacock-Pennebaker, 25, 26, 27, 59–60
Learning Channel, 81–82, 83–84, 101–2
Lears, Rachel, 174
Leary, Timothy, 59
Leboyer, Frederick, 66t
Lebrecht, James, 160
Lee, Spike, 92, 102, 110

Legend of Cocaine Island, The, 161–62
Leipzig, Adam, 123
Leiterman, Doug, 29
Leopard Son, The, 134–35
Lerner, Murray, 26–27, 57
LeRoy, Mervyn, 18n.16
Lester, Richard, 25–26
Let's Get Lost, 95–96
Letter from Siberia, 61, 66t
Let the Fire Burn, 160
Letting Go: A Hospice Journey, 107–8
Levine, Andrew, 180–81
Levy, Emanuel, 42
Lewis, Fulton, III, 19–20n.19
Lewis, Mark, 165–66
Lianna, 57
Liar Liar, 172n.35
Libra Films, 62–63
libraries (film), 137, 138–39, 144, 145, 155, 159, 191
licensing, 97, 111–12, 136–37, 175–76, 178
 Netflix and, 155–58, 159, 161, 163, 167, 173, 186
 public television and, 70–71, 76–77, 83–84, 85–86
Liddy, G. Gordon, 59
Life (magazine), 13–14
Life and Times of Grizzly Adams, The, 47–48
Life and Times of Rosie the Riveter, The, 55t
Lifetime, 101–2
Lilyhammer, 156
Lin, Justin, 195
Linfield, Susan, 51–52
Lionsgate, 99, 112, 119, 126–27, 134–35
Lipscomb, James, 18
Little Carnegie, 21
Little Three, 23, 38
Litvak, Anatole, 11n.3
Liu, Bing, 168–69
Living Camera, The, 18
Livingston, Jennie, 88–89, 90
Living Undocumented, 165
Loader, Jayne, 66t
local stations (public television), 70–71, 73, 75–77, 85–86
London International Doc Fest, 129
Lonely Boy, 18

Long Tail, The: Why the Future of Business Is Selling Less of More, 117
Look of Silence, The, 182
Lopez, Norberto, 34n.62
Lorber, Kino, 156–57, 191–92
Lorber Media, 140
Lorentz, Pare, 14–15
Los Angeles, 39–40
Los Angeles Plays Itself, 162n.16
Los Angeles Times, 1–2
Lotz, Amanda, 159, 167
Love, Theo, 161–62
Lowenthal, John, 43*t*
Lowry, Rich, 124
Loxton, David, 78

MacArthur Foundation, 75, 81, 83–84, 149
MacDonald, Heather Lyn, 96–97
Machover, Robert, 33–34
MacQueen, Angus, 165
Mad Hot Ballroom, 121–22
Madonna: Truth or Dare, 88, 90
Magnolia Pictures, 119, 125–26, 133–34, 135, 144–45, 149–50, 154, 171, 174, 182, 189–90
Making a Murderer, 163–64, 165–66
Malcolm X, 19–20n.19, 20
Maloof, John, 160
Mamas and the Papas, 27
Mannheim Film Festival, 9–10
Manning, Jon, 161–62
Manoeuvre, 75n.11
Manufacturing Consent, 95, 96–97
Maradona in Mexico, 165
March of the Penguins, 8, 119, 121–25
March of Time, The, 11, 13
Marcus, Bert, 161–62
Mariposa Film Group, 39–40, 43*t*, 47, 49–50, 66*t*
Marjoe, 60n.42
Marker, Chris, 66*t*
marketing. *See also* advertising
  of independent films, 47–50
  niche, 121–22, 145
Mass, 33–34
mass customization, 159, 186
Mass for the Dakota Sioux, 33–34
Matewan, 58

Matsushita, 94–95
Matters of Life and Death, 78–79, 83
Maurice, 58
Mayoux, Valérie, 66*t*
Maysles, Albert, 9–10, 13, 14, 17, 26–27, 46, 60n.42, 107–8
Maysles, David, 9–10, 13, 14, 26–27, 46
Maysles Film, 107–8
MCA Universal, 94–95
McBride, James, 18, 66*t*
McElwee, Ross, 55*t*
McGraw Hill / Pathe Contemporary, 34
McGregor, Conor, 161
McKnight, Bryan, 98
McNamara, Michelle, 169–70
Meat, 75n.11
Media Study / Buffalo, 81
Medved, Michael, 124
meetUp.com, 147
Mekas, Jonas, 17, 18, 32, 33–34
Memphis Belle, 11n.3, 162n.16
Men with Guns, 112
Mercury Records, 98
Mercury 13, 160
Metallica: Some Kind of Monster, 140–41
Metelus, Bob, 172–73
Meyers, Sidney, 14–15
MGM Home Entertainment, 140
MGM/UA, 116, 119
Milk, Harvey, 58–59
Miller, Jonathan, 176
Millhouse: A White Comedy, 61, 66*t*
Mills of the Gods, 19–20n.19
Minding the Gap, 168–69
Miramax, 64, 89–90, 93–95, 100, 108
Miss Americana, 3, 161
Mission Blue, 160
Mitchell, J. Terrance, 43*t*
Model, 75n.11
MoMA's documentary fortnight, 129
Mondo Cane, 7, 21–22, 24, 55–56, 120–21
  Academy Award nomination, 21
  adult themes in, 10, 21–22, 31–32
Monterey Pop, 14, 26–28
Moore, Michael, 39, 40, 88, 99n.21, 116, 120, 126–27, 179
"More" (song), 21
Morfoot, Abbie, 180

Morris, Errol, 63–64, 66t, 99–100, 99n.21, 112, 161, 169–70, 182
MoveOn.org, 147
Moving the Mountain, 99
Mr. Death: The Rise and Fall of Fred A. Leuchter, Jr., 99n.21, 112
Mr. Dynamite: The Rise of James Brown, 171
Ms. Magazine, 103
MTV, 98
Mubi, 176–77
"Murder: No Apparent Motive" (*America Undercover* episode), 103, 106
Murderball, 141
Murder on a Sunday Morning, 138
Murray, Susan, 162
music documentaries, 7, 10, 26–27, 56, 57, 65–67, 139–40, 161
Muska, Susan, 96–97
Musser, Charles, 55t
My Architect, 116, 133–34
My Best Fiend, 112
My Kid Could Paint That, 135, 136
Myrick, Daniel, 100–1

NAACP Image Awards, 110
Napalm, 19–20n.19
National Educational Television (NET), 19, 73–74
National Endowment for the Arts, 50–51, 78
National Endowment for the Humanities (NEH), 77–78, 80–81
National Film Registry of the Library of Congress, 9–10
National Geographic Feature Films, 122–23
National Geographic Society, 122, 171
National Review, 124
National Talent Service (NTS), 9–10, 31, 49
Nava, Gregory, 58
NBC, 13, 107–8
NEH. *See* National Endowment for the Humanities
NEON, 174, 189–90
neorealist films, 15–16
NET. *See* National Educational Television

Netflix, 1–2, 6–7, 8, 137–38, 146, 149–50, 152–77, 186, 191–93
 during coronavirus pandemic, 188–89
 distributor function, 142–46
 documentaries added to streaming (2014-2020), 164t
 DVD delivery, 142–46, 154–56, 157–58
 expansion of original content and exclusivity, 163–67
 switch to streaming and original content, 154–59
 types of documentaries on, 159–62, 186
Netflix First, 143–44
Netflix Originals, 156–57, 159–60, 163, 165–66, 169–70, 174, 185, 186
Netflix's Watch Instantly, 154–55
Netherlands, 129
Neuman, David, 19–20n.19
Neuwirth, Bob, 138–39
Neville, Morgan, 177, 181
Nevins, Sheila, 1–2, 104–5, 110–11, 133–34
New American Cinema, 16–18
New American Cinema: A Showcase of Premiere Films, 50–51
Newark Community Union Project, 33–34
New Cinema Playhouse, 33–34
New Day Films, 36–37, 153
New Directions / New Films, 69
New Horizons, 23
New Line Cinema, 94–95
New Line Home Entertainment, 143–44
Newman, Michael, 44–45
Newmarket Films, 134
Newnham, Nicole, 160
Newport Folk Music Festival, 26–27
Newsreel, 33–37, 34n.61, 37n.69
Newsreel: Report from Milbrook, 33–34
newsreels, 10, 11
New Video, 156–57
New Wave films, 15–16
New York City, 9–10, 21, 27, 39–40, 46, 51–52, 125
New Yorker Films, 17–18, 39–40, 53–54, 56, 112, 119, 133–34
 case study, 60–65
 contracts for documentary films, 66t
New Yorker Theater, 16, 17–18

New York Film Festival (NYFF), 16, 17–18, 19, 33–34, 129–30
   The Celluloid Closet, 100, 109
   Dark Circle, 68–69
   Titicut Follies, 75
New York State Electronic Media Organization, 74
New York Times, 19, 20, 106, 125–26, 169–70, 188
niche audiences, 118–19, 121, 123, 159
niche marketing, 121–22, 145
Nichols, Bill, 35
Nierenberg, George, 57–58
Nilsson, Rob, 43–44, 43t, 53
Nixon, Robert, 160
No, Lincoln, 182n.57
No End in Sight, 144–45
"nonfiction television," 102–3
Non-fiction TV, 77, 78, 80
nonprofit organizations, 2–3, 7, 50–53
nontheatrical market
   for Direct Cinema, 30–37, 38
   for independent films, 49–50
   New Yorker Films and, 60–61, 62–63, 64–65
   for small distributors, 176–77
Northern Lights, 43t, 50, 53
The Notorious Bettie Page, 134
Noujaim, Jehane, 156, 169–70
Nova, 70–71, 73
Now, 19–20n.19, 20
Now Do You See How We Play?, 33–34
NPR, 1–2
NTS. *See* National Talent Service
Nunez, Victor, 43–44
Nutty Professor, The, 172n.35
NXIVM cult, 169–70
NYFF. *See* New York Film Festival

Obama, Barack, 152, 153
Obama, Michelle, 152, 153
observational documentaries, 11–14
Ocasio-Cortez, Alexandria, 1–2
Ochs, Jacki, 55t
O Cinema, 190
October Films, 94–95, 99
O'Grady, Gerry, 81
O.J.: Made in America, 190–91

Olafsdottir, Greta, 96–97
One Child Nation, 168–69
"One Man's Fight for Life" (*America Undercover* episode), 103
One of Us, 160
One Year in a Life of Crime, 107–8
online shopping, 140
On the Pole, 13–14
Open Society Foundation, 130
Open Solicitation of the Corporation for Public Broadcasting, 72–73
Ophuls, Marcel, 60n.42
Oppenheimer, Joshua, 182
Oprah, 121–22
"Ordinary People, European-Style" (Insdorf), 43–44
Orion, 41–42
Orion Classics, 41–42
Orson Welles Theater, 46, 48–49
Ortner, Sherri, 179
Oscilloscope Laboratories, 192
Osder, Jason, 160
Outfoxed: Rupert Murdoch's War on Journalism, 147
output deals. *See* pay-one deals
OVID.tv, 192
Ozu, Yasujiro, 60

P&A, 48, 53–54
Painleve, Jean, 14–15
Painters Painting, 61n.43
Palme d'Or, 126–27
Paradise Lost: The Child Murders at Robin Hood Hills, 109–10, 146–47, 166, 169–70
Paramount Classics / Vintage, 94–95, 119
Paramount Home Entertainment, 140–41
Paris Is Burning, 8, 88–91, 162n.16
Paris Was a Woman, 96–97
Participant Media, 151–54, 177, 179–80, 182, 183–84, 185, 186–87
Passion, 57
Pathe-Contemporary, 31, 49
Pavarotti, 172–73
pay-one deals (output deals), 156–57, 174–75
PBS. *See* Public Broadcasting Service
Peabody Awards, 69, 103, 110

Peacock, 191
Peck, Raoul, 160
Pennebaker, D. A., 13, 14, 17, 25, 28, 92, 99–100, 134–35, 138–39, 146–47
Pepe, Stefan, 140
Peppercorn-Wormser, 26–27
Perren, Alisa, 137
personal memoir documentaries, 85
Peter, Paul & Mary, 27n.42
Pfeiffer, Carolyn, 59
Pi, 100–1
Pierce, Kimberly, 112
Pincus, Ed, 19–20n.19
Place Called Chiapas, A, 96–97
Poetic License, 139
Point of Order, 17–18, 34
Poison, 95–96
Poitras, Laura, 177
political documentaries, 4–5, 7–8, 10–11, 65–67, 75–76, 96–97, 171
 distribution experiments, 34–37
 Netflix and, 159–60, 165, 186
 streaming services and, 168–69
PolyGram, 94–95, 98
Porn Star: The Legend of Ron Jeremy, 138
Porter, Dawn, 182
Portrait of Jason, 33–34, 61n.43
Portugal, 129
Potter, Bridget, 105–6
P.O.V., 7–8, 85–86, 103–4, 160, 184–85, 194
 importance to airing of independent films, 68–69, 70
 original title of, 84
 path to, 82–85
Presidio, 25
Press, Richard, 96–97
Prestige Films, 89–90
Pretend It's a City, 165
Price, Sarah, 100
Primary, 13–14, 17, 18
Primate, 75n.11
Prison in Twelve Landscapes, A, 176–77
private investment, 151–52, 153, 177–85, 186–87, 188
 commercialization and, 179–80
 filmanthropy, 178–79
 promise and limits of, 185

shift to, 177
producers, streaming video and, 169–73
Program Fund (of CPB), 77–78, 80
"Program of Restricted Nazi Propaganda Films," 14–15
Projectr.tv, 192
Project XX!, 11–12
Prosperi, Franco, 20–21
Psihoyos, Louie, 177
Public Broadcasting Act of 1967, 73–74
Public Broadcasting Service (PBS), 7–8, 19, 37–38, 39–40, 46, 68–71, 76–77, 81, 82–84, 88, 90–91, 158, 160, 161, 169–70, 190–91, 194–95
 AIVF *vs.*, 71, 72, 82
 Amazon and, 168–69
 creation of, 73–74
 in docbuster era, 139
 funding sources, 71
 HBO compared with, 102, 103–5, 106–7
 importance of place in the ecosystem, 194
 independents win airtime and funding from, 85–87
 lobbied for funding and airtime, 7–8, 69, 71, 72–73
 Netflix and, 143
 refusal to air funded films, 79
public-service agenda, 3, 4–5, 10–11, 69
Public Telecommunications Financing Act of 1978, 72, 85–86
public television, 2, 5, 7, 68–87, 188
 barriers to accessing, 69–71, 72–75
 controversy feared by, 70, 73–74, 77
 Doerfer Plan on, 11–12
 financing of independents feared by, 73, 74–75
 legal requirement to fund independents, 72
 local stations, 70–71, 73, 75–77, 85–86
 schedule disruption feared by, 73
publishing market, 31–32
Pulcini, Robert, 134
Pull My Daisy, 17
Pulp Fiction, 92
Putin, Vladimir, 168–69, 193

qualifying runs, 108–9

Quarters of Paris, The, 18
Queen, The, 31–32
Queen of Versailles., 177
Quiet One, The, 14–15
Quinn, Gordon, 19–20n.19
quiz-show fixing, 11–12

Radio City Music Hall, 59
Rafferty, Kevin, 66t
Rafferty, Pierce, 66t
Rape: Cries from the Heartland, 107–8
Raymond, Alan, 99n.20, 104–5, 108
Raymond, Susan, 99n.20, 104–5, 108
RBG, 1–2, 177, 182, 187
Reaching Audiences: Distribution and Promotion of Alternative Moving Image (Knight and Thomas), 6
Reagan, Ronald, 77–78
Real Cancun, The, 116
Real Sex, 103, 110–11
Real Women Have Curves, 134
Reclaiming Popular Documentary (collection), 193
Red Envelope Entertainment, 144–45, 154, 155–56
reenactments, 106
ReFocus: The Films of Barbara Kopple (Jaeckle and Ryan, eds.), 4–5
Reggio, Godfrey, 59, 66t
Regional Report, 73–74
Reichert, Julia, 36, 51, 147, 151–52, 153
Reinventing Cinema: Movies in the Age of Media Convergence (Tryon), 6
Rendezvous, 131
Resha, David, 4–5
Return Engagement, 59
Return of the Secaucus Seven, The, 41–42, 44–45, 55–56
revival houses, 16
Revolution Studios, 127
Ricciardi, Laura, 163–64
Richter, Richard, 106
rich uncle / grant pictures, 44–47, 48–49
Ride, The, 85
Riding Giants, 132
Riefenstahl, Leni, 14–15
Riggs, Marlon, 82
Ringer, The, 1–2

Rivette, Jacques, 60
Rizzo, Sergio, 120
RKO-General, 13
Roach, Hal, 18n.16
Roadside Attractions, 119, 145
Robin Williams: Come Inside My Mind, 171
rockumentaries, 26–27, 55–56
Rocky Flats Nuclear Weapons Facility, 68–69
Roger & Me, 39, 40, 88, 90
Rogosin, Lionel, 16, 32
Rolling Stones, 26–27
Romero, George, 43–44
Room with a View, 58
Rooney, David, 100
Rosenberg, Robert, 55t
Roses in December, 77–78
Rothschild, Amalie, 36–37
Rudolph, Alan, 59
Rumsfeld, Donald, 161
runtimes (as indicator of target market), 113–14
Rush to Judgment, 34
Russo, Emily, 95–96, 97, 175
Ryan, Susan, 4–5

Sackman, Jeff, 141
Safe, 95–96
Saidman, Aaron, 165
Salesman, 9–10
Sánchez, Eduardo, 100–1
San Francisco, 39–40
San Francisco Film Festival, 26–27
Sans Soleil, 61–62, 66t
Sapadin, Lawrence, 77–78
Sarandos, Ted, 145, 154, 155, 157–58, 159
Savage, Steve, 138, 143–44
Say Amen Somebody, 7–8, 57–58
Sayles, John, 44–45, 57, 58, 112
Schiller, Greta, 55t, 96–97
Schroeder, Barbara, 165–66
Schroeder, Barbet, 66t
Schulberg, Sandra, 50–51
Schwartz, Russell, 90
Schwartzman, Arnold, 57
Schwarz, Shaul, 165
Scorsese, Martin, 165, 192
Secret Honor, 58

Seed&Spark, 195
Seeger, Pete, 27n.42
Seeing Red, 39–40n.1, 51
See It Now!, 11–12
Sehring, Jonathan, 112–13
self-distribution, 7–8, 10–11, 36–37, 75–76, 89
   continued use of, 88–89
   of independent films, 40–41, 45–46, 47–48, 50, 65–67
   in the internet age, 146–47
Selling of the Pentagon, The, 34n.62
Selma, 158
Sembene, Ousmane, 60
September 11 terrorist attacks, 126
Seventh Art Releasing, 93, 98–99
sex, lies, and videotape, 92
sex-themed content. *See* adult content in films
SF Docfest, 129
Shadow Distribution, 119
Shadows, 17
Shaffer, Deborah, 43t, 45, 53, 55t
Shaman, Robert, 81–82
Sharma, Sudeep, 142–43
Sheffield International Documentary Film Festival, 129
Sherak, Tom, 127
Sherman's March, 55t
She's Gotta Have it, 92
She's Nobody's Baby: American Women in the Twentieth Century, 103
Shirkers, 160
Shoah, 66t
Showman, 18
Showtime, 169–70
Sicko, 119
Sigel, Newton Thomas, 66t, 79
Silber, Glenn, 43t, 46, 48–49, 50
Silver, Joan Micklin, 46
Silverlake Life: The View from Here, 96–97
Simone, Nina, 161
Sinai Field Mission, 75n.11
Sinatra: All or Nothing, 171
Sington, David, 160
Sinofsky, Bruce, 109–10, 140–41, 146–47
Siskel, Charlie, 160

Sissel, Sandi, 55t
Sivan, Daniel, 165–66
60 Minutes, 104–5
Skoll, Jeff, 182
Skoll Foundation, 182
Sky above, the Mud Below, The, 20–21, 21n.24
Smith, Chris, 100, 161–62
Smith, Herb E., 50–51
Smith, Howard, 60n.42
Smithereens, 41–42
Social Cinema in America, 19–20, 28–29, 129–30
social issue documentaries, 19–20
Soderbergh, Steven, 92, 112
soft documentaries, 159–61, 168–69, 186
Soldier Girls, 55t
Soldier in Hiding, 108
Solo: A Star Wars Story, 172–73, 172n.35
Some Nudity Required, 138
Some of These Stories Are True, 78–79
Sonnenfeld, David, 98
Sons and Daughters, 19–20n.19
Sony Pictures Classics, 56–57, 62–63, 64, 93–96, 100, 109, 119, 135, 141
Sopranos, The, 109
Soros Documentary Fund, 130
Sorrow and the Pity, The, 60n.42
Southern Comfort, 138
Spears, Ross, 55t
specialty labels, 94–95, 98–99
Spellbound, 116, 121–22, 123–26, 133–34
Spielman, Fran, 53–54
sports documentaries, 165
Spotlight, 182n.57
Square, The, 156, 169–70
Standard Operating Procedure, 182
StartUp.com, 100–1
Statement of the New American Cinema (manifesto), 16
State of the Documentary Field, The: 2018 Study of Documentary Professionals (Borum Chattoo and Harder), 196
Stations of the Elevated, 55t
Step into Liquid, 116
Stern, Bert, 66t

Steve Jobs: The Man in the Machine, 161, 171
Stevens, Fisher, 160
Stoll, Jerry, 19–20n.19
Stone, Bernard, 77–78
"Stoned: Kids on Drugs" (*America Undercover* episode), 103
Stoney, George, 14–15
Stop Making Sense, 7–8, 58
Story, Brett, 176–77
Story Of, The, 12n.6
Strand Releasing, 175–76
Stranger Than Paradise, 41–42
Streamers, 57
streaming services, 1–2, 5, 7, 8, 167–69
streaming video, 8, 142–43, 148–49, 151–87
   consequences of, 167–77
   Netflix's switch to, 154–59
   private investment and (*see* private investment)
   theatrical release and, 152–54, 174
stripping, 86
Strong Island, 165–66
studio classics divisions, 55–60, 93–94, 99
studio specialty divisions, 93–94, 98
Study of Documentary Professionals (Center for Media and Social Impact), 187, 190
subscription video on demand (SVOD), 152–54
Sundance Artist Services, 156–57
Sundance Channel, 97, 139
Sundance Channel Home Entertainment Documentary Collection, 139
Sundance Documentary Fund, 130
Sundance Film Festival, 41–42, 83, 88–89, 100, 113–14, 129–30, 131–32, 183
   American Factory, 152
   Bisbee '17, 184–85
   Blue Vinyl, 138
   Buena Vista Social Club, 100–1
   Capturing the Friedmans, 125
   The Celluloid Closet, 100, 109
   Dark Circle, 68–69
   The Dissident, 192
   documentaries at (1986-2001), 114*t*
   documentaries at (1996-2006), 132*t*
   Knock Down the House, 1–2, 174
   My Kid Could Paint That, 135
   Paris Is Burning, 89
   Southern Comfort, 138
   When We Were Kings, 98
   Who Killed Vincent Chin?, 69
Sundance Institute, 130, 149, 151–52
Sunn Classics, 47–48
Super High Me, 145
Super Size Me, 116
Superstar: The Life and Times of Andy Warhol, 66*t*
Sutcliffe, David Felix, 160
SVOD. *See* subscription video on demand
Swift, Taylor, 161
Swimming to Cambodia, 58
Switzerland, 129

Tajima-Pena, Renee, 51–52, 69, 104–5, 107
Takei, George, 161
Talbot, Daniel, 16, 17–18, 60
Talking Heads, 58
Tan, Sandi, 160
Tarantino, Quentin, 92
Taxicab Confessions, 103, 110–11
Taxi to the Dark Side, 170–71
Taylor, Elizabeth, 57
Taylor Chain: Story of a Union Local, 36–37
Teleculture, 58–59
television. *See also* cable television; public television
   advertising on, 47–48, 56–57
   Direct Cinema on, 11–14, 18
   financing theatrical released films, 90–91
   HBO emphasis shift to film from, 108–11
   Netflix and, 156
   tension between cinema and, 2, 8, 37–38, 88–89, 101–2, 190–91
Television Week, 133
Tell No One, 155
Temaner, Gerald, 19–20n.19
tentpole films, 4, 40–41, 123–24
Territory, 76

(T)ERROR, 160
theatrical release, 7, 92–101
  banner year for documentary (1967), 24–28
  cable television's use of documentaries to enter, 133–36
  core of documentaries, 95–97
  of Direct Cinema, 20–29
  in docbuster era, 118–27
  First Run Features and, 53
  general documentary, 98–101
  of great-man history, 23–24, 38
  of independent films, 47, 49–50
  limited support for, 10
  Netflix and, 144–45, 157, 165
  New Yorker Films and, 62–63
  to qualify for Academy Award nominations, 8, 91, 91n.6, 92, 102, 108–9, 111, 112–13
  risk of for small distribution companies, 175–76
  streaming video and, 152–54, 174
  television funding of films, 90–91
  types of films favored for, 10
They Shall Not Grow Old, 1–2
Thin Blue Line, The, 63–64, 90, 124–25, 166, 169–70
ThinkFilm, 119, 121–22, 125–26, 133–34, 141, 145
Third Independent Film Award, 17
13th, 188–89
35 Up, 90
30 for 30, 161, 165, 167–68
34th Street East, 25
Thomas, Bob, 74–75
Thomas, Peter, 6
Thompson, Molly, 135–36, 168–69
"Three Faces of Cuba" (*Changing World* episode), 73–74
Three Identical Strangers, 1–2, 195
ticket contests, 96
Tiger King: Murder, Mayhem and Madness, 3, 165, 188–89
Tillman Story, The, 136
Time, Inc., 13, 18
Time of the Locust, 33–34
Times Film Corp., 15–16, 21–22
Times of Harvey Milk, The, 58–59

Time Warner, 94–95
Titicut Follies, 19–20n.19, 20, 20n.21, 31, 75
To Be and To Have (Être et avoir), 116
To Be Takei, 161
Today Show, 107–8, 121–22, 125–26
Tonight Show, 13
Toni Morrison: The Pieces I Am, 190
Toronto Documentary Forum, 131
Totally Under Control, 171, 182
Touching the Void, 116
"tourist gaze," 20–21
touristic documentaries, 7, 10, 20–22
Trials of Alger Hiss, The, 43t
Trials of Henry Kissinger, The, 170–71
Triton Pictures, 62–63, 64, 99
Triumph Films, 41–42
Triumph of the Will, The, 14–15
Troublemakers, The, 31, 33–34
Trouble the Water, 95
true-crime documentaries, 163–64, 165–66, 172–73
True/False Film Festival, 129
Truffaut, Francois, 57
Truly Indie, 146
Trump, Donald, 169–70
Tryon, Chuck, 6, 117, 147, 148
Tuckman, Michael, 184–85
Tupac Resurrection, 116
Turner Broadcasting, 94–95
TV Lab (of WNET), 77, 78
Twentieth Century Fox International Classics, 41–42
28 Up, 55t, 90
20 Feet from Stardom, 162n.16
Tzioumakis, Yannis, 56–57, 94–95

UA Classics, 41–42, 56–58
UCLA Center for Social Impact Entertainment, 182
Un Chien Andalou, 18n.16
Uncovered: The Whole Truth about the Iraq War, 147–48
unions, 77
Unique War, The, 19–20n.19
United Artists, 23, 41–42
United Kingdom, 129
Universal, 23, 41–42, 48–49, 94–95, 98, 99

Universal Classics, 41–42
University of Wisconsin-Madison, 46
Unknown Known, The, 161, 182
Unsolved Mysteries, 166
Up the Yangtze, 95
Urman, Mark, 121–22, 145
USA Films, 94–95
US Film Festival (later Sundance Film Festival), 83
US Techniques and Genocide in Vietnam, 34

Van Peebles, Mario, 139
Van Sant, Gus, 134
Varda, Agnes, 96–97
Variety, 20, 23–24, 28–29, 31–32, 42–43, 46, 50, 53, 62, 73–74, 95–96, 117, 121–22, 136, 139–40, 144–45, 180
  on *Buena Vista Social Club*, 100–1
  on *The Celluloid Closet*, 100
  on *Dont Look Back*, 25–26
  on *The Endless Summer*, 24
  on *European Nights*, 20–21
  on *Mondo Cane*, 22
  on *Monterey Pop*, 27
  on *Paradise Lost: The Child Murders at Robin Hood Hills*, 109–10
  on *Salesman*, 9–10
  on *The War at Home*, 48
  on *Woodstock*, 28
Venice Film Festival, 9–10, 18, 27, 100, 109, 110
Vernon, Florida, 63–64, 66t
Veronika Voss, 57
Verrell, Addison, 46
VHS, 137, 142
Victory at Sea!, 11–12
Victory Will Be Ours, 19–20n.19
video streaming. *See* streaming services; streaming video
Vietnam: The Secret Agent, 55t
Vietnam War, 34, 46, 73–74
Vigo, Jean, 14–15
virtual cinemas, 189–90
Virunga, 195
Visions du Reel, 129
von Einsiedel, Orlando, 156, 195
Vow, The, 169–70

Vulture, 188–89

Waiting for Superman, 177
Walsh, Heather, 160
Walter Reade-Sterling, 34
Walter Reade-Sterling / Continental, 17–18
Wang, Nanfu, 168–69
War at Home, The, 7–8, 43t, 46–47, 48, 50, 53, 72–73, 147
war documentaries, 10
Warhol, Andy, 33–34
Warner Bros, 27–28, 40, 47–48
Warner Independent Pictures, 119, 122, 123
Warner Strategic Marketing Home Video, 139–40
Warrendale, 19–20n.19, 20, 28–29, 31–32, 120–21
War Room, The, 99–100
Way, Chapman, 161–62, 165–66
Way, Maclain, 161–62, 165–66
Weavers, The: Wasn't That a Time!, 57
Weber, Bruce, 95–96
Weinstein, Bob, 90, 126
Weinstein, Harvey, 90, 126
Weisenborn, Christian, 66t
Weiss, Marc, 83, 84
Welfare, 75n.11
Welles, Orson, 57
Wenders, Wim, 88–89, 100–1
West, Betsy, 177
We Steal Secrets: The Story of Wikileaks, 171
WGAE (Writers' Guild of America-East), 193–94
WGBJ, 80
What Happened, Miss Simone?, 161, 169–70
What's Happening: The Beatles in the USA, 14
What the #$! Do We Know*, 116
When Billy Broke His Head...and Other Tales of Wonder, 85
When the Levees Broke: A Requiem in Four Acts, 110
When the Mountains Tremble, 61–62, 66t, 79

224 INDEX

When We Were Kings, 8, 88–89, 98, 99
"When Women Kill" (*America Undercover* episode), 103
While Brave Men Die, 19–20n.19
White Helmets, The, 156
Whitney Biennial, 110
Who, The, 27
Who Killed Vincent Chin?, 68, 69
Whose Streets?, 160, 190
Why We Fight, 11n.3, 162n.16
Wild, Nettie, 96–97
Wild Parrots of Telegraph Hill, The, 119
Wild Wild Country, 165–66
Wilinsky, Barbara, 22
Willis, Jack, 19–20n.19
Wilson, Cis, 106–7
Wilson, Lana, 161
Winged Migration, 116, 119, 123–24, 140, 141
Winston, Brian, 75
Wintonick, Peter, 96–97
Wired, 155
Wisconsin ETV, 72–73
Wiseman, Frederick, 19–20n.19, 75–76, 82, 170
With All Deliberate Speed, 134–35
Withers, Bill, 98
WNET, 72–74, 75–76, 77, 83
WNYC, 90–91
Wobblies, The, 43t, 45, 53, 55t
Wohl, Ira, 43–44, 43t
Wolper, David, 12n.6, 18n.16, 23
Woman Under the Influence, The, 46
Women of the World, 20–21, 21n.24
Wong, Lexine, 139–40, 141
Won't You Be My Neighbor?, 1–2, 177, 181, 185
Woodstock, 26–28

Word Is Out: Stories of Some of Our Lives, 7–8, 39–40, 43t, 46–47, 50, 61, 66t, 72–73, 147
publicity for, 48
subject of, 39–40
theatrical release of, 49
Workman, Chuck, 66t
World, 80
World According to Sesame Street, The, 182
World Magazine, 124
World of Tomorrow, The, 51–52
World War II, 11
Wormwood, 165–66, 169–70
Writers' Guild of America-East (WGAE), 193–94
WTTW, 77, 81–82
WTVS, 69
Wyatt, Justin, 47–48
WYES, 76–77
Wyler, William, 11, 11n.3

Yates, Pamela, 66t, 79, 82
Year of the Horse, 99
York Theatre, 61–62
Young@Heart, 145
Yousafzai, Malala, 161
youth culture documentaries, 7, 10, 26
YouTube, 188–89

Zeitgeist Films, 93, 95–97, 98–99, 119, 156–57, 175, 192
Zero Days, 171, 182
Zero Gravity, 13
Ziering, Amy, 169–70
Zipporah Films, 75–76
Zwerin, Charlotte, 9
Zwigoff, Terry, 66t, 88–89, 100

Printed in the USA/Agawam, MA
March 5, 2024

862203.007